The Spycatcher Affair

Also by Chapman Pincher

TOO SECRET TOO LONG
THE SECRET OFFENSIVE
TRAITORS: THE ANATOMY OF TREASON

The Spycatcher Affair

CHAPMAN PINCHER

St. Martin's Press/New York

Design by Judith Stagnitto

Library of Congress Cataloging-in-Publication Data

Pincher, Chapman.
    The Spycatcher affair / Chapman Pincher.
        p.   cm.
    ISBN 0-312-02290-5
    1. Wright, Peter, 1916-   —Trials, litigation, etc.   2. Trials (Treason)—Great Britain—London.   3. Wright, Peter, 1916-Spycatcher.   4. Intelligence officers—Great Britain—History.   5. Great Britain. M15—History.   6. Espionage—History.   I. Title.
KD373.W73P56 1988
345.41'0231—dc19
[344.105231]   88-16892
                                                      CIP

First Edition

10 9 8 7 6 5 4 3 2 1

The Spycatcher Affair is a revised edition of A *Web of Deception* © 1987 by Chapman Pincher, published in Great Britain by Sidgwick and Jackson.

To the Arbiter—for a singular service.

|Contents|

| Preface |

This book will, I believe, provide historic testimony of how people of the highest integrity, honestly trying to do their best for their country, can be ensnared by the cult of secrecy into situations that make them look inept, unprofessional, conspiratorial, deceitful, and untruthful. It offers fine-focus observation of the difficulties of knowing where the truth lies in secret affairs. It should serve to dispel some of the bewilderment of those who have followed the events but found them too complicated for easy understanding.

Historians have a phrase, "the fog of war," to explain apparent blunders by military commanders that are really due to the confusion and chaos inevitable in any widespread conflict. The Wright affair suggests that "the fog of secrecy" may be equally descriptive of apparent follies in the security and intelligence world, especially when deception operations are involved.

This account should help to undermine the fetish of secrecy in the administration of government, by exposing the danger it poses for those who have been trained to set such store by it.

| Introduction |

In 1987, Peter Wright, a retired counterespionage officer in the British Security Service—commonly known as MI5 and roughly corresponding to the FBI—published an account of his career with much detail about secret operations. His book, called *Spycatcher*, was first published in the United States, and it became a world best-seller. Wright, then seventy-one, was the first British secret serviceman ever to disclose such secrets to the public—although several had revealed them to the Soviet Union—and when the British government heard of his firm intention to "go public" under his own name, in 1985, it reacted strongly in every legal way open to it. It saw Wright's behavior as a breach of an almost sacred undertaking and as setting a dangerous precedent that other officers might follow with potentially disastrous results.

If Wright had been living in Britain, he would have been restrained under the Official Secrets Act because, on leaving MI5 in 1976, he had signed a declaration under that act acknowledging that he must keep secure all secret information he had learned during his work except any that might be made public officially. In Britain, where there is no Freedom of Information Act and no public right to know under a written constitution, no information of any consequence about the secret services is officially released if the government can avoid it. Wright, however, had emigrated to Australia, where the Official Secrets Act does not operate and from which extradition under the act is not permitted.

The British government was, therefore, restricted to suing Wright and his Australian publisher in a civil action in a court in Sydney to secure an injunction to prevent *Spycatcher* from being published there or (the government hoped) anywhere else. The action was based on the theory that Wright owed "confidentiality" to the Crown, his former employer, and that only the Crown could release him from his obligation, which it was not prepared to do. The case was comparable to a situation in which an employee of a pharmaceutical firm who knows the secrets of a manufacturing process moves abroad and sells those secrets to another company, which then makes profitable use of them. It is well established in international law that the aggrieved company can sue to injoin the rival from making use of the secrets and can claim damages from the firm and the renegade employee.

The trial, which attracted worldwide attention, opened on November 17, 1985. The principle of Wright's obligation of confidentiality made little impression on the judge for one particular reason: Wright had been one of my chief informants for a book on the British secret services that I had published worldwide in 1981 under the title *Their Trade Is Treachery.* There was little in Wright's proposed book that had not appeared in mine and Wright's young Australian lawyer, Malcolm Turnbull, argued that the government's failure to suppress my book or make any deletions when it had the opportunity to do so foreclosed it from now suppressing Wright's work.

The chief witness for the government was its most prestigious official, Sir Robert Armstrong, the Cabinet Secretary and Prime Minister Margaret Thatcher's chief adviser, especially on secret service matters. As will be seen, he was operating under a severe disadvantage: the real reason why *Their*

Trade Is Treachery had not been suppressed had been withheld from him by the secret services on unnecessary security grounds; and as a result Sir Robert misled the court, with fatal consequences for the government's case.

The government's lawyers labored under a further disadvantage. Wright was said to be so ill that he might die in the witness box if resolutely cross-examined. He was therefore permitted to present his evidence in the form of an affidavit, a sworn written statement that he was allowed to read in the court. This statement put forward the extraordinary claim that the government had conspired with me to produce *Their Trade Is Treachery* and that he had been entrapped into assisting me. He alleged that the government's purpose was to make public a number of secret security scandals so that it could dispose of them once and for all, rather than facing the repeated political embarrassment of dealing with them piecemeal as they were exposed by investigative writers. This fictitious operation was supposed to have been initiated by Lord Rothschild, the British head of that illustrious family, who had introduced me to Wright in the early autumn of 1980. In fact, the idea of writing a book was suggested to me by Wright, who was genuinely eager to expose some of the security scandals but was also in desperate need of money.

Because Wright was not effectively cross-examined, and since neither Lord Rothschild nor I was called to give evidence, his conspiracy story was widely publicized by the media, and many politicians affected to believe it, as a means of attacking the government. Lord Rothschild and I were accused of corrupting Wright and were eventually subjected to intense police investigation. Although we were exonerated, the whole *Spycatcher* episode proved to be something of a Bay of Pigs for the government in that it was ill-conceived and had disastrous political consequences. The Australian judge came out entirely in favor of Wright and his publisher in a long judgment that was very hostile to British interests. The government then became enmeshed in a series of appeals and consequent court cases involving British and Commonwealth newspapers that wanted to publish material from Wright's book. As a result, the reputations of the British attorney general and Sir Robert Armstrong were severely damaged, and in the minds of millions of people worldwide, the British legal system and government were brought into disrepute and ridicule.

It is widely believed that government ministers and their senior officials behaved foolishly and perhaps dishonestly, but the truth is that, without exception, they were all trying to do what they believed to be the best for their country. The disaster arose only because most of them had been kept in the dark by the secret services, which had ruled that some matters were so secret that not even the Prime Minister and her chief adviser could be told about them. They were ensnared by the cult of secrecy. In recent times there appear to have been comparable political circumstances in the United States, such as the current uproar over the sales of arms to Iran and the secret arrangements made to continue funding of the Contras.

In Britain and, I suspect, in the United States, the public rarely learns exactly what occurs at the highest levels when matters of extreme secrecy are being discussed, but the controversy concerning the *Spycatcher* affair is an exception. In revealing the details, as known to me through my involvement over eight years, I can be enlightening not only about the behavior of government ministers and officials in a parliamentary democracy under such circumstances but also about the response of political opponents in seeking to exploit the situation.

‖1‖

A Momentous Message

Who seeks, and will not take when once 'tis offer'd,
Shall never find it more.

—Shakespeare

Around 4 P.M. on the summery afternoon of September 4, 1980, the telephone rang at my retirement home in the quiet English village of Kintbury in Berkshire. It was a call I was not expecting, and it was to change my life by plunging me back into the mainstream of politics and intrigue, with national and international consequences involving some of the most senior politicians, civil servants, and legal authorities in the land. A few minutes later, I would have been on my way to the local river to fish for trout until late evening, and opportunity would have been ringing without response.

I recognized the voice as that of Lord Rothschild, an old friend with whom I had not communicated for some weeks. With his customary economy of words, he told me that he was being visited at his home in Cambridge by a friend from overseas who wished to see me and that, knowing my interests, he felt sure that I would want to meet him. The friend was due to leave on the following morning. Cambridge was a long way, and I was not prepared to drive so far on short notice. I therefore suggested meeting the individual in London on another day, but Rothschild said that would be impossible. He said that, if I could spare the time to spend the night at Cambridge, he would send a chauffeured car from London to pick me up and take me to his house in time for dinner. Then I would be driven back home the following morning.

From previous experience, I sensed that it was unwise to press for further details but felt confident that the mysterious friend was probably from the secret world in which Lord Rothschild moved—perhaps an Israeli intelligence officer. I knew that Victor Rothschild had served in MI5 (the security and counterespionage agency) with distinction during World War II and had maintained close connections with the British secret services as well as with Israel's intelligence service, Mossad. He was aware from my recent writings that I had retired completely from the general defense scene and was specializing in novels and occasional journalism about intelligence and security affairs. I also knew that he was not a man to waste anybody's time, his or mine. In any case, although I had visited the Rothschilds' London flat on several occasions and, with my wife, had vacationed with them in Israel, I had never stayed in their Cambridge house, so on that score alone the invitation was irresistible once I did not have to do the driving.

I arrived in Cambridge before 8 P.M., and was ushered into Victor's rather dark study, where he was alone, casually dressed without a jacket. Sitting me opposite to him, he explained that the friend, whom he declined to name, was a former member of MI5 whom he had known for many years and who was visiting from Australia. He then said that the friend, whom he called Philip, wished to talk to me about certain people and that, if I was interested, the friend would appear. ("They were two old spooks playing silly buggers," was how I described the situation later to my wife.) I expressed profound interest, and Victor left the room to be replaced by a smiling, blue-eyed man of medium height with a fringe of white hair. He was in shirtsleeves, tieless and leaning on a stick.

So far as I could remember, I had never seen him before. He had a memorable face and an inability to pronounce the letter "r"; and as a trained observer, I would have recalled both. This man was later to state in an affidavit in 1986 that he had refrained from telling Rothschild that he had met me. I am certain we had not met previously. He did not allude to any previous meeting, either to me or to Lord Rothschild.[1] Would he have agreed to be presented as "Philip" if we had already met? Further, when we met again at length in Tasmania, he made no mention of having encountered me before our meeting in Cambridge. All he told me then, in that respect, was that he had seen me once while lunching in London in the Ecu de France restaurant but had deliberately avoided being introduced to me by the friend who was lunching with him. As will be seen, there was some advantage to the case he would present to a court in Sydney in saying that we had met.

"Philip," who was sixty-four, explained that he was seriously ill, suffering from a blood-pressure problem that could be kept in check only by a strict routine of pills. He had retired from MI5 in 1976 and was living in Tasmania, where he was trying to eke out a miserable pension of £2,000 a year by running a small Arabian horse stud farm. He said that he was so perturbed about the security of MI5 that he had started writing a book to expose instances of treachery that, he claimed, had been consistently covered up to conceal the embarrassment of the secret services and of government ministers and officials, whose reputations could have been damaged had the truth been publicly known. He had a slip of paper with a list of names including Blunt, Philby, Maclean, Golitsin, a very important KGB defector to the CIA, and Sir Roger Hollis, the former Director General of MI5, and said that he had planned to deal with them all in his book. The handwriting was not that of Lord Rothschild, which is minuscule and spidery.

He explained that he had completed some 10,000 words in about ten chapters but was finding the task too onerous because of his deteriorating health and the need to devote more time to his stud farm than he had expected. His wife was already overworked on the farm, because of his infirmity, and in addition was having to type out his chapters. The small farm had suffered some serious setbacks, including the sudden death of the main stallion, and he urgently needed £5,000 if the stud was not to go bankrupt. He expressed concern that, in the event of his death, his wife would be left in very poor circumstances. He had hoped that his book, which would make new revelations about the Soviet penetration of MI5 and MI6, would be a best-seller, and in that connection he mentioned the sales of the book by the British author Andrew Boyle about the case of Sir Anthony Blunt, the KGB spy who had worked in Buckingham Palace. He feared, however, that he might not live to finish his book and certainly could not do so in time to solve his severe financial difficulties.

He suggested that I might care to develop and complete the book on the basis of information he would supply, saying that it would be far more revealing than Boyle's book. He declined to show me the chapters at that stage, but I learned that he had them with him and had shown them to Lord Rothschild, who was to tell me later that he had induced Wright to eliminate one chapter which dealt with Rothschild's secret services for MI5.[2]

"Philip," whose real name proved to be Peter Wright, was to state under oath at the Sydney trial that he did not suggest the idea of a book. I do not know what happened between Wright and Rothschild before I arrived at Cambridge but Wright certainly suggested the idea of a book to me, and it was immediately clear that this was the sole purpose of our meeting so far as he was concerned. He was also to state, under oath, that money had not been a prime motive, just an incidental benefit; but on that night in Cambridge, he stressed that the book would have to be produced at great speed, because of his urgent need for £5,000. He made me aware from the start that, if I wrote the book, he would want a substantial part of the proceeds and that, without an agreement on that score, he would not tell me anything. I was left in no doubt that, if I declined his offer, he would seek some other writer.

I did not know it then but, only three months previously, Wright had written to Lord Rothschild stating: "I am writing a book whose tentative title is *The Cancer in Our Midst*. It is about the penetration of our society by the Russians and how the Soviets have used it to manipulate us to achieve their ends."[3]

The fact that he had written 10,000 words of a book with a prospective title and had brought them with him to Britain disposes of the claim Wright was to make later that it was Lord Rothschild who suggested that he should write a book, during their conversation in Britain in August–September 1980.

It has now been established, and agreed to by Wright in court, that Rothschild had paid Wright's fare to London for an entirely different personal reason and that Wright then took the opportunity to mention his book to Rothschild (and later to me), though he persisted in referring to it in court as a "dossier."[4]

There can, therefore, be no truth to any allegation that Lord Rothschild and I conspired to bring Wright to Britain so that he could be induced to impart secrets to me. Rothschild had never mentioned Wright's impending visit to me and, until that chance telephone call, I had expected the quiet of my retirement to be disturbed only by the noise of shotgun cartridges.

As an interviewer of more than thirty years' experience, I was impressed by the fervor and apparent sincerity of "Philip," and this was not diminished when he said that, in the event of any collaboration, he would expect to receive 50 percent of any net profits that the book might bring. I had never paid for information in the whole of my professional life as a journalist and author, but I understood it to be a common practice in the production of a book; and if I was to make money out of the project, it seemed reasonable that he should, too. I was, of course, aware of the legal dangers, as was "Philip," and the need to avoid a situation in which I might be accused of securing secrets through bribery.

It was soon obvious from his conversation and use of certain names known to me that "Philip" had indeed been a career officer in MI5, more properly called the Security Service, which is responsible for countering subversion and espionage against the state. It was also apparent that he had enjoyed close connection with the sister service, MI6, properly known as the Secret Intelligence Service, which is responsible for intelligence operations overseas, corresponding closely to the CIA. To establish his bona fides, "Philip" gave me a few nuggets of information, on the understanding that I would not use them except in the content of the prospective book. They included the then-secret fact that Blunt had been "blown" by an American, Michael Straight, whom he had recruited to the Soviet service when both had been at Cambridge. "Philip" claimed that he had been chairman of an ultrasecret committee, called Fluency, set up to investigate suspected moles in MI5 and MI6. He confirmed what I had already learned about the case of Sir Roger Hollis from a different source, expressing surprise that I already knew so much.[5] He again declined, however, to let me see any of the chapters he had written, not wishing to show any substantial part of his hand until I had proved my serious interest by visiting him in the safety of Tasmania.

I will deal with the full significance of the Hollis case in the next chapter. Suffice it to say at this point that my knowledge of it when I first met "Philip" was substantial but my interest was limitless because the sheer possibility that the man who had been the head of MI5 for nine years—the British counterpart of J. Edgar Hoover—might have been a Soviet agent held enormous journalistic potential.

In my career as an investigative writer, a field in which I could be said to have been something of a pioneer, my principle had always been to discover everything possible and then to make a judgment about publication. I was not constrained by the Official Secrets Act any more than any other ordinary citizen and, while successive governments had often regarded me as a nuisance, my efforts had never been considered as dishonorable in a free society. While I may have been criticized for being overzealous, I had never been regarded as disloyal. I therefore agreed to collaborate in principle, provided that a book proved to be feasible and publishable.

Police who questioned me in 1986 found it hard to understand that I would make the journey to Tasmania in pursuit of information. They had no concept of the attraction of such a possible source to an investigative writer or of my long-established resolve to pursue and expose subversives and traitors, whether they be alive or dead. I felt that, if what Wright had hinted at was true, it could be in the national interest to expose it; but all writers, and I am no exception, are guilty of a certain amount of libertarian posturing on suitable occasions. I have no doubt, in retrospect, that what mainly motivated me to follow up Wright's offer was the prospect of an unparalleled scoop. I had, I suppose, been looking for someone like Wright for forty years, as had my rivals in Fleet Street.

Once I had agreed that I would seriously consider visiting him, "Philip" had to reveal his identity. I had never previously heard of Peter Wright, although it later came out that, through his professional work, he knew a great deal about me and my past career. He asked me to promise never to reveal his name as a source of information or that we had ever met. It was a promise I would keep until Wright himself revealed it to an Australian court six years later.[6]

Wright said that he lived in a small township called Cygnet, not far from Hobart, in Tasmania where he had moved after retiring from MI5 in order to be near his married daughter. He said that his visits to Britain were rare, and I appreciated at that stage that, if serious trouble arose with the security authorities over the book, I would be the one at the sharp end, for no criminal action could be taken against Wright so long as he remained in Tasmania. Extradition is not permitted under the Official Secrets Act, and even his pension could not be touched because the British government had ruled that no government servant can be deprived of his pension unless he is prosecuted and convicted.[7]

Wright explained that, for various reasons, he would be unable to see me until late October when, if I still intended to visit him, he could arrange for me to stay in a hotel near his house. I persisted in the hope of being able to avoid having to go to Australia and suggested that we should meet in London for a few days but Wright said that he dared not be seen there. He said he was highly recognizable, and if he were seen in London, his old office would wonder why he had not called in there and would become suspicious. In any case, Wright said that it would take a long time for him to explain everything to me and that I should be prepared to remain in Tasmania with him for at least two weeks and possibly three.

At that stage Victor Rothschild reappeared. I told him that it seemed that Wright would be helping me to write a book, and Wright suggested that I should sign a paper, with Lord Rothschild as a witness, to the effect that Wright, or his wife in the event of his death, should receive 50 percent of the net profits from the book. Lord Rothschild wanted no involvement, and I declined to sign anything, pointing out that the only arrangement to which I would be party would be through a properly constituted contract with a publisher, in which case, if such a contract could be secured, he could receive half the net profits, which would be paid by the publisher, not by me. Throughout our relationship, in personal contact and through letters, I told Wright that I could not possibly be involved in giving him any money, and I have copies of letters to that effect.[8]

When Wright pointed out that no publisher must ever

know his name, I said that I thought that could be arranged but he would have to set up some private banking facilities, in which I had no expertise, to get his share to him in Australia.

I was surprised that Lord Rothschild did not object to the collaboration, not only because of the great store he set by secrecy but because, a few weeks previously, when I had told him what I knew about the Hollis case, he had sent me a letter clearly trying to deter me from continuing with my inquiries.[9] Wright was to tell the Australian court that Rothschild had told him that his "dossier" ought to be published.[10] I find this impossible to believe because, as I discovered in Tasmania, the so-called "dossier" was not remotely publishable, containing very little meat and nothing whatsoever about the Hollis case. All that Wright and I ever talked about was a *book*, and the chapters had clearly been written as part of the book, *The Cancer in Our Midst*, which he had mentioned to Lord Rothschild in his recent letter.

Wright was also to tell the Australian court that he had brought the ten chapters to England so that Rothschild "could get them to Mrs. Thatcher," but for the same reason this made no sense either.[11] They would have told her nothing but very old and boring history.

These facts dispose of any allegations that I conspired with Lord Rothschild at any time to induce Wright to part with official secrets so that I could write a book. The proposal came from Wright. It was also Wright who insisted on a half-share of any net profits from the book. He was in financial difficulties; I was not and, until I met Wright, had no intention or prospect of writing any books, apart from novels, about intelligence affairs, although I would have written newspaper articles.

After my private talk with Wright in Lord Rothschild's study, we went in to dinner with Lady Rothschild, whom I knew as Tess, and there was no further conversation of consequence about the project. On retiring to my room I made a note of everything I could remember of our conversations, as has always been my habit. Wright did not appear at breakfast and I was not to see him or speak to him again until I visited him in October.

To suggest that there had ever been a conspiracy between Wright, Rothschild, and me, with our heads together, is entirely to misunderstand the nature of Lord Rothschild. If he had agreed to anything with Wright before I arrived, he would never have prejudiced his position by letting me know that. I did not "need to know" what, if anything, they had discussed and, with his penchant for secrecy, he would have operated as always on a "need-to-know" basis. (To restrict the spread of knowledge about secret operations, for security purposes, those involved are told no more than they need to know for their particular roles.) Wright's claim in the Sydney court that he felt he was being drawn into a "deniable operation"—meaning that our meeting was part of an MI5 deception plot that MI5 could later deny—has no basis in fact. [12] At no time during my association with Wright, in Cambridge, in Tasmania, or in any letters we ever exchanged secretly, did he suggest that Lord Rothschild had involved us in any "operation," deniable or otherwise. On the contrary, he consistently underlined the need for secrecy from MI5, which he believed would suppress the book if alerted to it. If I had been a conscious part of any MI5 operation, as Wright was also to suggest to the Sydney court, is it conceivable that I would have remained quiet while the Prime Minister, in Parliament, "rubbished" the book I eventually wrote, and while some newspapers went even further? [13] I owed MI5 nothing and would not have allowed my reputation to be sullied in its interests. The only commitment to secrecy I ever made was to Wright, to preserve his confidentiality as a source.

While that first meeting with Wright in Cambridge spun the first frame-threads of the web of secrecy that was to entrap some of the highest officials in the land, my involvement was less conspiratorial than it sounds. Though it was unusually secret, it was otherwise a normal progression of events in my long professional experience: a social introduction to a new contact, an offer of interesting information by the contact, a follow-up of the offer to secure that information under conditions of absolute confidentiality, and its conversion into salable copy.

On the way home, I tried to fathom Lord Rothschild's part in the procedure. I did not, at that stage, know why he had brought Wright over; and I simply assumed that Wright was just visiting his family in Britain and had contacted Rothschild. Throughout our friendship, Victor had always been extremely security-conscious. I had never questioned him about his MI5 days, and he volunteered so little that I recall telling my wife that, as a source, he was the "Great Clam of Chowder." He had been very concerned when I had mentioned a secret MI5 method of detecting Soviet intelligence officers, called Movements Analysis in my book *Too Secret Too Long*, published in 1984, and had written to me complaining about it. The reason I had done so was because it had already been "blown" by a Canadian author.[14] Rothschild had also tried to deter me from pursuing the Hollis case, even suggesting obliquely that it was untrue. I knew that he and his wife were close friends of Sir Dick White, a former head of MI5 and (later) of MI6, because we had all been together at a dinner to celebrate the publication of one of Victor's books. I therefore assumed that he might have passed on news of my interest in the Hollis case to White who would probably have fed it back to his old office. I knew, too, that Victor and Tess had been friends of Blunt and that the discovery of the latter's treachery in 1964 had been a great shock to them both.

Victor had always been encumbered by the fact that he had been a contemporary of Blunt, Burgess, and the rest of the Cambridge spy ring in the 1930s. Because of his brilliance, he had also been a member of the university's exclusive Apostles Club, which had become a haunt of communists and homosexuals. It was widely believed that during the war Rothschild let part of his London house in Bentinck Street to Blunt and Burgess and was involved in "orgies" there. The truth is that

Lord Rothschild and his first wife had offered accommodation to two former Cambridge friends, Patricia Parry (now Lady Llewelyn-Davies, the Labour peeress) and Tess Mayor. When Rothschild moved to another house, he wanted to dispose of the lease and offered it to the two young women. They could not afford the rent and, as the accommodation was on three floors, it was agreed that they could sublet to friends. One of these friends was Anthony Blunt, then in MI5 and totally above suspicion. Blunt suggested his companion, Burgess, as another tenant. At the time of the alleged orgies, which neither woman can remember, Rothschild was far from the scene.

Lord Rothschild has also been wrongly accused of being responsible for bringing Blunt into MI5; in fact, he has a letter from MI5 confirming that he did not do so. [15]

For these various reasons, it was inevitable that in the newspapers' intermittent search for the "fifth man" of the Cambridge ring, following the exposure of Burgess, Maclean, Philby, and Blunt as the first four, Rothschild's name should surface as a possible contender. It did not arise when Blunt was exposed to MI5 as a spy in 1964 because that was kept secret; but in 1979, when Blunt was publicly branded as a Soviet agent and his knighthood was withdrawn, the suggestion was resurrected. The intimation that Lord Rothschild was a Soviet spy was a monstrous smear of a most distinguished scientist and public servant, then aged sixty-nine, whose zoological work had earned him a Fellowship of the Royal Society, whose wartime work had merited the George Medal for bravery, and who had headed the research team for Shell International, chaired the Agricultural Research Council for ten years, formed and headed the government's first think tank, and been chairman of Rothschild's bank. I will deal with this unfounded smear in detail in chapter 19, but it is highly relevant to mention it here because it was the real basis of Wright's visit to Rothschild in 1980 and led, fortuitously, to my meeting him in Cambridge.

Lord Rothschild was deeply perturbed by various articles in magazines and newspapers that appeared after Blunt's public exposure. One of them in particular, by Auberon Waugh, in the *Spectator*, headed "Lord Rothschild Is Innocent," conveyed to Lord Rothschild the suggestion that perhaps he was not.[16] The security and intelligence services will never come to the rescue of one of their former officers who is being maligned because this would subject them to publicity. Rothschild therefore took legal advice and, in preparation for the possibility that he might have to take actions for libel if the smears continued, he needed some objective proof that he could not possibly have been the "fifth man" or any other kind of Soviet agent.

During his time with MI5 and on many other occasions after he left in 1945 to return to his scientific work, Rothschild had performed many services that were clearly against the Soviet interest. He could have made a list of these himself, but to be admissible and to carry weight in a court of law, such a list had to be prepared by someone else. The person best fitted to provide it was Peter Wright, with whom he had been personally involved in several endeavors.

Wright was later to tell the Australian court that he had been introduced to Lord Rothschild by Sir Roger Hollis, but Rothschild says this is incorrect.[17] Victor had been a senior figure in the Shell company on the research side and realized that one of the scientists employed there had special qualifications that might be of use to MI5. He therefore told Sir Dick White, then the head of MI6, who eventually arranged for Peter Wright to see Rothschild.[18] Later, when Wright was involved in the interrogation of Blunt, he went to see Rothschild, who was instrumental in inducing certain prominent figures who knew Blunt to talk to Wright; the two then became friends. A published statement that Lord Rothschild had been introduced to Wright by Blunt was a monstrous untruth.[19] Rothschild and Wright held each other in high professional regard, though they had no other common interests. Wright

also had first-hand knowledge of how Rothschild had so easily
defended himself when interrogated about his friendship with
Blunt.

When Wright moved to Tasmania in 1976, he was in
temporary need of capital, and Rothschild loaned him £5,000
because MI5 was delaying payment of that sum (which was
owed as part of his retirement arrangements). Wright repaid it
within a few months. [20] They remained in occasional communication by letter, and on June 25, 1980, following the *Spectator* article, Rothschild wrote to Wright saying:

> Things are starting to get rough. I cannot see that it
> would be a breach of the Official Secrets Act for you to
> put on a piece of paper *but not to send to anyone*, a
> detailed account of your relationships with me, in-
> cluding *all* details, and let me have it by a method
> which I shall let you know in due course. There is
> certainly a need to know and you would only be tell-
> ing someone something that, memory lapses apart, he
> could put down himself. I think it might be a good
> idea for you to come over to this country for a few days
> if you could bear it, but I shall think about that. [21]

What Rothschild wanted was an objective statement of
his various contributions to MI5 operations against the Soviet
Union, which had continued long after he had left MI5. On
July 16, he sent out one economy air ticket by mail—not a
first-class ticket by courier, as Wright later alleged. [22] He also
offered enough money to cover Wright's expenses on a round
trip to Britain that would enable him to see his children. [23]
Wright accepted and arrived in London on August 22, accompanied by his wife, Lois.

In his sworn affidavit to the Sydney court in 1986, Wright
stated that he received a first-class ticket and exchanged it for
two economy tickets so that his wife could accompany him, as

it was medically unsafe for him to travel alone. The bill for the ticket, which has been examined by the police, shows it to have been one economy-class ticket. Wright's reason for claiming that he had received a first-class ticket remains obscure.

Wright has stated publicly and in written statements to the Australian court that Lord Rothschild's need for the list of his achievements for MI5 was, indeed, the reason why he invited him to Britain.[24] On Lord Rothschild's part, it had nothing whatsoever to do with any book and no collaboration between Wright and me or anyone else was envisaged by Rothschild or myself at that stage. I knew nothing of Wright's intended visit or of his presence in Britain until Lord Rothschild telephoned me on September 4. It was a fluke of circumstance that I happened to be at home to take the call.

After a week in Yorkshire with a daughter, following his arrival on August 22, Wright booked into a London hotel and called at the Rothschilds' flat in St. James's Place. There they began their conversations about the list of Rothschild's security and intelligence contributions. The list has, so far, remained secret, and Victor has never told me what these contributions were; but from conversations with Wright in Tasmania and from other sources, I know some items on the list and will deal with them in chapter 19.

Wright is on record as saying that later, in the London flat, he raised the question of the Hollis case.[25] Lord Rothschild has no recollection of this. Wright also claims that he had begun a "paper" on the case and showed it to Lord Rothschild, seeking advice as to how to draw it to the attention of Mrs. Thatcher.[26] Rothschild cannot remember this either, and when I was given the chapters of Wright's book in Australia, there was no mention of Hollis in them because he had not reached that stage of his story. As our time together there was limited, he would surely have given me his "dossier" on Hollis to read, had it really existed. Instead he had to recall all the Hollis material, and I had to make notes of it.

Wright was to tell the court in Sydney that Rothschild had told him that Mrs. Thatcher had recently been sitting in his London flat talking about intelligence matters.[27] In fact she has never been to the flat. Lord Rothschild had referred to a brief call paid by Mrs. Thatcher to his Cambridge home during an interval in a visit to a Cambridge laboratory on August 27, 1980. She had been accompanied by her husband, Denis, and her political assistant, Ian Gow, so it is hardly conceivable that intelligence matters were discussed. This has been established to the satisfaction of the police, with evidence from the diaries of Number 10 Downing Street. The police told me, in the course of questioning me, that Wright was clearly wrong about this statement concerning Mrs. Thatcher.

I did not know, until late in 1986, that Rothschild had been aware of Wright's intention to write a book for some ten years. Wright had first told him about the project in a letter from Tasmania as early as November 1976, in which, referring to Anthony Blunt, he wrote, "He shall have a special place in my memoirs."[28] Rothschild had been so perturbed by the prospect, in MI5's interest, that he had quickly sent a letter to the Director General of MI5, then Sir Michael Hanley, warning him that Wright was "going bad" and that it was a dangerous situation. He coupled this with a plea for a better pension for Wright, because he could see what might happen to such a man as he became isolated and embittered on the other side of the world. MI5 had taken no action, although it eventually sent Wright the standard warning, beginning "Dear Pensioner," that former officers remain bound to secrecy.[29] Since MI5 displayed so little interest, it is understandable that Lord Rothschild took no further action when Wright wrote to him again about the book, giving the title, in June 1980.

I have often been tempted to ask Lord Rothschild why he involved himself in the book project at all, but as those who know him will agree, he is somewhat inscrutable, and I never managed to secure a full, first-hand explanation. I now have good reason to believe, however, that the explanation for his sudden decision to introduce Wright to me was his conviction, when shown the ten chapters, that Wright was determined to produce his book somehow and was being forced by financial pressures to do it quickly. He felt that a book under Wright's name would have such credibility that it would be totally believed by the Soviets and would do much greater damage than a book by a professional writer, which the authorities could ignore or dismiss as speculation—as they eventually did. I believe he also calculated that there was some very "hot" information that Wright might publish under his own name in the safety of Australia but would not give me to publish in Britain or that I would not use if he did give me it—a supposition since justified by events. Clearly, with Wright in Tasmania, I would be the person to decide what went into the book and what did not. Rothschild had despaired of securing any action from MI5; Sir Michael Hanley had not even acknowledged his warning. So when Wright showed him the chapters, he may have decided to take the initiative—a book by me, which would limit the damage, being the lesser of two evils. It must have been a sudden decision, given the circumstances under which I was summoned by telephone.

Such an action would have been almost instinctive in a former MI5 officer as loyal as Rothschild and as committed to belief in the paramount importance of counterintelligence. When suppression of a dangerous situation proves impossible, damage control becomes the immediate objective. Whatever the reason, Lord Rothschild would not have brought me into the situation without the most careful thought. He has always been noted for his razor-sharp intellect and does nothing impetuously. Nor could he be talked into doing anything against his own reasoning.

Wright's lawyer, Malcolm Turnbull, was to argue in a telephone conversation with me in 1986 that, if Rothschild had wished to stop Wright from producing a book under his own name, he could simply have given him the £5,000 that he needed or even the £30,000 plus that he eventually obtained. I told Turnbull that most rich men do not behave that way, especially in old age when they have made most of their money over to their dependents. Turnbull's suggestion was telling evidence of the financial motive on Wright's part.

Of one thing I am absolutely certain: Lord Rothschild did not contact MI5 or any other authority to secure approval for his action. Nor was he knowingly part of any secret MI5/government deception plot to involve me with Wright without my knowledge. He was eventually subjected (at the age of seventy-six, when he was not well) to lengthy police interviews that he found undignified, unpleasant, exacting, and dangerously debilitating. I do not believe that he would have tolerated them and the attendant publicity had he really been doing MI5 a service. He could simply have told the police to go away and privately consult MI5. If I was conned into such a project without my knowledge, which in view of the known facts I find inconceivable, then Lord Rothschild was, too.

Why did Rothschild choose me, rather than any other writer, to meet Wright? In the first place, we were friends. He knew of my current interest in the Hollis case, and he was aware that I already knew a lot about it because I had recently tried, unsuccessfully, to secure more information from him. He knew that my politics were not suspect. He believed that I could be trusted to keep secret Wright's identity and his involvement, whatever might happen. He knew that I had long experience in handling sensitive situations involving the Official Secrets Act, having safely negotiated myself through the tribunal investigating aspects of the case of John Vassall, a naval spy; the inquiry into the surreptitious examination of private telegrams by the government; and other brushes with the "authorities," which remain private.[30] There had also been a previous occasion on which Lord Rothschild and I had collaborated successfully, though this had nothing to do with MI5.

In 1972 he had asked me if I would go to Tehran and interview the Shah, who was a personal friend of his. While no announcement had been made at that stage, the Shah intended to (and in fact did) visit Britain the following June, staying with the Queen at Windsor and attending the Ascot races. The Shah felt that he had been subjected to unfair criticism by the British media and wished to give an interview that would present his aims and attitude to Britain more favorably. I learned that the most important part of his visit would be an attempt to pave the way for very large arms sales; being then a Fleet Street defense correspondent, I was particularly interested in that. I agreed to go.

The Shah gave me a splendid interview, with so much new information that the British ambassador in Tehran was rather perturbed.[31] I received a message that His Imperial Majesty was well pleased with my efforts, as was the editor of my newspaper. The success of that mission may well have contributed to Rothschild's opinion that, if Wright was determined to publish his information, I was professionally fit to deal with it.

Whatever the reasons, his totally unexpected telephone call to my home proved to be momentous, and not only for me.

‖ 2 ‖

The Hollis Affair

> How can we expect another to guard our secret if
> we have not been able to guard it ourselves?
> —La Rochefoucauld

Mrs. Thatcher had not needed Peter Wright
to tell her about the Hollis case in August 1980. More than six
months earlier, on January 31, Jonathan Aitken, the Conservative MP for Thanet, had written to her in secrecy, warning
her of "certain developments and possible new disclosures arising out of the Blunt affair." These included the cases of Hollis
and his former deputy, Graham Mitchell, about which Aitken
had surprisingly detailed information. The letter was marked
"Strictly private and confidential," but it has since been made
available to the Australian court. It is so important to an understanding of the events that, with Aitken's permission, I have
reproduced the whole letter in appendix A.

It warned Mrs. Thatcher, the Cabinet Secretary, and any
ministers they cared to alert that a great deal of information on
the subject was "circulating among journalists on both sides of
the Atlantic." Aitken suggested that the Prime Minister should

brief herself fully "on all aspects of this material in order to be able to make an immediate and appropriate response should the need for public comment arise." What he had in mind was a sudden disclosure by a journalist or author. Aitken said that his information had come from both American and British sources, which I know to be the case. "I hope you will at least find it helpful to receive prior warning of possible press disclosures, principally from American sources," his letter stated.

It went on to explain that there were strong suspicions that Soviet agents had penetrated the Security Service at the most senior level and that the two chief suspects were Sir Roger Hollis, the Director General of MI5 from 1956 to 1965, and his former deputy, Graham Mitchell, who was then still alive. The damaging activities of Hollis were alleged to include warning Philby of his imminent arrest in 1963; thwarting the investigation and interrogation of Mitchell, and destroying significant documents about that case; and thwarting the interrogation of Blunt.

Aitken's letter also revealed that he knew that the former Cabinet Secretary, Sir John Hunt, had asked his predecessor, Lord Trend, to undertake an inquiry into the Hollis case and related issues. Aitken had been told, as I was later, that Trend's report on the matter had concluded that high-level Soviet penetration had taken place and that Hollis was probably the Soviet agent responsible.

The letter also warned that Hollis and Mitchell may have recruited other Soviet agents, so the secret services might still be penetrated.

Aitken then provided further information suggesting that the Hollis "story" might break at any time. To forestall the problems that this might cause for the government, and for the Prime Minister in particular, Aitken suggested an independent inquiry, the reappraisal of MI5 officers recruited during Hollis's time, and the planning of major reform of the secret services.

While the Prime Minister was taking advice on the letter,

she must have been astonished, if not shocked, by the extent of Aitken's knowledge of matters that had been kept tightly secret. He had in fact stumbled on the story by chance while visiting Washington in December 1979, shortly after his marriage. He chanced to call on James Angleton, the former chief of counterintelligence in the CIA, because he had been an old friend of Aitken's late father. While discussing the recent Blunt case, Angleton hazarded the opinion that Mrs. Thatcher had decided to make a statement about Blunt because it was the first phase of a move to stage a full inquiry into the state of MI5 and MI6. Angleton believed that such an inquiry was necessary and, when Aitken asked him why, he said that he would think about some way of answering the question and that perhaps Mrs. Thatcher ought to be warned.

When Aitken returned to London he found a letter from Angleton giving him the names of Arthur Martin, a retired MI5 officer, and Christopher Phillpotts, formerly of MI6. Aitken asked them to the House of Commons for a drink and Martin, in particular, collaborated in bringing the explosive Hollis situation to the Prime Minister's notice, along with the related case of Graham Mitchell who had been Hollis's deputy.[1]

Aitken received no response for several weeks and, after making inquiries, eventually received no more than a brief acknowledgment from the Prime Minister saying only that she was aware of the allegations. The delay had, no doubt, been occasioned by MI5's tardiness in deciding what to advise the Prime Minister to do. No action of consequence seems to have been taken by MI5 except, perhaps, to trace the source of Aitken's information. The Prime Minister accepted the advice, which was to do nothing.

On April 29, 1980, Aitken and I were guests at a dinner given for ex-President Richard Nixon at the Hyde Park Hotel in London. Aitken was a member of Lord Beaverbrook's family, with which I have been associated for many years, and was also a journalistic colleague. Concerned and frustrated by the lack of action, he urged me to look at the Hollis case and, in a brief conversation, gave me some of the information contained in the letter to Mrs. Thatcher and some additional details. He named two British journalists who were investigating the Mitchell story and said he thought that the Hollis affair might break in the United States.[2]

Over lunch at the Café Royal on May 8, Aitken gave me much more detail and explained how he had come by the information. Later he showed me the letter to the Prime Minister—of which he would not then let me have a copy—and we discussed the issue on several other occasions.

On May 19, I met Lord Hunt of Tanworth at a reception. As Sir John Hunt, he had been the Cabinet Secretary who had initiated the Trend Inquiry. To engage him in conversation, I told him that the British journalist Duncan Campbell was getting his teeth into a story about a former Director General of MI5, making it clear that I meant Hollis. He did not comment until he was leaving, when he said, "I'm sorry to hear that Campbell has got hold of that story." Hunt may or may not have then alerted MI5.

It was not until almost seven years later, in February 1987, that Aitken told me that Arthur Martin had known by the summer of 1980 that he was briefing me about the Hollis case. Aitken felt certain that Martin fed that information into the MI5 office, as would be normal practice in that world. No action of any consequence was taken against Martin.

Wright was to tell the Sydney court that I had been "particularly well-informed about the Hollis case" before I went to see him and indicated, damagingly, that I had received my information from Lord Rothschild.[3] This was totally untrue. Lord Rothschild never told me anything about Hollis and affected to know nothing about the case when I asked him about it. The only action he ever took was to send me a note trying to deter me from pursuing it further.[4]

Wright's evidence for assuming that Rothschild had given me information about Hollis was singularly unscientific for a professional scientist. In his affidavit to the Australian court, he referred to a passage in my book, *Inside Story,* published in 1978. There I told how one senior officer of MI5 had become so incensed by the activities of two Labour ministers that he believed it to be urgently in the national interest that they should be exposed. I had been told that this officer, whose name I did not know and have never been told, was prepared to go public provided he could be assured of a livelihood— since dismissal from MI5 would have been inevitable. He therefore approached a senior Whitehall personality who, I was told, had agreed to see what could be done. This personality contacted a well-known figure in the City who was sympathetic but proved unable to find the MI5 man any assured employment. In his affidavit, Wright clearly identified himself as the dissident officer and assumed that it must have been Rothschild who had told me about the episode. He conveniently ignored the possibility that the information could have come from the City figure, which in fact it did, for this man, who is exceptionally eminent and greatly respected, was also a friend and told me the details over lunch. Lord Rothschild told me nothing about it whatsoever and denied knowing anything about the incident when I asked him about it.

Though I had heard vague rumors of the suspicion about Hollis in the 1970s, my active curiosity about the case derived from what Aitken had told me. That curiosity, in 1980, had induced me to ask Lord Rothschild about it, with the result that, while he pretended to know nothing, he was aware of my interest. Thus, a chance conversation between Aitken and Angleton in America was the seminal event leading to my involvement and all that flowed from it.

As will be seen, Wright was to tell me a great deal more about the Hollis and Mitchell cases and other related events, and I was to discover additional information through my own researches. There was little doubt in the minds of the other secret service officers who had been involved in the long investigations that one or more Soviet agents had been operating at a high level in MI5. The intelligence evidence, showing that the preponderance of the probabilities pointed to Hollis, had been recorded at length in my book, *Too Secret Too Long,* and need not be repeated here.[5] Graham Mitchell, Hollis's deputy, was the only other candidate who was seriously considered and nobody with professional competence doubts that he was effectively cleared of the very thin evidence against him.

The Hollis case is not closed, as the public has been led to believe. In the Sydney court on November 24, 1986, Sir Robert Armstrong said: "It is possible that further information will come to light which would prove guilt. It has not. If there was more information the investigation would have to be reopened."[6] Sir Robert also admitted that the question of whether or not Sir Roger Hollis was a Soviet spy is "a question of abiding public interest."[7]

In his judgment on the Sydney court case about Wright's projected book, Justice Powell argued that "the public interest in preserving confidential information should be overridden by the public interest in knowing the whole story." Regarding the Hollis case, I agree with that assessment and will continue my efforts to provide it.

‖ 3 ‖

Encounter in Tasmania

No memory of having starred
Atones for later disregard.

—Robert Frost

|A|fter considerable thought about the merit of traveling 12,000 miles to Tasmania to see Wright, my wife and I decided that we would make the trip (for which I would have to pay) a potential holiday. We had a standing invitation to stay with friends in Hong Kong, which was on the way, and had a daughter living in Sydney whom my wife was particularly anxious to visit. So if the project came to naught because Wright was ill or had changed his mind, the journey would not have been wasted.

We left on Monday, October 6, for Hong Kong, where I put some research in hand concerning Hollis's early days in China; we then left Hong Kong for Sydney on October 11, arriving on October 12. I telephoned Wright, cryptically, and in the agreed interests of secrecy booked a passage to Hobart, Tasmania, under the name of Dr. Chapman, Pincher being such a rare and peculiar name as to be too easily recognizable.[1] My wife remained with our daughter.

I was met at the airport by Wright's wife, Lois, a pleasant woman two years older than her husband. It was about an hour's drive to the small township of Cygnet through hilly country very reminiscent of Scotland. I was rather shocked by the Wrights' home, which their lawyer, Malcolm Turnbull, was to call a "three-room shack" made, apparently, from two apple-pickers' huts. It was pleasantly situated in a few acres of grassland, formerly an apple orchard, which provided grazing for the small Arabian stud farm, but it was certainly not the kind of home in which a secret service officer would be expected to end his days.

I felt sorry for the Wrights' having to live permanently in what were little better than cramped trailer conditions, but I was soon feeling sorry for myself when I checked in at the hotel where Wright had booked a room for me. The hotel seemed to cater mainly to lumberjacks. My bedroom had a window looking out onto the corridor leading to the bathroom, and the various male residents gave me a "Hiya, cobber!" each time they patronized the lavatory. The single bed had been shaped over the years to the contours of much heavier men. Fortunately I had elected to have only breakfast at the hotel; after the first morning the landlord's wife, who was not an early riser, asked me: "Do you mind cooking your own igg? I can't cook iggs." I agreed to perform this task but soon dispensed with it because the kitchen was so littered with last night's unwashed dishes and pint glasses that I had no appetite.

Instead I read over the previous day's notes while I waited for Wright, who picked me up each morning in the utility truck he used for his business, having bought it on an extraordinary installment arrangement peculiar to Australia.

I enjoyed my time with Wright because he had so much of the kind of information I had been pursuing all my professional life, but he displayed the personality traits common to those who have spent too much time isolated in the secret world. He was calculating and intensely suspicious, with an air of cunning and a habit of narrowing his eyes. In describing his exploits, he repeatedly emphasized the need for ruthlessness. He was highly intelligent and vainly aware of it, which had not endeared him to some of his colleagues, as I was to discover later when I spoke to them.

He was smoldering with resentment at the unjust way in which he believed he had been treated by MI5, both as to the manner in which his efforts to uncover moles in the secret service had been dismissed and as to his poor financial circumstances. He expressed deep disappointment that, while MI5 always had a resident liaison officer in Melbourne, no effort had ever been made to contact him. But his main motive for cooperating with me was his conviction that MI5 had cheated him on his pension, and his desire and need to recompense himself on that score.

As I was to write in *Too Secret Too Long*, the experience of listening to Wright, and later to others, was like being taken into an Aladdin's cave with nuggets and jewels sparkling everywhere. It soon became clear that much treachery and incompetence inside both MI5 and MI6 had been concealed. I was astonished by the depth of Wright's knowledge and his involvement in so many interesting cases that had provided evidence of Soviet penetration. His years as assistant to the Director General had given him the closest insight into security and intelligence relations with the United States, Canada, Australia, and New Zealand. He told me that he had established liaison with many foreign intelligence officers, including James Angleton, with whom I was in occasional correspondence.

I was even more surprised by his willingness to tell me secrets for publication on a scale that I knew to be unprecedented in the entire history of the secret services and, almost certainly, in British history as a whole. As had happened during our brief meeting in Cambridge, he did not attempt to conceal the obvious fact that he was committing a massive

breach of the Official Secrets Act, but he always justified this
on the grounds that the penetration of the secret services by
Soviet agents had never been sufficiently appreciated by successive governments. He was particularly incensed by the way
the Hollis case had been "swept under the carpet," as he put it.
But at no time did he suggest, as a reason for breaking his bond
of secrecy, that he believed that MI5's methods, such as bugging and surreptitious entry, should be exposed because they
were morally wrong. He believed then, as I did, that legal
restraints would tie the hands of MI5 in its unceasing secret
battle against a ruthless adversary. He was to take a different
view six years later in *Spycatcher*.

I quickly came to agree with Wright that the only way of
securing some action to improve the efficiency of the secret
services against the Soviet intelligence offensive was through
publicity, because the services would continue to convince
whatever government was in office that nothing needed to be
done.

Wright began my briefing by handing me about 9,000
typewritten words, in eight or nine chapters, one chapter having been removed by Lord Rothschild for reasons of his personal security. At no time did he refer to these as part of a
"dossier," but as part of a book that he had originally intended
to complete himself. The chapters, apart from one entitled
"The Klatt Affair," were quite unsuitable as they stood, and I
realized that the whole book would have to be reorganized and
written by me from scratch. Wright would not let me keep the
chapters, so I had to make notes from them. Reports that I
eventually returned from Australia with Wright's manuscript
are entirely untrue. He was most anxious that I should have
nothing that was traceable to him, such as a script typed on his
machine, if I were to be searched by customs on my return to
London, as he warned I might be.

I saw that, to make the book salable and especially to
secure serialization by a newspaper, it would be necessary to
open it on the Hollis case. There was no mention whatsoever

of Hollis in the 9,000 words. Wright had not reached that far
in his narrative. He was later to tell the court that he had taken
a paper on Hollis to Britain and shown it to Rothschild, but
Rothschild does not remember it, and I saw no sign of anything written about the Hollis case when I was with Wright in
Tasmania. I do not believe that it existed. If it had, why did he
not show it to me when we both wanted to cut down the verbal
interrogation, which was particularly wearing for him? Almost
everything he told me that eventually appeared in *Their Trade
Is Treachery* was given to me verbally and had to be noted
down and then copied out in longhand late at night when I
was back at the hotel.

Wright was genuinely concerned about the Soviet penetrations of the secret services, and he described in great detail
the activities of the mole-hunting Fluency Committee and its
findings. This, without doubt, was a major motive for breaking his obligation of lifelong secrecy, of which he was fully
aware; but he was also very concerned about money and in
desperate need of £5,000 before the end of 1980 if his stud was
not to go bankrupt. He constantly reminded me of this
urgency, although he did not need to because the conditions
under which he and his wife were living were eloquent
enough. Lois looked desperately tired and worn and was having to do far too much of what her husband called "horse
business"—putting mares to the stallion and keeping the stables clean and the horses in good order. Wright, who firmly
believed that he was living on borrowed time and took about a
dozen pills a day, was understandably concerned about leaving
his wife in near penury. Wright was to assure the Sydney court
that money was not an important consideration, but history
shows that most men who betray their country's secrets for
money claim a more laudable motive.

I also have reason to believe that Wright's aspirations had
been fired by the success of Boyle's book about Blunt. He had
realized that he could write a much more exciting book about
Hollis and related cases, including that of Blunt, and make a

lot of money from it. I had some difficulty in convincing him that Boyle had not made £1 million and that, because the subject was parochial, sales of my book would be largely limited to the British market, which was pathetically small.

Wright produced no documents apart from some small diaries that were helpful in stimulating his memory by reminding him where he had been on various dates throughout his career. He gave me the impression that he had no official papers, but in 1987 I was to learn that in a letter he had written to Lord Rothschild about Anthony Blunt on November 3, 1976, he had stated, "I've still got my notes of my talks with him." Later, in the Sydney court, Wright was to state that he had brought no notes from England to Australia. In conversations with me, Wright repeatedly referred to tape recordings of his long interrogations of Blunt, but if he had them, he never produced them.

There was no doubt that his memory was exceptional, because I was able to test it at frequent intervals by asking questions to which I already knew the answers and was able to check out most of what he told me with other sources after my return to Britain. "I'll back my memory against any documents, and the access is quicker," he remarked. It was a symptom of self-delusion that motivated me to make so many checks. Of course, if Wright was able to refer to records, it would explain his seemingly total recall of events. It would also explain how, six years later, he was able to give specific dates of events and reproduce conversations in his book, *Spycatcher.*

I worked a ten-hour day in Wright's company. At some points he would disappear for a couple of hours with his wife to assist in the service of a mare or to meet someone. I learned that the stud had recently suffered another setback when a promising young Arabian horse had died after being bitten by one of the very poisonous snakes that are common in Tasmania.

Like most of the secret service officers I have met, Wright

liked a drink. He consumed a fair amount of Australian wine while bemoaning his inability to afford whisky, of which I eventually provided a couple of bottles, not being a whisky drinker myself. But he had no need of alcohol to loosen his tongue: he liked to talk. A former Canadian intelligence officer described his loquacity in uncharitable terms: "Peter Wright was one of the greatest blabbermouths around once he had gained confidence with his audience; it was part of his ego trips to show the extent of his knowledge, in order to impress people." Wright himself confessed to me that he had sometimes broken a ban of silence imposed by his MI5 superiors to brief foreign intelligence cronies, especially in Canada and the United States.

On the third morning, Wright insisted that we should spend some time dealing with his pension position, and he gave me a rundown of his career. He was born in Essex on August 9, 1916; his father, Maurice, was at that time an electronics engineer. I had heard of his father because he had invented the antidote to "Satyr," a most ingenious Russian eavesdropping device that, for the first time, had allowed a room to be bugged without the need for any wires or batteries. When this device was discovered in the British and American embassies in Moscow, every relevant office in Whitehall and Washington was searched, and the need for a cheap countermeasure that could be installed as a routine precaution was immediate. In my book, *Inside Story*, published in 1978, I recorded that G. M. Wright, who was just a name to me, had been responsible for the solution; I had then never heard of either of his two scientist sons, Peter and Paul.[2] I certainly did not know that Wright claimed to have been responsible for discovering how "Satyr" worked, as he eventually did in *Spycatcher*! He never mentioned it to me, although he was not backward in describing his achievements.

After education at schools in Chelmsford and Bishop's Stortford, Peter worked on a farm and then studied forestry at the School of Rural Economy in Oxford but left in 1940 without taking a degree. Through the influence of his brother, who was employed by the Admiralty, Peter worked in the Royal Navy's scientific service during the war and then moved to the Marconi electronics company.

In 1950, Sir Frederick Brundrett, the chief scientist in the Defence Ministry, set up a committee to improve the scientific resources of MI5 and MI6, and Wright was selected to serve as a part-time, unpaid adviser. He helped to develop improved eavesdropping techniques, working in the Marconi laboratory at Great Baddow in Essex.[3]

Wright never held high rank in MI5 but, because of his scientific and technical experience, he enjoyed a perhaps unprecedented degree of access to important cases. He entered MI5 as a scientific adviser in July 1955 at a salary of £1,700 a year, rising by annual increments of £75 to £1,950, and signed the Official Secrets Act. In 1958 he was appointed to the established staff. He was promoted in 1963, and in the following year Dick White, a senior MI5 officer, asked him to put his major effort into helping D Branch on the Soviet problem. In this he worked closely with Arthur Martin and, when Hollis dismissed Martin, with his successor Barry Russell Jones. Wright was a founding member of the Fluency Committee, which investigated Mitchell, Hollis, and other suspects, and was sometimes its chairman (a position that rotated). He became number three in the counterespionage branch and held the same position in K Branch, following a reorganization. He was then given the special post of counterespionage adviser to K Branch and to the Director General. He retired early, at his own request, in 1973 to start a farm in Cornwall because his pension prospect was so poor but was reemployed half-time as consultant to the Director General.

When he retired completely, on January 31, 1976, six months short of his sixtieth birthday, he had been involved in Russian counterespionage from 1955 to 1976, longer than any other MI5 officer. He had been actively concerned with the surreptitious entry of properties and the bugging of embassies, an expertise that had taken him abroad on some assignments.[4]

In the six years he spent as special assistant to the Director General, he was privy to ultrasecret matters involving intelligence relations with the United States and with the Commonwealth nations of Canada, Australia, and New Zealand.

Wright emigrated, almost immediately, after signing the usual declaration that he would preserve the secrets he had learned during his MI5 career. That document, signed on January 30, showed that he understood that the Official Secrets Act still applied after his retirement and that it was an offense, making him liable to prosecution either in Britain or abroad, if he ever revealed any information he had acquired through his employment. It was produced at his trial in Sydney and showed that he had already given his address as Cygnet, Tasmania.

In spite of efforts made on his behalf by Lord Rothschild, who felt he had been unjustly treated, his pension was only 60 percent of what he believed it should have been.[5] Wright told me that it was only £2,000 per year in 1980 because the MI5 management had failed to keep verbal promises made to him when he entered the service on transfer from the Civil Service, when he relinquished his previous pension rights. Treasury officials who examined his case decided that he was receiving his full entitlement according to the rules and that it could not be increased without creating a precedent that others might exploit. His entitlement was small because of his broken service and because he never achieved high rank—that of Assistant Director, printed on the cover of *Spycatcher*, being much more modest than it sounds and having been held by Wright for only a short time.

There was a distinct air of vengefulness as Wright blamed the MI5 management and the Whitehall establishment for his predicament. He did not tell me that he had also been given a lump-sum payment of £5,000.

Lord Rothschild seems to have been alone in foreseeing the danger of allowing such a man, with so many salable secrets, to stew in resentment "out in the sticks," 12,000 miles away, immune from the Official Secrets Act.

In view of all that has happened since, the possibility that Wright went to Australia to put himself outside British jurisdiction cannot be discounted.

In 1986, according to Wright's affidavit to the Sydney court, his pension rose to £600 per month, presumably having been substantially increased in line with inflation, in spite of MI5's knowledge of his leakages to me.

It has been said that Wright went to Australia "in frustration and disgust," but he never expressed such feelings to me; instead, he gave me to understand that he had gone to Tasmania because his daughter was living there, the climate would suit his indifferent health, and the climate was also better for his Arabian horse project. It has also been stated that hanging on a wall in his house is a framed Latin quotation from Pope Gregory VII that translates, "I have loved justice and hated iniquity, and therefore I die in exile."[6] I saw no such notice when I was there, and Wright did not regard himself as being in exile.

One of his major reasons for preserving the secrecy of our joint venture was that he did not want to be prevented from visiting Britain, although he had no intention of returning there to live. The other was his fear that, small though his pension was, MI5 would terminate it if it could prove that he had been the source of massive leaks. I assured him that MI5 had no such power, but he insisted he had been told that the Director General could do what he liked.[7]

While Wright was anxious that MI5 should not know of our meeting, if only because of the threat to his pension, he expressed even more concern about the KGB. He believed he had done the KGB so much harm that its assassination squads would take their revenge on him if they could, and he gave this as another reason why he wanted his identity and address kept secret. Looking around in the uneventful peace of tucked--away Cygnet, this seemed unlikely, but stranger things have happened in the intelligence world.

Wright's cover was very nearly blown toward the end of my stay when he was driving me to a liquor store. He grazed the rear bumper of a station wagon traveling at considerable speed, and the driver stopped to examine the damage. Fortunately it was minimal, and he waved us on. It could have been a serious accident involving the police; had I been injured or required as a witness, the local newspaper might have secured a considerable scoop.

It is not impossible, in view of an event that I will describe later in this chapter, that MI6 and possibly MI5 already knew that I was with Wright and why. I did not suspect this at the time, but when any stranger called at Wright's house I ensured that I was not seen. I have to confess to having felt some element of conspiratorial apprehension during my stay with Wright and my visits there and back.

I had intended to stay for at least two weeks and possibly three, but after eight or nine days we were both mentally exhausted and I felt that I had secured the main information and that we were already tending to go over the same ground. I had also taken as much of the rough living as I felt inclined to do. I knew that, with information I already had, Wright's material would help to make a remarkable book, but I still had serious doubts about the problems of publishing it safely. Wright said that, if MI5 found out about the existence of the book in advance of publication, it would do everything possible to suppress it. But if the authorities could be presented with a *fait accompli*, they would accept it rather than create a public fuss. He said that I should take every step to ensure complete secrecy until publication day. Wright warned me that MI5 had avenues into publishing houses and, on occasion, had made use of eminent lawyers to secure advance proofs of books they had heard about.

It was clearly understood that I would be entirely responsible for writing the book and would not be referring to him concerning its format or any editorial matters. He did not ask to see a synopsis or expect to see and comment on parts of the book as it progressed, and I would not have been prepared to write the book under such circumstances. Nor were there any specific agreements or arrangements concerning expenditures that would clearly be necessary in checking the information he had given me and in securing additional information from other sources. As I was the sole author, in whom the copyright would be vested, it was clearly understood that the judgment and decisions on all editorial matters and additional research would be left entirely to my discretion.[8] He had never had a book published and knew nothing about the process.

I asked Wright what he would do if MI5 approached him, having got wind of the project. He said he would simply deny any involvement. These facts make nonsense of Wright's claim at the Sydney trial that he had sensed, when meeting me and Lord Rothschild, that he was being drawn into a deniable operation that had MI5's blessing. Had this been so, he would not have given me so many instructions for keeping the project secret from MI5. These included destroying original letters he sent me and making photocopies because they were more difficult to trace to an individual typewriter. He urged me to use plastic tape for sealing all the edges of envelopes. This would not stop MI5 from opening letters but we would be able to tell if they had done so. When communicating by letter, we should use accommodation names and addresses and write cryptically—not to fool MI5 but so that the contents would be meaningless to any ordinary person who might read a stray letter. He advised me not to bother to look for bugs in my home because I would never find them, MI5 being so professional in this respect.

Wright had also warned me not to put my notes in my main luggage because, if MI5 had got wind of my venture, they might ask the Heathrow customs officers to search my bags and do a quick photocopy of the notes, for which they had permanent facilities. I therefore posted the notes piece-meal in envelopes to accommodation addresses. Whether MI5 intercepted them and read them I shall never know.

My last words to Wright before his wife drove me to the airport were that, in view of all that he had provided and confirmed, I was not much of a writer if I could not place the book with a publisher and secure an advance that would give him the £5,000 he needed so urgently.

My wife and I left Australia for Hong Kong on October 22, and after spending one day in Hong Kong—where I made further arrangements for certain research into Hollis's Chinese days—we arrived in London on October 24.

On my return home, I learned from the housekeeper that telephone repairmen from the Post Office, which then ran the telephone system, had made an excuse to enter the house in my absence. They had insisted that the telephone was out of order, although the two lines had not been used in my absence. They examined the various telephones and extensions and spent a long time in the attic, which made no sense at all—if they were ordinary Post Office engineers. I took Wright's advice and did not look for the bugs but assumed that they were there, as they still may be. If bugs were planted then on behalf of either MI5 or MI6—I suspect the latter—the authorities knew of my visit to Wright before I reached him.

How could this have happened? Only too easily. For many months before meeting Wright, I had been in regular contact with a retired senior officer of MI6 and had discussed the Hollis case with him many times, especially after my briefing by Aitken. I knew he was in touch with his old office and expected that he would have warned MI6 of my interest. He knew that I was going to Australia at fairly short notice, ostensibly on holiday, and MI6 may have made the right deduction. It would seem to be more than coincidence that MI6, not MI5, later made the running regarding the book that was to be called *Their Trade Is Treachery*.

‖4‖

Secret Intervention: Enter MI6

An official secret is any official information which has not been officially released.

—Lord Normanbrook

On my return from Australia, I sought advice in various professional quarters and then went to prodigious effort and expense to check and extend the new information that Wright had given me. As I did not know Wright well and was aware of his mercenary motive, I could not safely assume that what he had told me was true. In view of this and of the need for speed, I engaged a professional researcher whom I knew I could trust with extremely confidential matters to assist me: my son Michael. Later events were to show that my prudence was justified.

Having confirmed most of Wright's information, I decided to write the book and attempt to have it published, even though I knew that, technically, it would offend the Official Secrets Act on every page. I accepted this risk as a routine

occupational hazard—a legal tightrope that British investigative writers in the secrets field walk almost every day. Although the Official Secrets Act is widely discredited, it is still a
technical offense merely to be in possession of official information that has not been officially released. So the genuine
investigative writer has no alternative but to operate in the
hope that, in a true democracy that prides itself on a free press,
the government will not move against him for discovering information by talking to people who have it, so long as his research does not involve seeing classified documents. This has
been accepted by every British government since the end of
World War II and is the basis of the background briefing and of
the submission of books and articles for clearance. In realistic
terms, in the 1980s, any credible offense for a genuine writer
lies in the publication of secret information, not in its possession. I therefore concluded that, provided that I omitted anything that could prejudice current operations or endanger
officers who were still serving, publication of the information I
had acquired could be regarded as being in the public interest.[1] I was also aware, of course, that such omissions would
reduce the risk of injunction.

Before I left Tasmania, Wright suggested that I use the
title he had in mind for his book, *The Cancer in Our Midst*,
but I rejected it as quite unsuitable. Instead, during the journey home from Australia, I decided on a title that was not only
apt and all-embracing but would give me some personal satisfaction. In 1964, MI5 had prepared a booklet for restricted
circulation among government officials with access to secret
information. Entitled *Their Trade Is Treachery*, it described,
with case records, the methods used by the Soviet bloc to trap
the unwary into serving as spies, saboteurs, and agents of influence. After securing a copy I wished to give its message wider
publicity, but MI5—acting through various Whitehall departments—did all it could to stop me, finally resorting to threat of
prosecution under the Crown copyright laws. So, as titles cannot be copyrighted, I decided to publish my own version of

Their Trade Is Treachery, with rather more detail of Soviet penetration of the secret services than MI5 had dared to reveal.

I took reasonable security precautions, in view of what appeared to be the surreptitious entry into my home by "telephone repairmen," and my wife and I took note of strange cars parked outside the house. Letters were carefully examined for signs that they had been opened. To judge from what was going on behind the scenes, without our knowledge, our fears were justified. There is, however, a limit to the deception techniques available to a lone investigative writer. I had to consult other retired secret service officers to check statements that Wright had made, and I was aware that they may have sensed that I was busy with a book and that they could have relayed their suspicions to MI5 and MI6, particularly the latter. In addition, it proved impracticable to make every telephone call from a telephone booth or a friend's house, although I made many that way; in any event, some of the incoming calls would have been highly significant to any eavesdropper.

These concerns, which occasionally loomed large during sleepless nights, would not have arisen had I been party to any deniable MI5 operation, as Wright eventually alleged.

I contacted William Armstrong, the managing director of my British publisher, Sidgwick and Jackson, toward the end of November and asked him, casually, how long it would take to produce a book from a finished manuscript. We then had a discussion about the book I had in mind. He was immediately interested. I prepared a detailed six-page synopsis of what I was writing, which is a standard requirement for a publisher, and this intensified his interest. He realized that it would breach the Official Secrets Act in a major degree but believed we could claim publication to be in the national interest because of the apparent persistent cover-up of Soviet penetration. We were also, of course, aware that the book could be a big seller and could enhance the reputation of both author and publisher.

Armstrong agreed with me that, if the book were submitted for clearance through the official channels, such as the secretary of Whitehall's D-Notice Committee, who would have passed it on to MI5, it would certainly be suppressed. The only way it could be published would be to print it secretly and suddenly offer it to the bookshops for sale.

In retrospect, I do not think that either of us was lacking in courage; we faced a situation that was unprecedented for both of us and we were alone. Because of the extent of the disclosures, prosecution was a distinct possibility and, as Armstrong recalled recently, "we indulged in some gallows humor as to where we might be incarcerated if an Official Secrets prosecution was successful." From previous experience, I was aware that the official reaction was likely to be sharp, since no MI5 officer had ever leaked in such a massive way before; in fact, the actual reaction was so intense that the Prime Minister, the Home Secretary, the Cabinet Secretary, and chiefs of the secret services became personally involved.

Armstrong was more immediately concerned about the heavy loss that the firm would sustain if an injunction were issued against publication and 10,000 books or more were impounded on publication day or sooner, should MI5 get wind of the project. [2]

We both knew that we desperately needed independent advice about the wisdom of proceeding, and we needed it in a hurry. There was no point in approaching an ordinary lawyer at that stage, as he would simply have told us what was already obvious. The requirement for absolute secrecy seemed to rule out securing advice from any other quarter. Eventually Armstrong suggested that we should seek it from one of the distinguished people who occasionally served Sidgwick and Jackson, in absolute confidentiality, as arbiters of taste and prudence concerning new book projects. The man he nominated happened to be an old and trusted friend of mine, with whom I had been involved professionally in the past on matters involving confidentiality, so I agreed with alacrity. I felt that, while his unquestionably wise advice might carry no weight in any eventual court action, I would probably sleep more soundly if it favored publication. I would not have been experiencing any of these very real fears had I been a witting party to any plot that had MI5's blessing.

Armstrong left me in no doubt that, if the advice was firmly against publication for legal reasons or on convincing grounds of national security, he would have to reject the book. I would then be free to seek another publisher, but I said that it was most unlikely that I would do so, because I would encounter the same problem. We agreed that we would accept the advice and resolve the dilemma, whichever way it went.

The person whom Armstrong consulted was told that we would both rely on his judgment and had put the fate of the book in his hands. He fully appreciated the heavy responsibility and accepted it only on condition that his involvement would be completely secret in the event of any court action or publicity. That condition still stands, and I will, therefore, refer to him simply as the Arbiter.

When given a verbal outline of the book, including the material concerning Hollis, by William Armstrong, the Arbiter expressed immediate concern about the danger that the book might pose to national security and to the government. He also believed that it might put Armstrong and me at real risk of prosecution. He therefore told Armstrong that he would need more information about the book before he could make a useful judgment.

On November 29, the Arbiter telephoned me at my home to discuss these concerns, which I did my best to allay. The following day I wrote to him explaining that the book's purpose was twofold: "to reveal the true extent of the insidious Russian and Communist effort to undermine British institutions and to show the supreme importance of effective Security and Intelligence organizations in combating this menace." I assured him that the book would deal with old history and that there would be no criticism of the present state of either MI5 or MI6. (Wright had convinced me, for reasons I will reveal later, that, after Hollis retired, MI5 was clean at the top, and I had no reason for any doubts about the leadership of MI6.) On December 3, William Armstrong asked me to prepare a synopsis outlining the main themes of the book, for him to show to the Arbiter. He advised me to leave out all mention of the Hollis case—which he regarded as the most sensitive and most interesting part of the book, and which he had already discussed with the Arbiter—in case anyone else might chance to see the synopsis.

On December 5, I posted William Armstrong a two-page synopsis which he sent to the Arbiter on December 8, 1980, with a brief letter confirming that they had discussed the Hollis affair previously. A further letter gave an assurance that, when the Arbiter eventually received a copy of the typescript of the book, I would be delighted to consult with him concerning any problems.

A provisional contract was then drawn up by Sidgwick and Jackson in such a way that Wright would receive 50 percent of the net profits on all book sales and serializations, to be paid directly by the publisher to a company representing Wright's interests. A clause stated that I, the sole author, was entitled to claim my editorial and research expenses, which would be deducted before the royalties were shared. This was an obvious requirement since my small company, Summerpage Ltd., to which my book and newspaper earnings were normally paid, would incur substantial overheads and other expenses involving libel insurance, travel (including the visit to Australia and other expeditions), research fees, and legal fees; there would also be expenses involved in the photographs and the promotion of the book. The expenses were to continue into 1982 and 1983 in connection with the paperback version, foreign editions, and a promising television project. It would have been quite inequitable for Wright to have been paid half the gross royalties when he was incurring no expense and no legal hassle or libel risk in the safety of Tasmania. Further, he had undertaken no liability for losses in the event that I was successfully sued for libel or prosecuted and heavily fined.

On Wright's instructions, which I had received in Tasmania to preserve his confidentiality, he was not named in the contract which, being something of a deception document, referred only to "consultants." The company representing his interest was an existing offshore organization named Overbridge International, based in Curaçao in the Netherlands Antilles.

Sidgwick and Jackson had no knowledge of Wright's involvement in *Their Trade Is Treachery* before the publicity of the Sydney trial in 1986. I was never asked about the identities of my sources and would not have revealed them anyway. Sidgwick and Jackson was also unaware that the Overbridge International arrangement had been organized by Lord Rothschild to ensure that the royalty share would eventually be paid into Wright's bank account at Huonville in Tasmania. Lord Rothschild had asked a colleague at Rothschild's bank to make the arrangement and then had had no further connection with it. Overbridge International was not a Rothschild company. This was normal banking practice in a case where a client, who was a friend, had requested complete confidentiality.

Lord Rothschild distanced himself from the project completely. He did not see a synopsis. He never saw the typescript or page proofs and never asked to see them. I did not brief him about the book in any way. Nor did Peter Wright ever correspond directly with him about *Their Trade Is Treachery*.[3] In fact, Lord Rothschild has told me that, since Wright visited him at Cambridge in September 1980, he has never heard from him or been in any kind of communication with him.

I had no contractual responsibility for the payments to Wright and no part in forwarding money to him. Other considerations apart, the receipt by me of any payments for Wright could have presented tax problems and occasioned explanations to the Inland Revenue involving Wright's identity.

The advance on royalties was fixed in the contract at

£30,000 specifically so that Wright could get the £5,000 he needed urgently. An advance is usually paid in three equal parts, the first being paid shortly after signature of contract. Five thousand pounds of the first installment came to me and £5,000 went to Wright. There were other consultants, but Wright was the only one who had insisted on payment. The contract was dated December 12, 1980, but it was not signed by me, and therefore did not become valid, until December 23.

While I was arranging the contract and before the publishers had time to pay the advance, I received frantic cables from Wright pleading extreme urgency but I ignored them. On one occasion, well-remembered by those who witnessed it, my wife appeared in the middle of a partridge drive on a shoot near my home clutching one of these prepaid cables, which had just arrived. After all his conspiratorial advice about secrecy, Wright was so pressed that he had risked sending an open cable, knowing that all cables are available for examination by the security authorities. Whether they spotted the cable and realized its significance I shall never know.

On seeing the two-page synopsis, the Arbiter had been even more concerned about the danger of publishing the book. He thought that William Armstrong and I might be deceiving ourselves about the public benefits of publication or were, at best, being too courageous—or too imprudent—for our own good, a view which turned out to be totally correct. By happenstance, he had a purely social friend in the secrets world called Sir Arthur Franks who by then was chief of the Secret Intelligence Service (MI6). The part played by Sir Arthur Franks has been officially revealed in documentary evidence submitted by the government during the Wright trial in 1986, has been commented on by the judge, and has been widely publicized by the media.[4]

The Arbiter took the opportunity of a social occasion to show Sir Arthur the two-page synopsis and to tell him about the Hollis implications, seeking guidance on a completely unofficial and totally confidential basis. He needed high-level professional assurance, from a friend with authority and whom he could trust completely, that the book would not be damaging either to the interests of the nation or to the government. He made it clear that he was acting on behalf of Sidgwick and Jackson and that, because of the deference paid to his views in the past, he was in a position to prevent publication of the book if there were serious objections to it. When explaining his initial action to me, much later, when I had learned about it from someone else, the Arbiter said, "You are a dear old friend of mine, but my country comes before my friends"—a sentiment that entirely accords with my own view of loyalty.[5]

Sir Arthur said that he could not offer a worthwhile view until he had seen the full text of the proposed book and, as the synopsis indicated that it would be wide-ranging, it might have to be shown to other experts for their opinion. The Arbiter took the point and, since no other solution to the task for which he had accepted responsibility was possible, he agreed to provide a copy when one became available.

Neither the Arbiter nor Sir Arthur Franks has revealed details of their extremely confidential conversations, but two facts crucial to the whole saga have emerged from documents and information disclosed during the Sydney trial.

Before he agreed to supply the typescript, the Arbiter secured some kind of understanding to ensure that neither I nor William Armstrong would be at personal risk if objection were made to the text. The Arbiter would effectively be submitting the material for official appraisal, and it is standard practice that when this happens the author concerned runs no risk of prosecution; otherwise texts would never be submitted. Sir Arthur Franks was, arguably, the most senior authority in the secret service world, and—should the law officers later disapprove of the way I had been virtually given immunity to prosecution for being in possession of secret information—his undertaking would have to stand. Quite fortuitously through a social contact, Franks had been presented with an opportunity of substantial potential benefit to the secret services and to the government, and he felt that he had no alternative but to accept it.

Second, from the moment that Sir Arthur Franks, the MI6 chief himself, became involved, the issue was automatically enveloped by official secrecy to a degree that prevented the Arbiter from telling either William Armstrong or me what had occurred, even though it had been done expressly in our interests. He, too, was entrapped in the web of secrecy. This must have caused him some disquiet, but secrecy had sealed his lips.

As indicated by a letter dated December 15, 1980, and produced to the court in Sydney almost exactly six years later, Franks told senior colleagues in MI6 and MI5 that Sidgwick and Jackson intended to publish a book by me about the security services in February or March 1981. A copy of the synopsis was sent to MI5 on December 15, perhaps the same day that MI6 had received it from Sir Arthur.[6] In doing this, MI6 was abiding by the established protocol. It is MI5, the Security Service, not MI6, the Secret Intelligence Service, that has responsibility for taking any action over security infringements. It is MI5 that has links to Scotland Yard's Special Branch in the event that any police action may be required.

MI5 and MI6 decided to keep the information "in house" until the typescript had been received and analyzed. No copy of the synopsis was sent to the Cabinet Office or anywhere else. This not unreasonable decision enabled Wright's lawyers and the media to accuse Sir Robert Armstrong of misleading the court in Sydney. At an early stage in the trial, Sir Robert stated, in all honesty, that he had first become aware of the existence of *Their Trade Is Treachery* in or about February 1981. He was later to make it clear that Franks, specifically, had not given him any early indication of the book. When asked if anyone else in the service of the government had known in late 1980 that I was writing a book about Hollis, he replied, "Not to my knowledge." He was telling the truth, but when a summary of documents that he had never seen was released near the end of the trial, showing that MI6 had a synopsis of the book in December 1980, it was inferred that he had lied. It would not be the last time that he would pay a personal penalty for the requirements of official secrecy.

The fact that the authorities received only the two-page synopsis is significant evidence that neither MI5 nor MI6 had been party to the inception of *Their Trade Is Treachery*. Had they been, I would have ensured that they saw the full six-page synopsis, which was never seen by anyone but William Armstrong and me. In the Sydney trial, Wright's lawyer, Turnbull, was to argue that the synopsis seen by the authorities was worded in such a way as to assure them that the book would not be excessively critical, but it never occurred to me that they would see it. The six-page synopsis, of which copies still exist, was anything but reassuring to either MI5 or MI6.

I wrote the book at great speed, incorporating Wright's information with what I already knew. My son and I checked whatever we could with other sources. On December 23, I wrote to William Armstrong telling him I was "nearing the end of my labors," and he appointed his senior editor, Margaret Willes, to edit the book, with instructions that she had to work on it at home and that the copy must not be brought into the office. I delivered the typescript to Margaret Willes on January 13, with the proviso that deletions and changes would, no doubt, be required by the lawyer. I recall that Margaret told me she was keeping it locked in her wardrobe.

The book was known only as Project P. Lord Longford, then Chairman of Sidgwick and Jackson, read the text and bet William Armstrong "a medium-priced bottle of medium-quality sherry" that news of the project and some of its contents would leak. Armstrong was to collect on the bet, although in reality Longford had won it.[7]

A full, edited typescript, with the required legal changes, became available to the Arbiter early in February 1981 and, as promised, he passed it to Franks via an intermediary who called for it.[8]

The clear understanding was that, if there were serious objections to the book, the Arbiter would give the publisher such an adverse opinion that the book would be rejected. There was no question of the need for an injunction or legal action of any kind.

When selected MI6 officers studied the typescript, they quickly realized that much of the information must have come from members or former members of the security and intelligence services. Having noted—with some relief and, perhaps, satisfaction—that the strictures on MI5 were far greater than those on MI6, they made photocopies and passed one to MI5 without further delay.

As soon as the typescript reached the secret services, it became subject to the "need-to-know" restriction that applies in all properly run organizations dealing with secret matters. It is generally accepted by almost all intelligence officers whom I have questioned that, when Sir Arthur Franks was in charge of MI6, it was run with competence. So it can safely be assumed that only those there who needed to know the contents of the typescript were allowed to see it.

Sources of information are absolutely sacrosanct in intelligence work because they are its lifeblood; and though the Arbiter was probably unaware of it, he was, inevitably, treated as a secret source. This meant that his identity could never be revealed to anybody who had no need to know it. Few, if any, needed to know it, and the evidence of the Sydney court was to show that few, if any, were told.

These events, occasioned by men of the highest integrity who were doing what they had been trained to do for proper, patriotic motives, inadvertently spun the first viscid threads of the trapping zone of the web of secrecy begun by Wright and me in Cambridge and Tasmania.

Meanwhile, I had contacted my old colleague, Andrew Edwards, the legal manager of Express Newspapers, with whom I had negotiated on libel and Official Secrets issues over many years. Andrew, who was to figure in the publicity surrounding the Wright affair as the "mystery lawyer," lunched with me in London on January 7 so that I could brief him about the book and ask him if he would vet it, which he kindly agreed to do. On January 18, I journeyed down to Edwards's home, near Frome, Somerset, taking the typescript with me. He insisted on the removal of many names of living people known to have been involved with Soviet agents, because my sources could not give evidence in the event of a libel action. The deletions included Michael Straight, Leo Long (later a self-confessed spy), Alister Watson (an almost certain Soviet agent), and Flora Solomon (a friend of Philby's who eventually betrayed him). The removal of these names weakened the book considerably, but I had already devised ways of securing the quick disclosure of some of these identities once the book was published, as I will explain later.

Though I had omitted all material that I felt might be prejudicial to current or future intelligence operations, I appreciated that the book still offended the Official Secrets Act on almost every page. Edwards realized this, too, and said that, as I was the one at risk, I would have to make the decision on that score. He said that, as far as the operation of the Official Secrets Act was concerned, nobody in the law or anywhere else had as much day-to-day experience at operating within it successfully as I. Edwards agreed with me that the odds were against suppression if the book could reach publication without falling into the hands of MI5. He judged that, in the current political climate, any action by the government was most unlikely because the material was historical and care had been taken to avoid giving any information that was not already known to the Russians, while the criticisms were in the public interest.[9] Nevertheless, with all the responsibility on my shoulders, I felt more inclined than ever to accept the advice of the Arbiter, whatever it might prove to be.

In his report submitted to William Armstrong on February 6, 1981, Edwards remarked with regard to official secrets: "It is not really a question of law at all. It is a matter of judgement. There is an increasing feeling among responsible people that the public has a right to know within limits what is going on. I share that view. I do not believe that publication will do any damage to the country and I would be surprised if the book did any more than to cause annoyance in some official quarters."

Edwards later went to the office of Sidgwick and Jackson to discuss the report. The results satisfied William Armstrong and the others involved.

In the event that the book went ahead, Sidgwick and Jackson had meanwhile taken the initiative in trying to sell the serial rights of the book for publication shortly in advance of the book's appearance, which is standard practice. Because of the immediate news value of the material, it was not possible to put the book out to several newspapers for competitive offers. William Armstrong, who took responsibility for disposing of all serial rights, favored the *Daily Mail*, and a lunch, which I attended, was set up with the editor of that newspaper, David English. He expressed immediate enthusiasm, and once he read the typescript he must have taken the view that publication was in the national interest. A letter from me to Armstrong dated January 23, 1981, shows that a contract with the *Daily Mail* had been signed but, presumably, could be canceled without penalty if the book had to be suppressed. I was not involved in the financial negotiations, but the *Daily Mail* wanted me to concern myself, journalistically, in the day-to-day presentation of the material in the newspaper.

The *Daily Mail* must have been supplied with printed page proofs as soon as these were ready, and—as it was repeatedly stated in the Sydney court that the security authorities obtained page proofs (as well as the earlier typescript)—journalists have suspected that the secret services obtained these from the *Daily Mail*. According to the judgment in the Sydney court case, Sir Robert Armstrong asserted that neither the typescript nor the page proofs had been stolen. So did the *Daily Mail* supply page proofs voluntarily after a request from the security authorities? In retrospect, I must say that the newspaper's behavior was odd. I was in the *Daily Mail* office day after day helping to prepare and oversee the serialization, yet the lawyers did not seem to query anything concerning the Official Secrets Act. This was remarkable because the *Daily Mail* was to be the first publisher; in the event of legal action, it would have been impossible for Sidgwick and Jackson to be prosecuted without the newspaper's being charged as well.

It now seems certain, however, that the *Daily Mail* did not supply the security authorities with any documents or information. Sir David English, who remains editor, has assured me that he and his senior staff were quite unaware that the authorities had possession of the text in any form. The newspaper's lawyers had taken the view that, since no secret documents were quoted in *Their Trade Is Treachery*, the Official Secrets Act was not being infringed. "We just decided to print it because it was a good story," Sir David wrote.[10]

Page proofs could not have been obtained from *The Times*, because they were never supplied to that newspaper, which simply reprinted, one day later, what appeared in the *Daily Mail* under second serial rights.

It remains remotely possible that MI5 obtained a set of page proofs surreptitiously from some source, but various witnesses in the Sydney trial were probably in error in talking about page proofs at all. The typescript and page proofs seem to have been confused in witnesses' minds. Whether the authorities received printed page proofs or not is quite academic, however. The typescript provided them with all they needed to know, and it was with respect to the typescript that the truly fateful decisions were made.

I was particularly pleased and relieved by the *Daily Mail's* purchase of the serial rights. It would clearly be difficult for the government to prosecute Sidgwick and Jackson and me because the *Daily Mail* would be the first publisher, and I thought that the government would be loath to prosecute one of its major supporters and its editor.

Meanwhile, as I continued to beaver away, complacently confident that we had deceived the security authorities, events involving the chiefs of MI5, MI6, and others of the highest rank were unfolding in the most rarefied areas of Whitehall.

‖ 5 ‖

A Perilous Web of Secrecy

The easiest person to deceive is one's self.

—Bulwer-Lytton

Afterward copies of the text of *Their Trade Is Treachery* had been studied by senior officers of both MI6 and MI5, and before any outside officials were told about it, the legal advisers to those services, who are full-time career officers, were asked for their opinion as to what could be done.[1] As evidenced by a summary of documents eventually produced in the Sydney court on December '10, 1986, "it was generally agreed that there would be no point in trying to encourage specific deletions or changes in the text."[2] No reasons were given for this view in the summary, but they were obvious. If the authorities were going to object at all, they would have to object to the whole book—which they certainly could have done because the Arbiter had assured Sir Arthur Franks that, if there were serious objections, he could ensure that Sidgwick and Jackson would not publish it.[3]

It was decided, mainly by the legal advisers and, later, with the agreement of the Treasury Solicitor, that it was not in the interests of MI5 and MI6 that the book should be restrained.[4] These authorities believed that to restrain the book would require an injunction, and they could not risk entering into legal argument that might expose the source of the typescript. This conclusion was to mystify the judge in the Wright trial in Sydney and many others. Why was it reached?

After an exhaustive study of all the available evidence, I regard it as certain that the legal advisers and the Treasury Solicitor had not been told exactly how the typescript had been obtained. They had no "need to know" the identity of the source who had supplied the text, and it was, I believe, withheld from them for this reason. Nor would they have pressed to be told it—knowledge of the identity of sources being so inviolate. For sound security reasons, MI6 and MI5 have never been in the habit of revealing their sources to one another, and when MI6 passed the text to MI5 for action, information as to how it had been obtained would almost certainly have been restricted to a statement that the circumstances precluded any restraint. This strict limitation would also have extended to the Director General of MI5 who, knowing how he himself would behave in such a situation, would not have sought the identity of the source.

During his cross-examination in the Sydney court, Sir Robert Armstrong made a highly significant statement to the effect that, in any legal action to secure an injunction against *Their Trade Is Treachery*, MI5 officials would need to be more specific about the source "*than they were in a position to be.*" I believe, therefore, that the legal advisers only knew that the typescript had been obtained without my knowledge or the knowledge of Sidgwick and Jackson's managing director and that, in the process, some kind of commitment not to take any action against us had been made and had to be honored to protect the source. As they were aware of the kinds of subterfuges used to obtain such documents in the past, they could be excused if they assumed that the typescript had been obtained surreptitiously and, perhaps, illicitly.

Once the legal advisers had made up their minds, about ten photocopies of the typescript were made and passed to a few other interested parties, again in extreme secrecy. These included the Cabinet Secretary, Sir Robert Armstrong, who later confirmed in the Australian court that he had a copy early in February, supplied to him by MI5, not by MI6.[5] Sir Robert was told, orally, by an MI5 official only that the typescript had been obtained *"on conditions which made it impossible to take any action about it."* This fact, later revealed in the summary of relevant documents submitted to the court in Sydney, is evidence that the Arbiter had protected William Armstrong and me, as described in the last chapter.[6]

As Sir Robert was at pains to point out in the court, the inability to take action did not necessarily mean legal action, but any kind of restraint. The authorities could not, of course, ask Armstrong or me to abandon the book without letting us know that they had it, and the legal advisers insisted that this could not be done without prejudicing the identity of the source of the typescript. They argued that, if I knew they had the text, I would make efforts to discover how they had acquired it. And not knowing the true identity of the source or why he had provided it, they assumed that, if my efforts were successful, the source might be in danger of being exposed and might suffer professionally.

The judge in the Sydney trial, Justice Powell, could not understand why the authorities had not "hot-footed it to the Law Courts to secure an injunction" as soon as the typescript became available. Sir Robert and the Treasury Solicitor's representatives, who were in court, were not in a position to explain the peculiar circumstances that had made that impossible.

Sir Robert's statement to the court that no restraint of any kind was possible, though made in good faith through ignorance, was grossly misleading. All that was needed to stop the book in its tracks was a telephone call or a letter to the Arbiter, whose very purpose in submitting the typescript had been to give the authorities the chance to veto it if they could convince him that it would be seriously damaging. Clearly Sir Robert, who consistently gave evidence to the best of his belief, could not have known that simple fact, as he was to confirm, emphatically, in the High Court in London in 1987. He, too, had not "needed to know" how the typescript had been obtained and so he had not been told—the golden rule governing the ultrasecrecy of sources being applied even at his level. This was made clear in the early stages of Sir Robert's cross-examination in the Sydney court when, on being asked how the text had been obtained, he replied, under oath, "I don't know where it had come from." Later, he indicated that the source had not been exposed publicly or to him.

The identity of the person who had been detailed to brief Sir Robert about *Their Trade Is Treachery* shortly before its publication early in 1981 is unknown to me, but it was revealed in the Sydney court case and confirmed later in the High Court in London, that he was from MI5, not MI6, so he could not have been Sir Arthur Franks. Once the text had been passed to MI5, it was MI5's proper responsibility to sort out the problem and, having reached a conclusion, to pass it to the Cabinet Secretary as a recommendation for action by the senior ministers responsible. This means that it is unlikely that Sir Arthur had any direct dealings with Sir Robert on the issue and was not put in a position where he could be asked about the source or had any reason to volunteer it. He is not the kind of man who would try to gain personal credit with the Cabinet Secretary for securing the typescript. Once the text had been passed to MI5, he remained distant from the action, as he was entitled to do. Later he was to be criticized by politicians for doing so.

There is no evidence that Sir Robert was ever even aware of Sir Arthur Franks's personal involvement. All his dealings were with MI5, which would be unwilling to volunteer any suggestion that the credit for obtaining the typescript belonged to MI6. So Sir Robert had no reason to question Sir Arthur about the circumstances when they happened to confer about other issues.

Sir Robert's MI5 informant had not been told exactly how the typescript had been secured and so was not in a position to tell him. The evidence indicates that Sir Robert was only told that certain conditions made any action impossible, and (not unnaturally at that stage) he, too, assumed that the text had probably been obtained in some surreptitious way that had to be concealed. He may not even have been told then that MI6 had originally secured the text. Clearly, if Sir Robert did not know how the book had been obtained when questioned in court about it in 1986, he could not have been told when briefed in 1981. This situation, engendered by the rules of secrecy, was to prove extremely damaging to Sir Robert.

As I was to discover soon after the book's publication, various former officers and senior civil servants named in the book, including the previous Cabinet Secretary, Lord Hunt of Tanworth, had also been given copies of the typescript to read under conditions of secrecy so that they could comment on it.

While the arrangements ruled out any action against me or Sidgwick and Jackson, they did not preclude action against my informants, and inquiries were set in motion by both MI5 and MI6 to discover the sources of the information I had used in the book. The summary of documents submitted by the government to the Sydney court revealed that, on or about February 12, 1981, Sir Robert Armstrong and the Home Office were told that the information in the book must have come from former MI5 and MI6 officers. By March 12, "several sources had been identified but it was stated in writing by an officer of the service [presumably MI5] that the service was a long way from obtaining hard, usable evidence on sources." In fact a former officer who had been in touch with Sir Dick

White, a retired chief of both MI5 and MI6, told me that as soon as Sir Dick had read the typescript he had remarked, "It has to be Peter Wright!"

The senior serving officers of MI5 should have been even quicker on the ball because they had been warned in writing by Lord Rothschild that Wright had "gone bad" and was preparing a book.

Sir Robert is on record in the Sydney court as saying that no attempt was made to interview any of the suspected informants before the book was published. Arthur Martin, the retired MI5 officer living in Britain, was an obvious suspect, as was Stephen de Mowbray, another retired officer who had been deeply involved in the Hollis case, although neither had ever met me or given me any information. Why were they not interviewed before the book was published? Why was no attempt made to interview me?

These questions also puzzled the judge in the Sydney court case. The answer would seem to be obvious. Everything had to be subservient to one overriding consideration: nobody outside a very small charmed circle in the security-intelligence world—and it may have been only one, Sir Arthur Franks himself—could be allowed to know the secret of how the book had been obtained in advance, although it could hardly have been more prosaic. A solemn promise had been given to the source, and it had to be kept. To have set inquiries in motion before its publication could have prejudiced that secret. They did not come to see me and warn me of any damage that they believed the book might inflict because that would have revealed that they already had the typescript, and I would then have begun a search to find out how they had acquired it. This belief was confirmed by Sir Robert during his cross-examination in the Sydney court, when he repeatedly explained that Sidgwick and Jackson and I had to be kept in ignorance "to protect the confidentiality of the source."

The same argument applied to the suspected informants because, if they had really been my sources, they could have warned me about what was happening. Wright would almost certainly have done so, and there was little to be gained from approaching him at that stage because no legal action could be taken against him, since he was outside the jurisdiction of the British courts.[7]

Further, once a decision had been made that suppression of the book was not possible, there was no hurry to discover the sources. The summary given to the Sydney court gave the impression that by March 12, 1981, when several sources had already been identified, the legal authorities of MI5 and MI6 reckoned that there was no action they could take without being absolutely sure about them. This, again, was inadvertently misleading because, had they been aware of it, they did not need to know anything to stop the book. Like almost everyone else, the legal authorities were stumbling about in the fog of secrecy.

The Attorney General of Great Britain was excluded from all the considerations so far described. Why? If the legal advisers of MI5 and MI6 had wanted an injunction to restrain the book, they would have needed to consult the Attorney General because his agreement would have been essential. But as they had been told that legal action was impossible, there was no point in involving him. He was, therefore, another individual with no "need to know" the circumstances, and he was not told them. Franks was to confirm to me personally on September 16, 1982, that "prosecution was never on."[8] The Attorney General might also have been incensed at learning that, because of the consequences of secrecy, I had been effectively given immunity from prosecution.[9]

Did the secret service legal advisers fear that the Attorney General might require an injunction that could lead to the exposure of the source? I doubt it. The transcript of the Sydney trial shows that, in retrospect in 1986, Sir Michael Havers thought that the recommendation against any restraint made by the legal advisers in 1981 was reasonable. This was his view even though he still did not know the identity of the source. So there are no grounds for believing that he would have disagreed with it in 1981, had he been consulted.

A further possible factor, associated with the Blunt case, may have strengthened the resolve of MI5 and MI6 to exclude Havers from the deliberations. When it had seemed that Blunt was going to sue Andrew Boyle for £100,000 in libel damages for indicating that he had been a Russian spy, Havers had told MI5 that a representative would have to appear and tell the truth. The MI5 management made it clear that they would not do so but would even stand mutely aside while Blunt collected his money rather than involve themselves in any court action that could lead to damaging admissions on their part. Havers had then induced the Prime Minister to read the famous statement confirming that Blunt had indeed been a spy and had confessed it. The MI5 management was furious, claiming that their promise to Blunt had been broken and that it would inhibit further spies from confessing. Even Peter Wright thought that Mrs. Thatcher's statement was "outrageous." To have brought Havers into the secret deliberations was, perhaps, to risk bringing in an independent spirit who might demand to know too much.

In view of what has since happened to Sir Robert's credibility and reputation in the Australian court, it seems unfortunate that no effort was made to ask whether the source of the typescript would have been willing to be identified confidentially to the few top people involved. The opportunity for such a simple and sensible solution was not allowed to arise because protocol, the "paramount need for secrecy," and the general mystique of the secret services had taken control of events. Total anonymity might not have been as essential as was assumed. I feel sure that the Arbiter would not have minded if senior people in the secret services of the government had been told because his motive was entirely patriotic and well-intentioned to all concerned. He, of course, was in no position to take any initiative because he had no idea of what was going on. Under the rules of secrecy, he had no "need to know" anything until a formal decision had been reached by ministers.

From the evidence dragged out of Sir Robert Armstrong in the Sydney court, it is now known that, finally, a high-level and very secret meeting was called to give the news of my impending book to the few politicians who were judged to have a "need to know." It was held at Number 10 Downing Street, probably in the Cabinet Room, in late February or early March 1981. Present were the Prime Minister (Margaret Thatcher), the Home Secretary (William Whitelaw), Sir Robert Armstrong, the Director General of MI5, and at least one other senior MI5 officer—an imposing collection of intellects with a wealth of experience and authority. Notably absent again was the Attorney General, Sir Michael Havers.[10] This exclusion spun another strand of the web of secrecy which was to entrap both the Cabinet Secretary and the Attorney General, most damagingly, in the Sydney court almost six years later.

The meeting had been called by Sir Robert Armstrong as a result of his discussions with his MI5 informant, and the decision to exclude the Attorney General was probably made during those discussions. In his evidence at the Sydney trial, Sir Robert confessed he had assumed that, before the legal advisers gave him their considered view, they had consulted the Attorney General and convinced him that there was no basis to restrain publication of the book. He therefore believed, not only that the Attorney General had approved the course of action proposed by MI5, but that, in doing so, the Attorney General had formally taken on the responsibility for it. This was a reasonable explanation of why he did not ask Havers to the meeting, but he had made a totally false assumption that was to shatter his credibility in the Sydney trial. Again, excessive secrecy was at the root of it. The meeting was judged to be so secret that no notes were ever made of it, and Sir Robert was unable to refresh his memory by consulting documents before he left for Sydney.

When Havers eventually learned that a decision about
Their Trade Is Treachery had been made without his participa-
tion, he followed protocol on secret matters and refrained
from demanding any explanation. As recently as late December 1986, nobody had ever explained to Havers why he
had been excluded, as he told me during a conversation in
which he asked me for an assurance that the typescript had not
been obtained by illegal means.[11]

To understand what happened at the Downing Street
meeting and to appreciate why it happened, one must put
oneself in the position of the people involved and appreciate
the extent of their honest ignorance of the facts.

Sir Robert told the meeting that a senior MI5 officer had
informed him that the legal advisers to MI5 and MI6, who had
consulted the Treasury Solicitor, had concluded that there was
no basis for restraining *Their Trade Is Treachery*.[12] Sir Robert
had been told only that the typescript had been obtained under
conditions that precluded prosecution, injunction, or any
other action about it. The explanation he apparently gave to
the meeting was that the government, meaning the administration, could not possibly admit that it had the text of the
book, erroneously suggesting that it had been obtained surreptitiously by one of the secret services. I believe that this was an
honest error and that Sir Robert made this reasonable assumption because he was not told how the typescript had been secured. It is possible that he was deliberately misled by his MI5
informant, who had been instructed to be economical with the
truth in the interests of preserving secrecy, but it is much more
likely that the MI5 informant did not know the truth himself.
It was therefore assumed by the politicians present that the
typescript had been obtained by secret (and possibly illegal)
means that had to be concealed at all costs. As Sir Robert
Armstrong was to tell the Sydney court, the authorities went to
"desperate lengths" to protect the name of the supplier of the
typescript, suggesting that he or she might be in trouble if it
leaked. What seemed to be in the minds of those at the meet-

ing was the possibility that the typescript had been stolen by MI5 or provided by an employee of the publisher who might be fired if exposed.

By the time Sir Robert appeared in the court action in Sydney in 1986, he had been assured that the typescript was not obtained by illegal means, but he did not know this when he addressed the top-level meeting at Number 10 early in 1981.

This may offer a further reason why the Attorney General was not present. If Sir Robert believed that the typescript had been obtained by an illicit method, he would have considered it improper for the Attorney General to participate in a discussion based on such an operation because he would then have become a party to it.

The meeting was not told that the book could still be stopped in its tracks simply by a message to the Arbiter, because no one present knew that. The Arbiter knew nothing about the meeting or its purpose until he read about it in newspaper reports of the Sydney trial in 1986.

Everyone at the meeting had already been assured that the book would inflict damage on Britain's security and intelligence interests. The Prime Minister had read a summary and extracts of the more contentious parts of it and knew the problem she faced in Parliament concerning the Hollis case. They all agreed, therefore, that it was preferable that the book not be published—a view I would have taken in their position.[13] Nevertheless these most senior people, including the Iron Lady herself, meekly accepted the MI5 recommendation passed on by Sir Robert. As he later put it to the court in Sydney, unanimous agreement "emerged" that publication of the book should not be restrained.[14]

The distinguished participants were then reminded of the need for extreme secrecy because of the way in which the book had been obtained.[15] This is evidence that none of those present knew how it had really been secured. The meeting and its conclusions were regarded as a deniable operation but proved

not to be once Sir Robert was under oath in court in a situation
that had not been foreseen. The fact that no minutes were
taken was fortunate for the government when Wright's lawyers
asked for them in 1986.[16]

Why did these powerful figures allow themselves to be
convinced, against their better judgment, and to be overborne
by advice that is now known to have been unsoundly based
and misleading? The factor that conditioned the ultimate decision is clear: politicians, however exalted, and civil servants,
however senior, will almost always defer to the view of MI5
and MI6 because of the mystique attaching to those departments. If the managements of MI5 and MI6 insist that a
course of action is in their interests, and that the paramount
need for secrecy prevents them from explaining why, that view
will almost always be accepted without argument—"in the interests of national security."

The managements were determined that the undertaking
given by Sir Arthur Franks to his unknown source should be
honored; and the Prime Minister and the Home Secretary,
who would have to deal with the inevitable consequences in
Parliament, do not seem to have required a fuller explanation.
Sir Robert Armstrong, who was opposed to publication himself, told the court that he did not query the view of the legal
advisers or take any steps to test it.[17] His evidence at the Sydney trial indicates that he accepted the advice because he
mistakenly believed that it had the Attorney General's
endorsement and protocol forbade that he should query a law
officer's decision.

The Prime Minister and the Home Secretary, while
strongly opposed to publication of the book, were overborne by
Sir Robert's purveyance of the legal advice, seemingly with
little argument.

I can find no evidence that those present at the meeting
were ever told that a likely alternative to a book by me was a
book by Wright himself. Had that occurred to them, it could
have been a factor influencing their decision because, from

what has been said since—in the court by Sir Robert Armstrong and in the House of Commons by the Prime Minister and the later Home Secretary, Douglas Hurd—it was generally accepted that there is a major difference between books written by outsiders and books written by members of the Security Service. Outsiders have not signed the Official Secrets Act, are under no bond of confidentiality, and do not carry the authenticity and credibility of former officers.

In the Sydney court case, Malcolm Turnbull, Wright's lawyer, called the Downing Street meeting a "conspiracy" that had the intention of ensuring the publication of my book. Nothing could have been further from the truth. Those taking part in a conspiracy must know what they are doing and why they are doing it. Those involved in the Downing Street meeting knew neither. There were no "conspirators": the only villain was secrecy, which blinded and deceived everybody.

It remains to be asked why the legal advisers of MI5 and MI6 had become so adamant that the book could not be restrained. In the first place, they had been told that legal action would not be possible because of the way in which the typescript had been obtained, although the precise details of that event were not explained to them and they were unaware that there was a simple way out of all the difficulties. Then, like anyone else in a similar position, they had searched for possible advantages in what appeared to be an adverse situation, and one was immediately obvious.

Ever since Jonathan Aitken's letter to the Prime Minister about the Hollis case in January 1980, the MI5 management had been aware that the story would break somewhere, perhaps in America, and had been waiting for the inevitable. The legal advisers were also aware, from Aitken's discussions with Arthur Martin, that journalists such as Duncan Campbell of the *New Statesman*, a left-wing crusading libertarian, were on the Hollis trail.

Second, the secret services' managements must have made contingency plans for dealing with such a break, and when they saw the typescript of *Their Trade Is Treachery* they knew that the moment had arrived. Unable to prevent or delay publication, they could console themselves that, at least, they knew in advance exactly what was coming and could make some dispositions. They knew, from my long Fleet Street record, that I was not politically suspect and that my intention was to improve intelligence and security, not to weaken it. I was told later by an MI6 officer that the security authorities took the view that, if publicity was inevitable, they would prefer that I should be the author.

Unlike the politicians, they knew that Wright intended to produce a book one day, if he survived, and a book by me was infinitely preferable—even if Wright had been a major source. With *Their Trade Is Treachery* disclosing so much, it would probably be several years before Wright could produce a salable book under his own name, and during that time he might die. A book by any investigative writer who refrained from naming his sources could be dismissed as speculation, as is standard practice with Whitehall leaks. The authorities could see that I had been at great pains to hide the identity of my sources, and my record showed that I would be unlikely to reveal them, even if hard-pressed.

A former MI6 officer told me that the advisers thought that, if a legal injunction had been possible, I and my publisher would have fought it in the courts, and that the MI5 and MI6 managements would have had to make too many damaging admissions about the contents of the book for their comfort. They feared that, in the event of a court case, the identity of the source who had supplied them with the typescript of *Their Trade Is Treachery* might have been revealed. In fact no such action by me or Sidgwick and Jackson was ever likely. It may not seem very courageous, but when a writer does not belong to a wealthy institution (as I did when I worked for Beaverbrook Newspapers but did not when I wrote *Their Trade Is Treachery*), he is unwise to take on governments.

I know that Sir Arthur Franks (and probably others) feared that, if Sidgwick and Jackson rejected the book, I might secure another publisher. This had been suggested to Franks by the Arbiter, even though I had assured William Armstrong that I would not continue to pursue publication if the Arbiter's opinion was negative. According to Sir Robert Armstrong's evidence to the High Court in London in 1987, the authorities seemed convinced that I would secure another publisher, and this factor added extra weight to their decision against trying to restrain the book. In fact, it was most unlikely, because I would have been duty-bound to tell a new publisher why Sidgwick and Jackson had withdrawn, and we would have faced the same problems. The authorities would, at least, have secured a breathing spell of several months by preventing Sidgwick and Jackson from publishing, and during that time they might have secured other information to use as grounds for a threat of prosecution under the Official Secrets Act, which might have frightened off any other publisher.

The legal advisers may also have believed that, in the event of the book's being stopped, there was nothing to prevent my releasing the information piecemeal in newspaper articles—not necessarily under my name—over a long period of time. It would have been difficult, if not impossible, to issue injunctions against several different newspapers. On the other hand, if the material appeared all at once, it might be a nine-day wonder—as, initially, it proved to be—whereas a long series of leaks through the media could keep the issues going for months.

While there could be some advantage in having all the secret service skeletons exposed in one swoop, suggestions that the book was initiated and engineered by MI5 to secure that result, as were made later in the Australian court and in the press, are preposterous. The idea that senior MI5 officers took the initiative to force the Prime Minister into agreeing that they should reveal their own extremely embarrassing secrets,

and that she should concur, is either the product of a strange
mentality or a deliberate concoction. Even the judge in the
Australian trial dismissed the concept.

In November 1986, the left-wing reporter, David Leigh,
who was covering the Sydney trial, wrote of an alleged plot by
intelligence officers that led Mrs. Thatcher to authorize MI5's
biggest leak. The story, which headed the *Observer*'s front
page, was inaccurate in almost all respects—partly due to ignorance, and partly due to half-truths deriving from some outside source.[18] Even the "mystery lawyer," Andrew Edwards,
who had no connection whatsoever with the secret services,
was dragged into the "plot" which never existed. All those involved in the decisions about *Their Trade Is Treachery* were
doing what they thought was best for their departments and for
the common good within their limited knowledge.

Shortly after the Downing Street meeting, the Arbiter was
told that there were no objections to Sidgwick and Jackson's
going ahead with publication without any deletions. He regarded the message as official approval, although he received
nothing in writing and, as is customary in the secret world,
was given no explanation. Both MI5 and MI6 had been
mightily relieved to find that there was nothing in the book
that they did not already know.

By his prudent and patriotic action, the Arbiter had
achieved the best of both worlds: he had secured safe publication of the book, after giving the authorities every opportunity
to suppress it if they so desired. Being bound to secrecy, he
simply let William Armstrong know that, after very careful
deliberation, weighing the advantages and the risks, he was
confident that publication would not damage the national
interest.

Armstrong and I were greatly encouraged. Events would
show, however, that, owing to the baneful effects of excessive
secrecy, the legal advisers' decision and its acceptance by civil
servants and ministers were generally disastrous. Both MI5
and MI6 got the worst of both worlds: a mass of disclosures

accusing them of incompetence and treachery, immediately followed by a Security Commission inquiry neither service wanted that revealed serious weaknesses in their precautions against Soviet penetration.[19] Sir Robert Armstrong was eventually to be sent to the Australian court not knowing the truth and, consequently, misleading it in ways that came to light during the trial and damaged both him and the government's case. The Attorney General was to suffer grievous damage to his reputation and even to his health. The government was to be accused in the court of having been party to a conspiracy to secure publication of *Their Trade Is Treachery*, with the judge commenting that what the government seemed to have done was very close to authorizing publication.

Further, it seems likely that, if my book had been suppressed, Wright would never have gone to court about *Spycatcher* in Australia. The original lawyers for Wright and Heinemann advised that the case could not be won; it was only when Turnbull conceived the ingenious idea of arguing the case that the government had acquiesced and even conspired to permit publication of my book that it went ahead. Without the Australian case, there would have been no international publicity; and without that, it might have been difficult to find an American publisher for the memoirs of a relatively minor British counterespionage officer, especially since his information had already been published.

As a result of the Downing Street meeting, the government faced the question of how to deal with *Their Trade Is Treachery* when it appeared. As Sir Robert Armstrong confirmed in the Australian court, the book was a "bombshell"; there had never been such a hemorrhage of secrets. So the objective was to achieve damage control by making the book appear to be speculative and inaccurate—in short, to "rubbish" it. The Prime Minister was provided with a summary of MI5's estimate of the damage the book would cause. Another extremely secret meeting was called, with the Attorney General present, and the Sydney trial evidence shows that there was general confidence that a statement made with Mrs. Thatcher's authority would counter much of the damage.

The draft of a Prime Ministerial statement was discussed by all the departments concerned.[20] This would mean MI5, MI6, GCHQ, the Home Office, the Cabinet Office, the Prime Minister's Office, and the Attorney General's Office. Sir Michael Havers was personally involved in preparing the statement and, once again following the rules of secrecy, did not ask why the book was not being restrained. He read the typescript and, being averse to the unnecessary censorship of investigative writers, was not opposed to the decision that it could be published. The treasury solicitors were also concerned. Some of the retired people to whom photocopies of the typescript had been sent, such as Lord Hunt of Tanworth, Sir Dick White, and Sir Michael Hanley, a former Director General of MI5, may also have offered advice.

The statement for the Prime Minister, which I shall deal with in chapter 7, must have been drawn up well in advance because Mrs. Thatcher was abroad during the few days before she made it.

An MI5 study of the typescript had shown that I was in error about some details of the Trend Report. Wright, who had given evidence to Trend, had told me that he was under the strong impression that Trend believed there was an a priori case against Hollis, and I reported that. Wright had misinterpreted Trend's remarks. I certainly erred in stating carelessly that Trend had spent only a few weeks on the case, when Aitken had told me that he had spent about a year on it. It was therefore decided to concentrate the discrediting attacks on that area and to decline to comment specifically on any other part, using the usual shield of the national interest.

As Sir Robert Armstrong admitted in the Australian court, the statement to be read by the Prime Minister was drawn up in the greatest secrecy; as with the decision not to prevent publication of the book, there were no minutes of the meetings, so no documents about them will ever come up for release. There were, however, departmental papers and when these were demanded by Wright's lawyer, there was consternation because some of them contained extremely embarrassing information that has still not emerged. The statement was to form another section of the web of secrecy in which several of the participants—Sir Robert Armstrong and Sir Michael Havers, in particular—have already found themselves injuriously entangled. Wright's book, *Spycatcher*, as originally written, devoted many pages to proving that the Prime Minister had been incorrectly briefed and that some parts of her statement were inaccurate, though this section was omitted from the American edition.

It has seemed odd that, when it was established some time after publication of my book that Wright had been a major source, nobody from MI5, which had a representative in Melbourne, went to see him or communicated with him in that respect. Even though he was then immune to criminal legal action, he could reasonably have been asked to answer questions. Again, the explanation lies in the intricacies of secrecy. If Wright had been informed, officially, that MI5 had proof that he was a major source but could take no action against him, he could have told me. Then, with no danger to either of us, I could have issued a much more credible edition of *Their Trade Is Treachery*, quoting Wright at length. This would have completely undermined the damage-control exercise, which was based on the claim that the book was all speculation by me.

‖ 6 ‖

A Letter from the
Cabinet Secretary

*Truth is the most valuable thing we have. Let us
economize it.*

—Mark Twain

For various reasons, the publisher and I agreed
that it was crucial to keep the existence of *Their Trade Is
Treachery* as secret as possible, and we wove our own web of
secrecy and deception—a web that, like the others in this extraordinary tale, could easily have entrapped us. Fortunately,
however, it was never as secret as we believed it to be.

To maintain exclusivity, it was essential that, once the
Daily Mail had bought the serial rights (for which it was to pay
£35,000), nobody apart from a very few *Daily Mail* executives
should see the text in advance because it was so milkable.
Other newspapers might claim that they had discovered the
Hollis material through their own resources, because a story,
once revealed, is easy to confirm from other sources, and even
easier to lay claim to as one's own discovery. We also believed,

at that stage, that it was essential to prevent MI5 from getting a glimpse of it.

All this meant that no review copies could be sent out in advance, as is normal practice. Nor could any be sent to the bookshops before publication day. The publishers therefore took the unprecedented step of announcing in the trade press, about a week prior to publication, that booksellers would be receiving "copies of a book that you haven't ordered and haven't even heard of" and that "the week after that will be a bestseller." There was a picture of the cover of *Their Trade Is Treachery* and an announcement that on Monday, March 23, three days before publication, the *Daily Mail* would begin a week-long serialization that would be promoted by television advertising costing £250,000. This announcement gave MI5 the warning to alert Lady Hollis that the press would be on her doorstep, and she was removed from her cottage in Somerset to a "safe house."

The first installment, which "blew" the Hollis case, appeared on March 23—three days before publication of the book. The banner headline read: "MI5 Chief Was Russian Spy Suspect." Late on the previous night, I had been telephoned by the *Daily Mail* to be asked if the headline could be hardened to say that Hollis had been a spy. I said no, forcefully.

Every rival newspaper picked up the story and the subsequent disclosures, which dominated the media for many days.

It is certain that the security authorities knew some weeks in advance that the *Daily Mail* would serialize the more sensational parts of the book, yet no action whatsoever was taken to curb the newspaper. It would have been normal practice for the Secretary of the D-Notice Committee, then Rear-Admiral Ash, to request the newspaper to submit its excerpts in advance so that they could be examined for possible security breaches, under the system agreed to by the media. No such request was ever made, and no complaint was ever received from the D-Notice Secretary following publication, although each day's excerpt clearly breached the general D-Notice referring to intelligence and security matters, which was in the possession of all newspapers. It so happened that Rear-Admiral Ash appeared as a witness in front of a Defence Ministry Committee on which I was serving in 1983, and I asked him if he had ever been approached by the security or defense authorities to make inquiries about *Their Trade Is Treachery*. He said that he had not.

On the day that the first installment of the serialization (the one about the Hollis case) appeared in the *Daily Mail*, the publisher, William Armstrong, received a personal telephone call from the Cabinet Secretary, Sir Robert Armstrong, to whom he is not related. Sir Robert explained that the Prime Minister would be required to make a statement about the book in Parliament and needed a copy of it, preferably two, so that this could be prepared. William Armstrong telephoned me for advice and, being totally unaware of what had occurred in secrecy, I expressed complete opposition on the grounds that it was ridiculous to present the government with evidence it needed in order to seek an injunction to prevent publication when we had gone to such lengths to avoid that. William said that he must make some response, so I suggested that we should offer to supply the books only if the Cabinet Secretary was prepared to provide a written promise that the government would not prevent publication. I felt confident that, as a civil servant, Sir Robert would be unable to give such an undertaking, and I knew that the Prime Minister, who I expected would have to be consulted, was abroad.

A note made later by William Armstrong records that he then telephoned Sir Robert and agreed to provide the copies on condition that Sir Robert would assure him that he would take no legal action against Sidgwick and Jackson or me. To our astonishment and gratification a letter signed by Sir Robert was delivered to the publisher's office guaranteeing that the copies would not go outside the Cabinet Office and that there was no intention of interfering with the book. It was not marked "Confidential."[1] Either the Prime Minister was a party to this deception device to secure a copy of the book and to provide the guarantee or Sir Robert assumed that she would have no objection to it.

William Armstrong has recorded that Sir Robert was "charming throughout the negotiations," and at no time did he give any impression that he already had the typescript of the book. He also recalls that Sir Robert indicated that he would call at the publisher's office in person to deliver the letter in exchange for the books. He believes that this occurred, for when he and a senior colleague were returning from lunch that day they saw a tall, elegant figure departing with the books and are confident that it was Armstrong.[2] The incident provides further evidence of the extreme secrecy with which the whole affair was being conducted.

I realized right away that Sir Robert's decision meant that we could not be prosecuted. The Attorney General could hardly instigate an action against me for revealing secrets when his colleagues had rejected the opportunity to prevent their full disclosure. But had the Attorney General been consulted about the letter? If so, did he assent to such a guarantee? Or was he, again, excluded from the decision because the Cabinet Secretary thought there was no need to consult him?

What I did not know then was that the Attorney General had not been involved in the decision to allow publication of the book. Nor did I know then that the decision had been reached six weeks previously.

The whole incident was an astonishing example of the level at which security deception games are played. In the Australian court Sir Robert admitted that his request for the book was made, essentially, to cover the fact that the security authorities already had it. The evidence also disclosed that the Prime Minister had already studied a summary of the book's contents, and there can be no doubt that her statement to Parliament had already been prepared. Sir Robert's admission proved to be a serious gaffe because it left him open to the charge that his letter had been a lie. His reply that it was not quite a lie but that he had been "economical with the truth" did great damage to the government's cause and, in the eyes of many observers, to Sir Robert's character. His admission was also unnecessary. He could have said, with some honesty, that the books were required because it was essential for the Prime Minister to be assured that there had been no important changes, omissions, or additions between the delivery of the typescript and the binding of the books.

"Economy with the truth" is a long-established practice in Whitehall, especially in the provision of answers to Parliamentary questions, and politicians who affected to be offended by Sir Robert's behavior were being hypocritical.

Sir Robert was not the only one to be stimulated by the disclosures in the *Daily Mail*. The editor of *The Times*, then Harold Evans, appreciated the uniqueness of the material and took an unprecedented step. By arrangement with the *Daily Mail* and with my publisher, *The Times* bought second serial rights and printed all the material one day after the *Daily Mail* for the remainder of the week. This further reduced any risk of prosecution since the government was hardly likely to take on *The Times* as well as the *Daily Mail*.

|| 7 ||

A Review by the Prime Minister

Truth is never pure, and rarely simple.

—Oscar Wilde

On the morning of March 26, a fleet of vans delivered the books to booksellers throughout the country. Many of them quickly ordered more. A very few took exception to the way the book was being marketed and returned the copies. Most proved to be very pleased with the way the book sold. The publishing world in general was impressed with the ploy, and Sidgwick and Jackson received an award.[1]

The first evidence in the government's move to trash the book took the form of leaks to political correspondents and MPs that Sir Roger Hollis had been cleared. When this appeared in various newspapers, I had little doubt that the Prime Minister would make a statement to the same effect. She did so on the afternoon of March 26 to a full House, creating literary history by, in effect, delivering a brief review of the book from the Despatch Box. It was a hostile review. While confirming that Hollis, who had served in MI5 for twenty-seven years, nine of them as Director General, had indeed been the subject of an internal inquiry, she told Parliament that it had been concluded that he had not been an agent of the Soviet Union. The Prime Minister then confirmed that, as this view had been challenged, Lord Trend, a former Cabinet Secretary, had reviewed the situation. She said that he, too, had concluded that Hollis had not been a spy, although it had not been possible to prove his innocence. Regrettably I had made some errors in reporting what I had been told about Lord Trend's effort. It has been stupidly suggested that my mistakes were deliberate, being part of a conspiracy between me and MI5 to get the skeletons out into the open and then provide an excuse for the Prime Minister to question their general accuracy. Sadly, I must insist that the mistakes were genuine. Some were Wright's; some mine. No sensible author of documentaries would deliberately impugn his own accuracy.

The collapse of cases and other security failures that the Fluency Committee investigators had blamed on Hollis were attributed by the Prime Minister to Philby or Blunt, although the dates connected with many of them made no sense at all under this alternative theory. While refusing to comment on any other aspects of the book, Mrs. Thatcher did what she could to denigrate them by referring to "allegations and insinuations."

It was soon to become apparent that the Prime Minister's statement was another dangerous example of advisers having been "economical with the truth." It ill accorded with Sir Robert's later admission to the Australian court that "Chapman Pincher has a good reputation for accuracy and good sources."[2] The statement, for which Mrs. Thatcher was in no way to blame, had been prepared by a group that this time included the Attorney General as well as Sir Robert Armstrong himself.[3] The deceptive information in it, however, could only have been supplied by MI5, which was undoubtedly responsible for inducing the Prime Minister to tell Parliament that the case against Hollis was based on certain leads suggesting that there had been a Russian intelligence service agent at a relatively senior level in British counterintelligence "in the last years of the war." In fact, the Fluency Committee had spent much time examining Hollis's behavior in the 1950s and 1960s.

In the Australian court, Sir Robert Armstrong admitted that the statement was not "comprehensive." In fact, by referring only to the war years, it was very misleading and deliberately so.

I was soon to receive a playback of the reaction of certain former members of the Fluency Committee to the Prime Minister's remarks, as well as hearing those of Wright who wrote to me about them. They identified several points in the statement that were badly flawed. According to evidence given in the Australian court, Wright devoted many pages in *Spycatcher* to demolishing it, but these were omitted from the book as it appeared in the United States.[4]

The firm belief of most of the MI5 and MI6 officers who were concerned is that the case is unproved either way but that the preponderance of probabilities still points to Hollis. I have recently been informed that the CIA has acquired new information "of a technical nature" pointing to his guilt.

After carrying out MI5's requirement to trash *Their Trade Is Treachery*, the Prime Minister announced the first independent inquiry for twenty years into the efficiency of the secret services' defenses against Soviet penetration. The inquiry was to be carried out by the Security Commission. As will be seen, it was far-reaching and even included inquiries into the homosexual behavior of the former MI6 chief, Sir Maurice Oldfield. Sir Maurice, who served for several years in Washington, was a lifelong bachelor whose compulsive homosexual behavior came to the notice of the police and the security authorities following his retirement from MI6 in 1978 and during his appointment, a year later, to an intelligence post in Northern Ireland. Scotland Yard detectives became concerned by the number and types of young men—waiters and others with no intelligence connections—visiting Sir Maurice's London flat. Inquiries showed that some of them were homosexual and functioned as male prostitutes. When confronted, Oldfield made no denials and confessed that he had falsified his positive vetting forms—an offense that would usually disqualify a person from continuing employment in the secret services. He suffered the indignity of having his access to top-secret information removed but, after promising to curb his compulsion, was allowed to complete his further brief tenure in Northern Ireland.

Whatever the merits and faults of *Their Trade Is Treachery*, there is now little doubt that but for its chance publication few of the far-reaching inquiries by the Security Commission would have been made.

Under the terms of the arrangements for invoking the services of the Security Commission, the Prime Minister was required to brief the leader of the opposition, Michael Foot, about her statement. He was relieved to find that it would not include any comment about the revelations in *Their Trade Is Treachery* concerning his late friend, Tom Driberg, the MP who had worked for both MI5 and Soviet bloc intelligence. He was therefore able to give Parliament the impression that these were among the inaccuracies and distortions. When Labour backbenchers were specifically asked about Driberg's treacherous activities, they were able to dismiss them as "fairy tales."

At a press conference called immediately after the Prime Minister's statement, I told the media that her brief had been badly flawed and that she would eventually regret having used it; all she needed to have said was that Hollis had been investigated and that the case remained unproved.

On March 27, 1981, Mrs. Thatcher revealed to Parliament that an inquiry into my sources for *Their Trade Is Treachery* was already under way. It was stated that any findings would be submitted to the Attorney General. Later information revealed that the inquiry had been set in motion shortly after MI5 had received photocopies of the typescript from Sir Arthur Franks. No doubt a report was finally submitted to the Attorney General, but I heard no more of it, and no question about it ever seems to have been asked in Parliament.

The book was, simultaneously, a *succès fou*, a *succès d'estime*, and a *succès d'exécration*, depending on who was delivering the opinion. Those in the media who had been envious of the *Daily Mail* joined wholeheartedly in trashing the book, mainly to counter the newspaper's circulation success. The *Daily Express* headlined its account of Mrs. Thatcher's statement "Wrong, Wrong, Wrong." [5] Television announcers repeatedly said that the Prime Minister had cleared Hollis when she had said only that Lord Trend had reached that judgment—a fact that would have been promptly recalled in the event of proof that Hollis had been a spy.

Subsequent events have shown that, in Fleet Street language, *Their Trade Is Treachery*, and particularly its paperback edition (a much-expanded version), was a succession of major scoops. Later books, including *Spycatcher*, while claiming all manner of new revelations, have done little more than add detail.

Their Trade Is Treachery remained high in the best-seller lists for several weeks, but in Britain, which has a tiny book-reading population, that does not necessarily imply massive sales. The Prime Minister's statement had such a negative effect that the publisher was left with 11,000 hardback copies that eventually had to be remaindered.

Wright made little comment on the book to me and none to Lord Rothschild—not even to express pleasure that the truth was finally exposed. All I can recall is his view that the paperback version, which contained much that the lawyers had originally vetoed for libel reasons, such as the names of several spies and suspects, was much better, as indeed it was. Later he was to tell the Australian court that he was very disappointed with the book because it did not call for an inquiry. His lawyer, Malcolm Turnbull, was to claim that I had gone against Wright's advice in that respect because that was part of my deal with MI5. The truth is that in his numerous letters Wright never expressed any disappointment to me, and my conclusion that MI5 was clean at the top by 1971, which made an inquiry seem unnecessary, was based on information supplied by him.

Wright had pointed out that when the KGB officer, Oleg Lyalin, defected in London in that year, he had already been working for MI5 for six months as an agent-in-place and that if there had been a spy at a high level in MI5, he would have been exposed. He said that the same applied in 1973 and 1974, when British intelligence produced the lead showing that Gunther Guillaume, a close adviser to the West German Chancellor, Willy Brandt, was a professional East German spy. Guillaume was watched and fed with false information for almost a year before his arrest in April 1974. Had there still been a spy at a high level in either MI5 or MI6, Guillaume would have been warned. Wright agreed with me that MI5 had probably been clean from the moment Hollis retired in 1965.

While we were together in Tasmania, Wright repeatedly expressed his opposition to the kind of far-ranging inquiry that had inflicted so much damage on the CIA in the 1970s. He wanted a limited inquiry into past Soviet penetrations of the secret services, to ensure that they could not so easily be repeated, but he seemed opposed to "putting a flue-brush" through the whole of MI5, as he put it.

Anyone who reads *Their Trade Is Treachery*, which was published in paperback in the United States by Bantam, will see that I left the question of an inquiry open, putting the case for and against one. Wright's alleged disappointment would seem to have been a late afterthought that suited the conspiracy argument put forward by Turnbull.

Within a month, I began to hear from secret service friends that our efforts to prevent the book from falling into the hands of MI5 had failed. Photocopies of the typescript had been circulating in the secret areas of Whitehall; former secret service chiefs and a former Cabinet Secretary had read the book in advance and had been asked to give their views about the truth and origin of the contents. In spite of Sir Robert Armstrong's eventual statement to the Australian court that the whole operation had been extremely secret, various people had been telling their friends about it.

As soon as the information reached my ears, I realized that Sir Robert's letter had been a deception. Sir Robert and I met socially when we were guests at a dinner given by Lord Zuckerman at the London Zoo restaurant on May 15, 1984. We were seated in close proximity, but I refrained from raising any controversial issues other than letting him know I would shortly be publishing a big new book, which caused him to raise his eyebrows quizzically in some amusement.

My immediate inquiries revealed that the legal advisers of MI5 and MI6 had been averse to any action that might involve their departments in public exposure, but it was to be several months before I learned exactly what had happened.

‖8‖

The End of a Relationship

> *No friendship can survive the gift of gold.*
>
> —William Smith

The serialization of the hardback edition of *Their Trade Is Treachery* gave me an opportunity to solve some of the libel problems that it had presented. The *Daily Mail* had an experienced journalist in Washington who, at my suggestion, approached Michael Straight and induced him to confirm his part in the exposure of Blunt. The ensuing article meant that Straight could then safely be mentioned in the paperback edition.[1] I applied the same technique to other names that had been barred by my lawyer, using other newspapers when the *Daily Mail* lost interest. This alone made the paperback more revealing, and in addition I introduced much other material that had come my way as a result of personal researches.

Once the danger of prosecution had passed, I began to correspond regularly with Wright, using the agreed accom-

modation addresses and a crude code intended to deceive any
ordinary person if the letters went astray. I was able to ask
Wright many questions that had come to mind after I had left
him. The answers were needed in my spirited campaign to
rebut the official rubbishing of *Their Trade Is Treachery*, in the
interests of foreign rights, television sales, and my reputation
for accuracy.

As Wright was so remote from his old colleagues, I included in my letters any items of gossip about them and other
matters that came my way. I never believed that these letters,
which I had written in extreme confidentiality and secrecy,
would ever be revealed, but he was to make them all available
to his lawyers for use in the trial both inside and outside the
Sydney courtroom.

I had told Wright, in Tasmania, that if the book was published it would surely become obvious that he had been a
source. He agreed but believed that if no documentary evidence fell into MI5's hands, nothing could be proved and it
would be safe for him to travel. I therefore destroyed almost all
of his letters as soon as I had read them and had noted anything of interest in my files. The fact that I did so (and that
Wright approved of it in writing) further undermines his contention that I was collaborating with MI5 because, in that circumstance, I could have kept the letters with impunity.

I was also anxious to preserve Wright's confidentiality for
professional reasons because I knew that rival writers would
soon be on his trail with offers if they heard about him—as
indeed they eventually were when his identity leaked from
MI5.

Wright did not suggest any amendments for the paperback, although he knew that I was doing a substantial rewrite
of the original edition. The only remark he eventually made
was that the paperback was much better than the hardback,
even though it still contained the chapter about the pros and
cons of an inquiry, which he was later to claim had offended
and disappointed him so much.

The paperback was published in November 1981, rather earlier than is usually the case because the hardback sales had collapsed. It reached the bestseller lists, but there were very few reviews because of the previous spate of publicity. Its day, however, would come.

Wright and I began to consider the possibility of a further joint effort and provisionally settled on a book with the working title *The Atlantic Connection*, which was to be about Anglo-American-Canadian links in the intelligence and security fields. It was understood that the arrangements would be as before—payment of 50 percent of net profits to Wright only by the publisher, if a publisher could be found.

After warning me that the authorities would be greatly perturbed by such a book, Wright sent me a few items of no great interest at lengthy intervals; clearly it was going to take a long time to produce a salable volume. He then suggested that I should write a quick book purely on the Hollis case, claiming that it was "bound to sell." He was unable to produce any new material, having already told me all he knew, as discerning readers of *Spycatcher* will appreciate. What had come to light about Hollis since *Their Trade Is Treachery* was published was the result of my endeavors. Nevertheless, he expected 50 percent of any proceeds. I told him that such a book would simply be dismissed by any prospective publisher as *"Their Trade Is Treachery* with knobs on," which I am sure was true. Wright then offered to provide new information for newspaper articles to produce some quick cash, but I rejected that, too, on the grounds that the proceeds, on which I had to pay a high rate of tax, were insufficient for sharing, and I was not going to involve myself in any direct payments to him.

Early in 1983 Wright ended our relationship simply by failing to answer my last letter. As the weeks and months passed, I thought that he might be too ill to write or perhaps had received a warning from MI5. There had been substantial gaps in our previous correspondence which he had explained as due to illness. There was no falling-out between us so far as

I was aware. He had found an alternative outlet, as will be explained in chapter 11. I never heard from him again.

In spite of the £31,827 which Wright had received as his share of net proceeds—including his share of paperback and serialization proceeds—made in six separate payments by Sidgwick and Jackson stretching over two years, Lord Rothschild has no record of any communication from him and is certain that, after the Cambridge visit, he never heard from him again. If Lord Rothschild had suggested the book, as Wright and his lawyer have claimed, one might have expected some letter, however cryptically worded, expressing gratitude for having saved him from bankruptcy.

Meanwhile, though MI5 had been able to prove to their satisfaction (by tracing my movements to Tasmania) that Wright had been a major source for my book, he was never interviewed or castigated in any way. In fact, it would seem that he was rewarded, if his original claim that his pension was £2,000 a year was true. His pension was considerably increased over the ensuing years so that in 1986, as he told the Sydney court, it was about £600 a month.

While Wright still maintains that he has been swindled, is there any other country that would continue to pay a steadily rising pension to a former employee who has leaked its secrets over so many years, on such a massive scale, and with so much consequential damage?

‖ 9 ‖

A Meeting with Sir Arthur Franks

In life there are meetings which seem
Like a fate.

—Meredith

On September 16, 1982, I took Sir Arthur Franks out to lunch at a small restaurant, convenient to us both, in Farnham, Surrey. "Dickie" Franks, as I knew him, had become chief of the Secret Intelligence Service (MI6) in 1978, succeeding my friend, Sir Maurice Oldfield. He had a distinguished war record and had joined MI6 in 1949, serving in the Middle East, Tehran, and Bonn.

Contrary to an impression given to the Australian court by Sir Robert Armstrong that Franks and I were regular acquaintances, we were not. Oldfield had told me that, when he was out of his office and I needed to speak to someone or leave a message, I should ask for Dickie Franks, who was then his deputy. I had done so on several occasions without ever meeting him.

I first set eyes on Franks at Oldfield's high-security memorial service on May 12, 1981, at Greenwich, and later met him briefly at a lunch that we both happened to attend on April 20 of the following year. He was a most pleasant person—quiet, distinguished-looking, and obviously sharp intellectually. Five months later, I asked him to meet me for lunch at Farnham because of documents I had received regarding allegations that Oldfield had been a practicing homosexual and that this had become known to the police and security authorities. As I have since reported in my recent book, *Traitors: The Anatomy of Treason*, this information was soundly based, but I did not know that at the time.

The documents were part of a projected book by two authors unknown to me. Franks read the relevant pages and told me that he had heard the allegations and that they had appeared in the Irish press but, pleading ignorance, he declined to comment on their accuracy. I was not aware then that he must already have known the full details of Oldfield's interrogation and his confession to homosexual practices, made in 1980, shortly before his death. In what was a mild deception —an understandable "economy" with the truth—he observed that Maurice had attracted young people and that many staff from the MI6 office visited him at his flat.

Having dealt with the Oldfield issue, I took the opportunity to raise the subject of *Their Trade Is Treachery*, and we discussed it. A quick note I made about the conversation immediately on returning to my car states, "All had been OK about the book."

Under my usual principle of observing confidentiality, I would never have publicly revealed the occurrence of this lunch but, sadly, I mentioned it in a confidential letter to Peter Wright, and this letter was made available to the media during the Sydney trial. It quickly found its way to Labour backbenchers, who made much of my association with Sir Arthur in Parliament.[1] Sir Robert Armstrong did not help matters by telling the Sydney court that he believed Sir Arthur and I "met from time to time."

In his judgment on the Wright case, Justice Powell said
that the evidence suggested that "at some time during January
1983" I had met Sir Arthur Franks and had discussed my
forthcoming book, *Too Secret Too Long*, with him. Like many
other statements in that judgment, based on faulty evidence
given to the court, this was completely untrue.[2] On August
26, 1983, I had written to Sir Arthur saying that I was interested in the pros and cons concerning the need for oversight of
the security and intelligence services by some independent
body, such as already existed in the United States, and would
welcome his views on the subject. He declined to give any.
Later, Justice Powell stated that Sir Arthur then "sought out
Sir Robert Armstrong and told him Chapman Pincher was
contemplating another book." Sir Robert's recollection of that
event evidenced serious confusion on his part, as I demonstrate more fully in chapter 13.

The total misinterpretation of my one lunch meeting
with Sir Arthur was exploited in the Sydney court by Turnbull,
with Sir Robert Armstrong's unwitting assistance. In the result,
the judge was misled.

|| 10 ||

The Security
Commission Reports

> *The Commission makes it clear that . . . the*
> *occasion of this reference to it was the publica-*
> *tion of a book which dealt with a number of*
> *cases of proven or suspected disclosures of sen-*
> *sitive information to Soviet bloc intelligence*
> *services.*
> —Margaret Thatcher, May 1982

When the Prime Minister set up the Security Commission's inquiry into the efficacy of countermeasures against hostile penetration of the secret departments in March 1981, following the publication of *Their Trade Is Treachery*, she promised to provide the Commons with an expurgated account of its findings. In the event, she did not do so. When the commission submitted its thick report early in 1982, after nine months of effort, the Prime Minister delayed any statement until May. She then issued a thirteen-page white paper entitled "Statement on the Recommendations of the Security

Commission," claiming that any expurgated text would give "a seriously misleading impression of the report."[1]

Normally this would have caused an outcry from her opponents, but the white paper had no political impact at all because it was issued in the middle of the Falklands War when Parliament was interested in nothing else.

The document was singularly uninformative in comparison to the full report, of which I was given a rundown by a source who had seen it. But it clearly indicated that a large number of recommendations for improvements in protecting the secret departments from infiltration had been made and put into operation.

In the statement, Mrs. Thatcher admitted that the report was the direct result of the publication of *Their Trade Is Treachery*. The commission had looked at the threat from all quarters, including the opportunities offered by technological advances such as computers and word processors for the storage and retrieval of classified information. It had paid particular attention to homosexuality as a threat through its potentiality for blackmail. It was not known in 1982 that the Security Commission had specifically been asked to consider the case of the late Sir Maurice Oldfield, following his confession to promiscuous homosexuality, a character defect that he had failed to admit during his positive vetting.

The extent of the recommendations in the unpublished report underlined the stupidity of a situation where so many improvements regarded as essential had to depend on the chance production of a book by an investigative writer.

Mrs. Thatcher had been advised to comment in her statement that the Security Commission had taken the view that the security procedures, as applied since 1962, had "worked well." Within two months, the Prime Minister was faced with the arrest of Geoffrey Prime, a Soviet agent entrenched in GCHQ. Two years later, an MI5 officer, Michael Bettaney, was jailed for espionage offenses. These two cases—and Bettaney's, in particular—are of special significance in the context of this book, for Peter Wright claimed that they had induced him to make a rather sensational television broadcast, which, in turn, is said to have steeled his determination to write *Spycatcher*. This broadcast is described in the next chapter.

The government's embarrassment over the Bettaney case was intensified by the appearance of three very revealing articles about MI5 operations in the *Guardian* in April 1984.[2] The Security Commission report on the Bettaney case (published in May 1985) and Justice Powell's judgment in the Australian trial made it clear that MI5 believed that the *Guardian* had obtained the material from Bettaney, who had somehow revealed it while he was in prison.

As Justice Powell commented, no steps were taken to stop further articles when they first appeared. No proceedings were ever taken against the *Guardian* or the authors concerned. MI5 had been averse to making any admissions and was probably highly embarrassed that Bettaney had been able to leak so much while in custody.[3]

Turnbull was able to make skillful, highly productive use of these omissions in the Sydney court to rebut the British government's argument that MI5 must be seen to be leakproof. They induced the judge to observe that MI5 had leaked like a sieve for years, and nothing had been done about it.

‖11‖

Enter Mr. Greengrass

> *Rashness is a quality of the budding-time of youth.*
>
> —Cicero

According to a letter that Wright sent me, he was approached by Paul Greengrass of Granada Television's *World in Action* program on November 23, 1982. Greengrass came armed with a letter from the writer Nigel West and said that *Their Trade Is Treachery* and a forthcoming book by West had stirred him to attempt a documentary about the high-level penetration of MI5 in which five other ex-members of MI5, with whom he was in touch, might appear. [1] West's letter told Wright that he had been identified as a source for *Their Trade Is Treachery* at a highly secret MI5 meeting.

Wright told me that he had then telephoned Arthur Martin, one of the five ex-members listed, who wanted more time to think about the project. The discussions with Greengrass lasted two or three days, during which Wright made it clear that he would want Granada to provide complete financial protection, both for himself and for his wife, and that he would require a letter guaranteeing this. Later he sent me a copy of a draft guarantee in which Granada had offered to pay all legal expenses if the government prosecuted him and to make up his pension if he lost it. The pension right would also apply to his widow.

I had never heard of Greengrass, who was well known in the TV world. He was to play an extraordinary role in the Wright trial and in the publication of *Spycatcher*, though at that stage Wright had apparently declined to appear on his projected program.

After the arrest of the MI5 officer Michael Bettaney in September 1983 and his conviction on a charge of espionage for the KGB, Greengrass approached Wright again and telephoned him regularly. Shortly before Christmas 1983, Wright agreed to give an interview, for which, he says, he received no payment. He had previously cut off communication with me, and he insisted that I should know nothing about the forthcoming program and that neither I nor *Their Trade Is Treachery* should be mentioned in it.[2] I suppose that his purpose was to make viewers believe that all he was saying was new when, in fact, almost all of it had already appeared in my book.

The interview was filmed in Tasmania early in January 1984, and supporting evidence was obtained from British and American sources.[3] Eventually the program appeared on Monday, July 16, 1984, under the title *The Spy Who Never Was*. If, by that, the producers meant Hollis, then Wright must have been even more disappointed than he said he was with me.

The program lasted an hour, during which Wright restated much that he had told me, only with greater certainty. He said, for instance, that he was 99 percent certain that Hollis was a spy. He also accused Mrs. Thatcher of having given false information to Parliament in her statement about Hollis on the day that *Their Trade Is Treachery* was published.

I was astonished to hear Wright mention a most secret

MI5 operation that he had told me about but that I had decided to withhold because I judged it to be really damaging to national security, since it was likely that MI5 was still engaging in similar operations. Called "Party Piece," it had been carried out in 1955 by MI5 officers to discover the identities of secret members of the Communist Party. A group of watchers and other specialists, including a locksmith and photographers, burgled a Mayfair flat where the secret membership files of the British Communist Party were stored by a wealthy party member. "In less than twelve hours—while the owner was away for the night—all 55,000 files had been stolen, their contents photographed and the files replaced." [4] Wright said that a series of public figures, including top trade unionists and thirty-one MPs, were covert members of the Communist Party. When we met in Tasmania, he gave me the names of some of these people, several of whom were still in the House of Commons or the House of Lords or were at the top of the trade union movement. He told me that all of these were overtly members of the Labour Party. [5]

In that program, as during my interviews in Tasmania, Wright gave no indication that he was in any way disenchanted with the methods used by MI5 in such operations, as he was to allege at his trial. His conversion to disapproval of them and to defense of civil liberties, if authentic, came afterward.

The most sensitive matter that Wright openly discussed on television (undoubtedly causing deep concern in Whitehall) was his description of certain extremely secret meetings of the security and intelligence chiefs of Britain, the United States, Canada, Australia, and New Zealand. I had written in *The Times* on December 12, 1981, that, at such a meeting in London, the visitors were given the facts about the investigation into Hollis so that they could make their own decision as to whether they needed to take any damage-control action, in case he had been a Soviet agent. It had already been publicly reported by the Canadian Solicitor General that Canada had done so. [6]

Government spokesmen had told inquirers that there was no truth to my statement in *The Times* and that such meetings did not occur—another deception—but Wright confirmed the essential details of the meeting with authority, even displaying a photograph of the venue.[7]

Wright had been allowed, perhaps encouraged, to appear in casual clothes, and this, coupled with his aged appearance and diffident manner, did not give a good impression. I heard much criticism of Wright as a typical MI5 officer. The program did not carry conviction and produced no political impact because Parliament was in recess. It should, however, have alerted MI5 to the probability that Wright might still be writing a book of his own.

On the day after the TV program appeared, I received a transcript of it, together with a letter from Greengrass apologizing for the fact that I had been kept in ignorance of it. The letter said that Wright had insisted on "putting distance between your very fine book and our programme."[8]

According to Justice Powell's judgment, MI5 was aware of the coming program and of Wright's appearance in it "some weeks" in advance. The summary of official documents submitted by the government to the Sydney trial revealed that MI5 had information by May 4, 1984, that there were plans for a *World in Action* program in which Wright was assisting and might take part. By July 3—thirteen days before the program was screened—MI5 knew that the program would center on an interview with Wright in which he would reopen the Hollis case; the Treasury Solicitor was immediately informed. Incredibly, the possibility of an injunction was not discussed by the Treasury Solicitor and MI5 until the morning of July 16. Then, following a *Times* report about the program on the morning before the broadcast, MI5 noted "the likelihood that Wright had breached the Official Secrets Act . . . and had taken the precaution of remaining outside the UK jurisdiction," indicating that he might be prosecuted if he were available for arrest. The legal adviser to MI5 discussed with the

Treasury Solicitor's department the possibility of issuing an injunction against the program. As could have been predicted, the legal adviser said that MI5's interests would not be best served by legal action at that stage. The summary stated, rather lamely: "The view was expressed that, if a preview was refused, going for an injunction would undoubtedly be a hard fight and, if a preview was agreed, the government could be put in the position of appearing to have approved it whether or not it asked for cuts."[9] There can be little doubt that the real reason was MI5's reluctance to be asked questions in court—especially about Party Piece!

Greengrass told me that nobody tried to interview him, and no action whatsoever was taken against him for patently taking the initiative to induce Wright to break his bond of confidentiality.

None of the vocal left-wingers in Parliament ever tried to make political capital out of the program or used it to secure publicity. It may be significant that *World in Action* has often taken such a left-wing, antiestablishment line that Alan Whicker, the well-known television interviewer, described its productions as "usually a sort of Marxist party-political."[10] I criticized their programs for their bias in my book, *The Secret Offensive*, published in 1985, to the annoyance of Greengrass, who telephoned me to complain, though weakly and long after the event.

In view of the government's stand in the Australian trial, it is remarkable that it took no action about the program that had the authenticity of Wright himself—a factor that the government was to rate as of such importance in the Sydney court. Wright of course was safe in the fastness of Tasmania, but Greengrass was not.

On July 30, 1984, Greengrass and his co-producer, John Ware, who had been with him in Tasmania, visited my home and stayed to lunch. Greengrass was a long-haired, bespectacled, mustachioed figure, then in his late twenties. They apologized again for excluding me from the Granada program but said that Wright had insisted on it. They told me that they had spent about three weeks with Wright, wisely staying in Hobart and motoring in and out each day. Each evening after a session with Wright, they went through the paperback edition of *Their Trade Is Treachery*, trying to check what was new but rarely finding that they had broken new ground. They realized that the only new aspect of their program was that Wright would be saying it. After leaving Tasmania, they did a lot of collateral research, especially in the United States, where they interviewed former officers of the CIA.[11]

Professionally, the Wright interview was a considerable media coup, and the program was well done aside from its lack of impact, which I attribute to its bad timing and to the adverse general reaction to Wright's appearance and personality.

From then on Greengrass and I talked occasionally on the telephone and had two or three lunches together in London. In September 1984, Greengrass told me that Wright was about halfway through writing a book of memoirs. While denying that he was ghosting the book, Greengrass said that he was helping Wright, and encouraging him to write as much as possible in the first person. He had urged him to keep the Hollis case until the last part of the book, which I understand Wright did in the version that he eventually submitted for review by the British government. Commenting, privately, on why Wright had been so forthcoming as a source, Greengrass said, "You have only to give Peter a few drinks, and he would tell you anything."[12] He indicated that Wright was still hoping to visit Britain one day but knew that he could not do so safely if he published his book under his own name.

At lunch on November 7, 1984, Greengrass told me that Wright had still heard nothing from MI5 about his TV appearance and so definitely intended to publish his book under his own name. I assumed that, having become too ill and frail ever to make the journey to Britain, he had decided that he had nothing to lose, since he was safe from prosecution so long as he remained in Australia.

On December 30, 1984, Greengrass told me that about a week previously he had spoken to Wright, who was now also suffering from diabetes. Greengrass also told me that Wright had shown him all of my confidential letters and had explained what they meant.

I saw Greengrass for lunch again in London on February 3, 1985, and he told me that Wright had an American publisher for his book and hoped to get it out that year. He said that he would show me a first draft of the book for my comments, but he never did so. He declined to say anything definite about a British publisher but I suspected that Wright had one. John Ware, co-producer of the television program, *The Spy Who Never Was*, has confirmed that Greengrass was ghosting *Spycatcher* when he visited Wright in the summer of 1985.[13]

Later, at the trial in Sydney, Greengrass was to be seen regularly on TV clips walking close to Malcolm Turnbull. The judge had granted him permission to function as part of Turnbull's legal team, even in the secret sessions. He was very active in the courtroom, repeatedly passing slips of paper or files to Turnbull to jog his memory.

According to a book on the Wright case written by an Australian journalist who appeared to have had access to the Turnbull team, Greengrass was a paid collaborator in writing *Spycatcher*. The journalist alleged that, for reasons of secrecy, Greengrass moved to an address in Amsterdam to which Wright's dictated material was forwarded by the managing director of the Australian subsidiary of the Heinemann publishing house. Some of the £18,000 advance that Wright told the court he had received allegedly went to Greengrass, with a royalty share later.[14] Greengrass was later to admit his part in writing the American edition of *Spycatcher* and his payment for it, in an interview with Andrew Lownie, the London representative of the National Intelligence Study Center in Washington.[15] Lownie reported that Greengrass told him that his job had been to "edit Peter's raw material and provide atmosphere" in what proved to be a substantial rewrite of the original book written for publication in Australia. Greengrass was reported as claiming that the legal process in Sydney had required him to halt the book at the first draft stage, which was why it contained some howlers. He was also reported as saying that he was being paid a share of the royalties.

He quickly confirmed his role in writing the American version of *Spycatcher* by allowing his name to appear on later editions. The delay in doing this had, apparently, been due to his fear of prosecution as an accessory to Wright's breach of the Official Secrets Act. He waited until I and Lord Rothschild had been cleared of any misdemeanor following police inquiries, as described in chapter 21. His assumption that he could not then be prosecuted may not be warranted. Because of the circumstances I have described, his case and mine are very different in law.

Greengrass's admission adds piquancy to the role he played in the Sydney trial. Though he was part of Turnbull's team, given judicial permission to be present even during secret sessions, he had a personal vested interest in the verdict. Was the judge aware of this? And would it have been considered ethical had he been legally qualified?

‖12‖

The "Dossier"

Silence is the gratitude of true affection.

—Sheridan

In the month after Wright's appearance on British television, he gave a 160-page report, entitled "The Security of the United Kingdom Against the Assault of the Russian Intelligence Service," to Greengrass to pass to a prominent Parliamentarian who, it was hoped, would bring it to the notice of the Prime Minister. The MP chosen was Sir Anthony Kershaw, Chairman of Parliament's Foreign Affairs Committee, who happened to be a friend of mine. The document was written in separate chapters, as though it had been dictated.

When Sir Robert Armstrong heard about it, he took the initiative and asked Kershaw for a sight of the document, which Kershaw referred to as a memorandum, but which was called a "dossier" by journalists to make it sound more exciting.[1] This was a quite different document from the "dossier" that Wright would later claim to have shown to Lord Rothschild in 1980. That was composed of ten chapters of his first draft of *The Cancer in Our Midst*. Sir Anthony took it to the

Cabinet Office, where he had a talk with Armstrong, who said he would return it. Armstrong said that Mrs. Thatcher would probably want to read the report but was unlikely to do so before MI5 had seen and commented on it.[2] Kershaw followed up the meeting with a long letter to Sir Robert dated August 10, 1984. It warned that even if the facts in Wright's memorandum were old "the problem will not be allowed to die down." Kershaw said that three publishing houses had approached him for help in securing rights to the report and anything else Wright might produce.

The report, which, according to Kershaw, was essentially a rerun of *Their Trade Is Treachery*, dealt with far more than the Hollis case.[3] It was studied by Sir Robert Armstrong, the Prime Minister, and the current MI5 management (then headed by Sir John Jones, perhaps the least known of all MI5 director generals). They claimed that there was no new material in it and were unmoved by Wright's thesis that "moles breed," meaning that any long-term Russian agent in MI5, such as Hollis, must have been pressured by Moscow to help insert others in order to continue the treachery after he had left the service. The Prime Minister and the officials were determined to prevent any inquiry involving MPs from any Parliamentary committee or any outsiders. Kershaw had seen Sir Michael Havers, then the Attorney General, who assured him that Wright would be arrested and prosecuted if he ever came to Britain. That decision had also been leaked to the newspapers.[4] Later, in a letter to Wright, Kershaw confirmed the danger of prosecution but said that it was the result of his TV appearance and had nothing to do with the submission of the memorandum.[5]

Kershaw proposed to press for an inquiry into the Hollis case and Soviet penetration in general and to use the debate on the Queen's Speech for this purpose.[6] (The Queen's Speech is the address that Her Majesty makes on opening a new session of Parliament, summarizing the government's program of legislation. Discussion of security issues during the debate about it is actively discouraged.) He saw Sir Robert Armstrong, Sir John Jones, and Jones's deputy at the Cabinet Office on September 24, 1984. The MI5 management gave Kershaw an assurance that it could produce more officers who thought that Hollis was innocent than could be found who were convinced of his guilt. This was an admission that many do consider Hollis guilty and at the same time an extraordinary argument in view of the golden security rule that, when doubt on such a scale exists, the benefit must go to the service and not to the individual, however senior. They discussed Kershaw's idea to press for an inquiry and for general oversight of the secret services in the debate on the Queen's Speech, and Kershaw offered to let Armstrong see his speech in advance, which inevitably meant that it would come to nothing. All of the officials present at the meeting were extremely bitter about Wright's behavior. [7]

By November 4, Kershaw had received "tough" letters from both the Prime Minister and Sir Robert Armstrong. The Prime Minister urged him not to make any intervention in the Queen's Speech, pleading that it would damage the morale of the services, which was at rock bottom following the conviction of the MI5 officer Michael Bettaney. Armstrong reinforced the request, ably maneuvering to prevent any resurrection of the Hollis case in Parliament. As a loyal high Tory, with much affection and regard for Mrs. Thatcher, Kershaw had to agree and was effectively stifled. He went on record as saying that he would require a statement in Parliament, but he failed to secure one.

He was not alone. In spite of much newspaper publicity about the "dossier," no Parliamentary questions were raised by any party, the whips (whose duty it is to keep their MPs in line) presumably having been at work. The MPs who usually latch onto any security breach or hint of incompetence were silent, while making every effort to capitalize on far less serious instances of civil servants who were alleged to have leaked documents to newspapers.

The memorandum was eventually returned to Kershaw, no doubt after it had been copied by MI5. He was surprised that it had not been classified. In turn, he gave the report back to Greengrass, who told me that he had sent it back to Wright, although he admitted keeping a photocopy. He confirmed to me that it had not been classified. I tried to secure a copy, with a view toward writing about it in *The Times*, but failed.

Kershaw recalls with certainty that Wright's report did not condemn the methods used by MI5 or urge the government to make them subject to the law in the interests of civil liberties. The whole of the "dossier" dealt with the question of moles and the obstacles that were put in Wright's way in his search for evidence.

Wright has given the impression that, if the government had set up some kind of further inquiry to study his allegations, he would not have written *Spycatcher*. I find that hard to believe for three reasons. First, Greengrass had told me, in September 1984, that Wright was about halfway through his memoirs, with which Greengrass was assisting.[8] Second, there was nothing in the "dossier" that had not been in *Their Trade Is Treachery*, and by that time the authorities were fully aware of the extent of Wright's involvement in providing information for it. Third, there were no new relevant disclosures in *Spycatcher*, a point made repeatedly by Turnbull in the Sydney court.

It is more than likely, according to my sources, that MI5 and the government knew that Wright had every intention of producing his memoirs, regardless of what happened to the "dossier." They were not going to give any credence to it by making it the basis for an official inquiry.

‖13‖

The Lunch That
Never Was

> *Memory, of all the powers of the mind,*
> *is the most delicate and frail.*
>
> —Ben Jonson

In the spring of 1983, Senator Malcolm Wallop, a Republican from Wyoming who is a friend of mine, suggested that I write a book about the urgent need for independent oversight (i.e., supervision) of the British secret services. He had spent several years on the U.S. Senate Intelligence Committee and was convinced that oversight was essential to the efficiency and general competence of secret services. He had been particularly incensed at how Geoffrey Prime had been able to sell American secrets to the Soviets while working in GCHQ. Prime was a relatively junior employee but had access to top-secret information about advanced American reconnaissance satellites. The cost of the damage he inflicted through espionage was estimated by the Pentagon at $1 billion. I was impressed with the senator's argument, and in further discussions he fired my enthusiasm. While wondering how to tackle such a project in an original way, I eventually hit on the idea of doing a retrospective examination of all the old spy cases to see what effect oversight might have had on them if it had existed at the time. Such a book would also be a plea for less unnecessary secrecy, which most authorities agree is now excessive. This was the whole basis of the book, *Too Secret Too Long*, as anyone who reads it can see. It was not just another book about Hollis, which Wright has attempted to claim. Indeed a government document produced during the Wright trial described it as "an anthology of espionage cases since the Second World War." I introduced new material about many cases, which I had acquired from my own resources. This included new material about Hollis of which Wright was ignorant.

I was by no means sure that the effort, prodigious as it was, would make a publishable book, since much of the material was old, and I did not secure a contract for it until April 26, 1984, by which time I had almost finished it. The truth about the origin and timing of *Too Secret Too Long* is highly relevant to the Wright affair, since much misinformation about it was given to the court in Sydney, where Malcolm Turnbull capitalized on it extensively, and has been repeated since.

According to a statement made by Turnbull during the Wright trial, and repeated many times, I met Sir Arthur Franks, the former chief of MI6, for lunch in January 1983, after which Franks gave Sir Robert Armstrong a verbal report of the meeting, indicating that I was writing another book and describing its contents.[1] Under belligerent cross-examination, Sir Robert, who said that his memory was hazy on the matter, eventually confirmed the allegation, saying that he supposed that the book in question must have been *Too Secret Too Long*, which eventually appeared in November 1984. Turnbull went on to question Sir Robert about his meeting and induced him to agree that Franks had given him a description of the book I had in mind. Turnbull's purpose was to convince the court that I had given the chief of MI6 the earliest possible warning —about twenty-one months—that I was going to write another book, thereby supporting his claim that I was working in close partnership with the intelligence and security services.

What is important about those exchanges, in such a celebrated and widely reported court case, is that they were based entirely on a myth and were typical of the statements made by Turnbull and then given official credence by Sir Robert because his memory was confused.

There was *never* any meeting between myself and Sir Arthur Franks in January 1983, as Sir Arthur could confirm, and therefore Sir Robert could *never* have received any report of it. I have never seen Sir Arthur since the lunch in September 1982 that I have described in chapter 9. I have contemporary records of all my dealings with Sir Arthur, and I did not tell him or indicate to him by letter or by telephone that I had another book in mind.

In a discursive letter I wrote to Wright on January 27, 1983, I stated, "I lunched with Dickie Franks recently." There was a reference to *Their Trade Is Treachery* and to the lunch the previous September, when we had discussed the book. Because of the lengthy postal service to and from Tasmania, and other built-in delays, my correspondence with Wright was at intervals of several weeks; in that context, September was recent. Turnbull wrongly assumed that I must have met Franks in January. Then, with his overbearing, hectoring manner, he bludgeoned Sir Robert into confirming this, and the court eventually accepted it as fact.

Sir Robert told the court that he had been "aware that there had been a meeting at that time" and that Sir Arthur had told him "briefly the information he had learned at it," along with several other confirmatory statements.[2] This suggested, of course, that through Sir Arthur I was also warning the government, with which I was alleged to be in close liaison concerning my writings.

The entire story was drivel, but Justice Powell accepted it and in his judgment stated as fact that after this meeting, which had never taken place, Sir Arthur Franks sought out Sir Robert and gave him an account of it.[3]

I wrote to Sir Arthur on January 4, 1983, seeking his advice in connection with positive vetting, following my appointment as adviser to the All-Party Parliamentary Committee on Defence, which had decided to examine the positive vetting system. He replied to me on January 12, declining to assist for various sensible reasons, and might have assumed, quite wrongly, that I was contemplating a book about positive vetting. I did not approach him about oversight, which is the subject of *Too Secret Too Long*, until August 28, 1983, and even then, in my letter, made no mention that I was contemplating a book on the subject. I asked for his views on the grounds that MPs would be raising the issue in Parliament, as they did, and I would be consulted by them for advice, which I was. Again, he declined to be helpful.

Sir Arthur was aware that I was maintaining my general interest in the intelligence field, and it is possible that he might have told Sir Robert, in a casual conversation at one of their routine meetings, that he would expect me to write another book some day. But he could not have told him anything about *Too Secret Too Long* because we never discussed it. I have always been aware that retired senior intelligence officers feed information back to their old service, and the last thing I would have wanted was to let the authorities know I was writing another book, particularly at such an early stage. It could only have led to a warning to intelligence officers not to be helpful to me, because neither the government nor the secret services wanted oversight.

I am quite sure that Sir Robert answered Turnbull as he did because he was recalling what had happened between Sir Arthur and me at our one and only lunch in September 1982. As I have described, that lunch was indeed about a book—but not one by me. It was about a projected biography of our mutual friend, Sir Maurice Oldfield, written by others. The only book of mine mentioned at that lunch was *Their Trade Is Treachery*. In view of my disclosure to Sir Arthur of the strong possibility that Sir Maurice Oldfield's alleged homosexuality would be exposed, he obviously had a responsibility to report that fact to the Cabinet Secretary and did so. Sir Robert had been informed of the several interrogations of Sir Maurice in 1980, which had resulted in a confession and the withdrawal of his positive vetting clearance. Both men were aware that, in the event of publicity about the issue, Mrs. Thatcher would be required to make a statement to Parliament, as she subsequently did when I disclosed the fact in 1987.[4]

Sir Robert eventually received some information about *Too Secret Too Long* from Sir Anthony Kershaw, during their meetings about Wright's "dossier," but that was late in 1984, when the book was close to publication. As Sir Anthony Kershaw was keen to promote oversight, I gave him a rundown of *Too Secret Too Long* on August 7, 1984, and he proposed to mention it in a speech to Parliament about the need for oversight.[5] On August 10, Kershaw referred to my book in a letter to Sir Robert Armstrong, saying, "As we both know, at least one very authoritative study will see the light of day before very long." The Cabinet Office then asked the Secretary of the D-Notice Committee to request an advance copy of the book from Sidgwick and Jackson. He did so but met with a refusal.

On September 24, when Kershaw saw Sir Robert Armstrong, Sir John Jones (the Director General of MI5), and Jones's deputy at the Cabinet Office, he mentioned my forthcoming book. As they had not been allowed to see it, all they could say was that they could not imagine what I had discovered that would be new to them.[6]

As late as October 1984, three weeks before publication of *Too Secret Too Long*, Sir Robert told Sir Anthony at a Downing Street dinner, "We shall just have to wait to see what Harry comes up with."[7] Kershaw himself did not see the book until October 29, when a copy was delivered to him at the House of

Commons. Early in November, Armstrong told Kershaw that he had not had time to evaluate the book or to have it evaluated.[8]

Sir Robert had, in fact, received his first intimation of the book from me directly on the evening of May 15, 1984, when we dined in close proximity in the London Zoo restaurant at a celebration for Lord Zuckerman, as described in chapter 7.

The summary of official documents revealed at the Wright trial stated that MI5 first knew about *Too Secret Too Long* on July 19, 1984, following a report about it in *The Times*.[9] It secured a copy of the book on October 26 with no difficulty, since, by that time, it had been sent out to booksellers. If Sir Robert had really known about the book in January 1983, he would undoubtedly have informed MI5; clearly, he did not.

In his evidence to the Australian court, Sir Robert claimed that, while he could not remember the analysis of the book done by MI5, there was very little in it of real significance that was new. Again his memory would seem to have been at fault. Justice Powell, having recently read the whole of it, disagreed and said in his judgment that it contained far more information than *Their Trade Is Treachery*, with much that was new. This included evidence of Hollis's communist connections in China and other matters. *Too Secret Too Long* was the authority most frequently referred to by Powell in his lengthy judgment. Turnbull also agreed that the book contained much new material and claimed that Sir Robert's dismissal of it was yet another lie.

Before the Australian trial, Paul Greengrass gave me an account of the reaction of Wright and his family to the book, and it was clear that they felt they should have had a share of the royalties, although there was no contract to that effect and although Wright contributed virtually nothing new to it. He had cut off communication permanently before I had begun serious work on it. In our conversations, Greengrass, who confirmed Wright's statement that Granada had paid him nothing for his efforts in making the TV program, kept referring to "poor Peter."

During the Australian trial, Turnbull was to ask, in a telephone call to me, why I had not sent Wright 50 percent of the royalties of *Too Secret Too Long*. I explained that, once material had been published, it was available for use by any author. Turnbull seemed to accept that, but it was clear that Wright, who claimed not to be particularly interested in money, wanted to be paid twice for the same information.

Turnbull's main interest in *Too Secret Too Long*, however, had been to use it as a means of convincing the court that I had been on such close terms with the former head of MI6 that he had, perhaps, assisted me with it and that the Cabinet Secretary had known this and had been aware of the book's contents for nearly two years without taking any action. These claims were without any foundation in fact but were made to appear true as Turnbull used his inquisitorial agility to capitalize on Sir Robert's flawed memory.

Many, including lawyers, may admire Turnbull for his cleverness in achieving this, trials being something of a game of wits. To me, it is a sad commentary on an accusatorial system of justice that it can be so abused that events that never occurred can be placed on what many would accept as a historical record.

‖14‖

Spycatcher

We *call it* Lie-Hatcher.
— Currently serving officer of MI5

A letter from MI5 to Wright as early as July 1981—only three months after the publication of *Their Trade Is Treachery*—shows that MI5 already had information that he was contemplating writing "an accurate history," although not for publication in his lifetime.[1] Before breaking off contact with me early in 1983, Wright told me that he was writing a book.

Wright's report, or memorandum, entitled "The Security of the United Kingdom Against the Assault of the Russian Intelligence Service," submitted to Sir Anthony Kershaw in 1984, was written in separate chapters and could have been a first draft of what was to become *Spycatcher*. In meetings with me in the autumn of 1984, and later in 1985, Paul Greengrass confirmed that Wright was far advanced with a book, which then had the working title, *I Was There*.

Wright had previously told me that he knew that the government would react strongly to such a venture, but he eventually secured a publisher—Heinemann (Australia), then a subsidiary of Paul Hamlyn. According to the trial evidence, Heinemann approached Wright after hearing that a book by him was possible. The contract was between Heinemann and a group called Project Tasmania Associates, one of whom was Wright. Attempts by the government to secure the names of the other associates during the Sydney trial were effectively blocked by Turnbull, with assistance from the judge. In one altercation, however, Turnbull intimated that at least one was a resident of Britain. A search in Tasmania has shown that the group is not a registered company or a business name.

Wright has stated that he was paid an advance of £18,000, with £9,000 presumably being paid on signature of contract and £9,000 on delivery of the typescript. Presumably the complete advance contractually due to Wright was £27,000, and he was to receive a further £9,000 on publication. The payment due upon publication may have been withheld pending publication of the book in Australia and Britain.[2] Whether this was the total advance or whether other "associates" received separate advances is not known. There was also the possibility of an American publisher and substantial royalties from serialization rights, both of which have been achieved at the time of writing.

Wright admitted in his affidavit to the Sydney court that the money was welcome but argued that it could hardly have been a major motive because of the hassle and costs of litigation. It would be interesting to know the extent to which Wright's publishers had underwritten his legal expenses or those of Project Tasmania Associates. Before undertaking the television program with Granada, he had insisted on a detailed agreement to ensure that, in the event of litigation, he could not lose financially.

In view of what Wright had told me of his financial fears and his wish to leave money for his wife and children, I am in no doubt that, with *Spycatcher*, money was *the* major motive. The book was essentially a commercial venture, and Wright's lawyer, Turnbull, was to make this obvious during the Sydney trial. He repeatedly argued that everything of significance in *Spycatcher* had already been made public to a wide audience by me and by others and that Wright should, therefore, be allowed to repeat it. This reasoning effectively demolished any argument that Wright was putting it on record for patriotic motives so that something could be done about it. In spite of all the publicity that has since been given to *Spycatcher*, the government has not been pressed to make further inquiries into the Hollis case or into any other aspect of Soviet penetration because the book contributed no new grounds for such investigations.

No doubt, having broken his cover (without legal penalty) through his appearance on the *World in Action* television program, Wright wanted the personal satisfaction of having his name on a book along with all the attendant publicity, which, from his numerous television appearances, he seems to have enjoyed. It would also seem, from the way in which *Spycatcher* was written, that there was a substantial element of revenge.

The parent Heinemann company in Britain quickly learned through its inquiries that publication would not be permitted in the United Kingdom and that the government would have no difficulty in securing an injunction that would effectively be permanent. The book was therefore transferred to the Australian subsidiary, which proposed to publish it in Australia and hoped to be able to export books to Britain. In October 1985, Wright's British attorney, David Hooper, confirmed to me that an American publisher had also been secured.[3]

To avoid an expensive court action, the publishers sent a copy of Wright's lengthy typescript to the Attorney General, Sir Michael Havers, with the proposition that he could remove any particularly offensive passages. Havers ploughed through it, describing it to colleagues as dull and very repetitive. He was concerned about further undeniable evidence of incompetence in MI5 and about disclosures regarding intelligence relations with foreign powers, but other ministers were not perturbed by the old allegations of dirty tricks that, if published, would be far more damaging to the Labour Party than to the Conservatives.

From the start, there had been fears that Wright might embroider the truth in much the same way that defectors try to improve their value. When senior MI5 officers read his original typescript, they assured the Attorney General that Wright had, indeed, introduced information that was untrue, and they were not prepared to concede that this might have been due to his age and infirmity. Since then, the Prime Minister has told Parliament that she has been assured that certain allegations concerning MI5's activities, which are said to have emanated from Wright—in particular, his statement that a "rogue" group of MI5 officers was trying to undermine the Labour government led by Harold Wilson—are false.

After consultation with MI5, it was decided that the book was so full of material still officially secret—even though I had previously revealed most of it—that it should be totally suppressed. The government's real objection of course was that no former officer should be allowed to publish, or even to leak, secret information that he has learned during the course of performing his duty. Heinemann's proposition was therefore rejected, and a protracted and damaging court action became inevitable.

The Attorney General let it be known through the Parliamentary lobby that Wright would be prosecuted if he ever returned to Britain—a decision later described by Wright on television as "outrageous." The Attorney General made the same statement to Sir Anthony Kershaw.[4]

In what the government understandably construed as a conspiracy orchestrated from Australia, some of the more sensational claims alleged to be in *Spycatcher* were leaked to left-wing British newspapers. The purpose was in part to generate public interest in the book, but mainly to suggest that the government was trying to ban it to prevent damaging disclosures, especially about the "criminal" behavior of MI5 in its allegedly illegal attempts to secure information—even though this related mainly to times when the Labour Party had been in office and had held responsibility for the Security Service. Information from the book, including the names of former MI5 officers, was also leaked to Labour backbenchers so that they could be disclosed in the Commons. For example, Dale Campbell-Savours, using the protection of Parliamentary privilege, referred to allegations that Harry Wharton, a distinguished MI5 officer, had been a "leading conspirator" in the "plot" to bring down the Wilson government and inquired whether disciplinary action would be taken against him.[5]

No such claim appeared in Wright's book when it was eventually published in America, though it, and other allegations, may have been in Wright's original typescript. Similar unsubstantiated allegations were made against other MI5 officers by Campbell-Savours, who was not prepared to repeat them outside Parliament.[6]

It was no coincidence that a general election was looming and that the Labour leadership saw the Wright affair as another banana skin on which the Prime Minister, as well as the Attorney General, might be induced to slide to defeat.

Injunctions were obtained by the government forbidding several British newspapers to give any details about the contents of Wright's book until further order, as described in chapter 22. Whether these injunctions applied to all the media was left in doubt but most media outlets assumed that they did. A dispensation by Sir John Donaldson, Master of the Rolls, exempted information that had already appeared in my books and those of other authors, but it could *not* be attributed to *Spycatcher*.

In spite of this, the orchestrated leakage to the media and to Labour backbenchers of allegations said to be in Wright's book reached flood proportions. *The Times* reported that among the victims of illegal bugging and letter interception were Harold Wilson; his secretary, Lady Falkender; his lawyer,

Lord Goodman; and his senior policy adviser, Bernard (now Lord) Donoughue.[7] It alleged that in the "spymaster's dossier on treason" was "an unsuccessful attempt by MI5 to lure the Labour Minister, Anthony Wedgwood Benn, into a sex scandal." Wright was reported as alleging that MI5 agents had fomented a general strike in Ulster in 1974 to destroy the government's power-sharing scheme. MI5 was also supposed to have leaked a file on a homosexual relationship between the former Liberal Party leader Jeremy Thorpe and his friend Norman Scott. None of these allegations was, in fact, in *Spycatcher* when it was eventually published in America.

Media reports, said to have emanated from the original version of *Spycatcher* or from Wright, provided the opportunity for other wild allegations, which were quickly proved to be false. The international financier Sir James Goldsmith was supposed to have been introduced to Wright by Lord Rothschild in the presence of others said to be plotting a paramilitary coup to overthrow the Wilson government. Sir James Goldsmith assured me that he had never met Wright and had no knowledge of any such coup. Lord Rothschild similarly described the story as a complete fabrication.[8]

The media were swift to recall a much ventilated tale of a plot to topple the Wilson government by means of a military coup in 1968. *The Times* suggested that *Spycatcher* would throw light "on this vivid interlude of our time."[9] The alleged plot had centered on a meeting between Cecil King, who then controlled *Mirror* newspapers, his associate Lord Cudlipp, Lord Mountbatten (the former chief of the Defence Staff), and Lord Zuckerman (then chief scientific adviser to the government). King, who wanted to be rid of Wilson as Prime Minister, was using the *Daily Mirror* to further that aim, which was being pursued by other proprietors and editors who felt that the British economy was sliding downhill, perhaps irretrievably, under Wilson's leadership. Such a meeting occurred, but Lord Cudlipp and Lord Zuckerman, who have told me about it in the past, said that it was of no consequence. I was seeing Lord

Mountbatten fairly frequently at the time and, while he wanted to discuss all manner of defense issues with me, he never mentioned the possibility of a coup. I was close to the chiefs of staff and intimately involved in defense affairs and am confident that the possibility of any military support for such a coup was nil.

The story, which has been widely reported, was linked in the public mind with various organizations set up by former military and intelligence officers to keep essential services going during a general strike. Extreme industrial action seemed possible because of the militancy of the trade unions, some of which were led by communists who seemed intent on wrecking the economy for political motives. I investigated and reported on the activities of all these organizations at the time. Though their objectives—such as operating power stations, keeping communication systems open, and preventing sewage from surging down the streets—were laudable, they were censured by the ignorant as "private armies," despite the fact that none had arms or need of any.

Spycatcher, as published in the United States, threw no light on any of these alleged conspiracies. Wright's alleged knowledge of a specific MI5 plot against Harold Wilson and his government will be considered in the next chapter.

Hoary stories that had been in books and newspapers for years were resurrected as being in Wright's book and were retailed with mock horror by Labour MPs. These included MI5's bugging of the hotel rooms occupied by the Soviet leaders Khrushchev and Bulganin when they visited London in 1956 —a common procedure invariably applied to visitors to Moscow and regularly practiced by MI6 as well. [10]

MPs even affected to be shocked at Wright's exposure of the bugging of embassies, which is standard practice worldwide when it can be achieved. Over the years, there have been hundreds of underhanded bugging operations in Great Britain, but they do not match the offensive mounted against Britain's embassies behind the Iron Curtain. The only way that visiting ministers can speak in secrecy inside the British embassy in Moscow is to sit in a wire cage cantilevered from the walls of the basement! The bugging of the new American embassy in Moscow reached such proportions that part of the building had to be demolished.

In previous books, I had related how even the corridors of political conference centers such as Lancaster House in London have been bugged to discover what delegates were saying among themselves. Suddenly MPs regarded this as monstrous when it was said to be in Wright's book.[11]

In his sworn affidavit to the Sydney court, Wright stated that the official but illegal operations in which he and his colleagues took part were the wrong way of doing things. His attitude when I saw him in 1980 was very different. He was proud of his part in surreptitious operations such as Operation Dew-worm (the implanting of microphones into the Soviet embassy being built in Ottawa following a fire in 1956) and Operation Mole (a similar operation against the Soviet embassy in Canberra), and in eavesdropping on the Soviet consulate in London. Wright's change of attitude to such operations may have been sincere, but it was also convenient for the image he wished to present to the court.

Dubious sources availed themselves of the ready publicity to appear on television to claim that they had been involved in various MI5 plots, especially in Northern Ireland. Though few of their tales made any sense, these individuals were given repeated opportunities to tell them.

It was not long before Labour politicians were joining spontaneously in the campaign to smear MI5. When Wright was reported to have written about various surreptitious entries into properties, Lord Glenamara, formerly Edward Short, a deputy leader of the Labour Party, claimed that he was convinced that two burglaries in his flat in London in 1974 had been carried out by MI5. It had been suggested that Wright's book would also disclose that an attempt to blacken Short, by means of forged Swiss bank statements sent anonymously to newspapers, was the work of MI5, but no such charge appeared in any published version of *Spycatcher*.[12]

Among the oldest of the recycled stories was Wright's alleged account of MI5's involvement in a plan to assassinate Egypt's President Nasser in 1956. The facts were widely known and had been described in some detail in *Their Trade Is Treachery* in 1981. My information did not come from Wright but from sources in MI6 and the SAS, which were more deeply concerned. The plan to kill Nasser, along with his bodyguards, was hatched in Whitehall following Nasser's seizure of the Suez Canal. It was known that he would be in a certain fortified building and that it should be possible to introduce canisters of a fatal gas through the windows. The Prime Minister, Anthony Eden, vetoed the scheme but turned a blind eye to an alternative operation in which the killing was to be accomplished by dissident Egyptian officers using a cache of weapons supplied by Britain and hidden in the sand. The officers bungled it and were executed. Again, for political motives, Labour MPs manifested outrage, as they also did over a revelation that MI5 had been involved in an abortive plot to ambush and kill the Greek-Cypriot leader George Grivas, who had a price on his head for his part in the murder of British soldiers.

Such plans, which are almost always vetoed by the Foreign Office, are regularly dreamed up by Whitehall departments for contingency purposes. In the 1970s, for example, MI5 and MI6 were involved in planning a full-scale Defence Ministry operation under the leadership of Air Marshal Sir Neil Cameron (later Lord) to topple Idi Amin during the height of his horrific rule in Uganda. A substantial airborne force was training to land on the runway at Entebbe and capture or kill Amin, but the Foreign Office vetoed it. When MI5 had been responsible for counterespionage in British territories abroad, it was involved in the planning of an astonishing operation against the Mau Mau insurgents in Kenya. Kew Gardens was asked to devise a way of causing a baobab tree, which is sacred to some Kenyan tribes, to wilt within one hour. Botanists supplied a liquid and syringes, and plans were laid to send out messages on the "bush" telegraph that the tribal ancestors, who are associated with baobab trees, were angry that people were being forced into taking the Mau Mau oath. A Dakota aircraft was to be sent up to stage a sudden display of fireworks over Mount Kenya and, while the tribesmen were wondering what it was, scores of baobab trees would quickly wilt. Fortunately for the trees, the operation was canceled.[13]

While the Wright trial was still in progress, several newspapers received anonymous documents listing suspected spies who were alleged to be named in *Spycatcher*, presumably in the hope that they would be printed and generate more interest and publicity. The names were identical to those given to me by Wright when I was with him in Tasmania, which I had judged to be unusable for lack of evidence or for libel reasons.

While every allegation, however wild, was given prominence, the interest of the media and anti-Tory politicians centered mainly on claims by Wright that a "rogue" group of MI5 officers had tried to undermine and even overthrow the Labour governments led by Harold Wilson. In April 1987, the *Independent* newspaper secured a copy of Wright's typescript—apparently the original one he had written—and printed the allegations under the banner headline "How MI5 plotted Wilson's fall," clearly implying that they were true. They will be dealt with in detail in the next chapter.

When Justice Powell, the judge in the Sydney trial, read Wright's typescript, he described it as being written in *The Boy's Own Paper* or *Biggles* style, while British officials found it dull and repetitive. The first edition to appear in the United States, however, had been completely rejigged and substantially rewritten by another hand, known to be that of Paul Greengrass.[14] Additional material that Wright had wanted to reveal had been eliminated in the interests of general readability and, perhaps, to reduce the risk of legal action. It was essentially a rerun of *Their Trade Is Treachery* with items that had appeared in *Too Secret Too Long*. There were, however, additional details of radio surveillance operations and the names of secret service officers, which both British and American security officials regarded as damaging to Western security.

Wright was described on the book's cover, deceptively, as "Former Assistant Director of MI5." There are many assistant directors in the various branches of MI5, but it was not long before local newspapers were describing him as the Deputy Director General, which hardly accorded with the fact that he had retired with such a small pension.

Understandably, the book was angled to show Wright as something of a scientific genius who had dragged an unwilling MI5 into the technological age. While promoting Wright's conviction that Hollis was a Soviet agent, *Spycatcher* made no mention of an inquiry that, if Wright had not muffed it, might have solved the case. In 1982, while I was studying the autobiography of Ursula Beurton, the Soviet agent code-named "Sonia" who is believed to have serviced Hollis during World War II, I noticed the name Arthur Ewert. He had been a firm friend of hers while she had been in China in the 1930s, contemporaneously with Hollis. I wrote to Wright, asking him if Ewert meant anything. He confessed, sadly, that it did and that he had "certainly missed something." Wright had heard of a retired Army officer, Anthony Stables, with whom Hollis had shared a flat in Peking and went to question him in the Cotswolds where he was living. Stables remarked that he had been worried about Hollis's friendship with Arthur Ewert, who was a well-known "international socialist." When consulting MI5's archives, Wright had looked up the name under *Ewart*, believing him to be British and, finding nothing there or anywhere else, dropped the inquiry without even leaving a note in the files. In fact, as I quickly discovered when I searched the plentiful literature, Ewert, who was German, was a professional communist and pro-Soviet agent of the highest rank, being close to some of the Soviet leaders. He was an ardent recruiter and had been involved in all manner of international revolutionary activities—in Canada, the United States, and Brazil, as well as in Germany and China—as I recorded in *Too Secret Too Long*. After being imprisoned and tortured in Brazil, he returned to East Germany, where he received a hero's funeral when he died in 1959. Had this been known to the MI5 officer who eventually interrogated Hollis, it could have been used as proof of a communist connection, and a much tougher line could have been taken. This gaffe is not described in *Spycatcher*.

Wright and his colleagues also failed to find another piece of evidence about Hollis that could have been crucial during the latter's interrogation. The Soviet defector, Igor Gouzenko, had revealed the existence of a spy inside MI5 with the codename "Elli." The few facts which Gouzenko knew about "Elli" fitted Hollis, save one: it was known that "Elli" had "something Russian in his background." While I was in Tasmania, Wright had described how he had failed to find anything really Russian in Hollis's background, in spite of an exhaustive search. Then, in 1985, while researching various books written by Hollis's elder brother Christopher that had long been available in most big libraries, I discovered that the whole Hollis family believed that they were descended from Peter the Great! *Spycatcher* makes no mention of this either, although I reported it fully in *Too Secret Too Long*.

There have been several disclaimers concerning the reliability of *Spycatcher*. Lord Mayhew has described Wright's references to a meeting which he had with him in 1969 as leaving him with doubts about his judgment and veracity.[15] Lord Rothschild has denied the truth of various references that Wright has made to him. There have also been American disclaimers concerning allegations about the CIA.

Several of Wright's former colleagues have publicly disowned him. Most prominent of these was Charles Elwell who, in a letter to *The Times*, described Wright as having "feloniously and treacherously" broken his trust and pointed out that the bond of silence prevented him and other former MI5 officers from "exposing their former colleague and his book for what they are." [16] Lord Noel Annan probably expressed the general view of the British and American intelligence communities when he wrote in the *New York Review of Books*, "Those who have worked in intelligence will say Wright is a shit and they will be right." [17] During the Parliamentary debate on the Official Secrets Act in January 1988, Dr. David Owen, a former Foreign Secretary, said, "Peter Wright is a skunk," and those present did not demur.

As for the general public reaction to Wright, the more money he seemed likely to acquire, the more public opinion turned against him—as people realized that it was their secrets that were being sold.

|| 15 ||

The Climate of Secret Suspicion

What is the point of spying on communists a thousand miles away and ignoring those just round the corner?

—A former FBI officer

In the 1960s and 1970s, no writer strove harder than I did to discredit the Labour government, which I believed (and still believe) was disastrous for the British people, socialism being an outworn and unrealistic doctrine suited mainly to the aspirations of the power-hungry, the envious, and the idle. Yet on no occasion did I receive any anti-Labour information directly from MI5. The information on which my many reports in the *Daily Express* were based came from sources in or close to MI6, from enemies of Harold Wilson in the Labour camp, such as George Wigg (Wilson's former confidant and adviser on security affairs) and George Brown (Wilson's Foreign Secretary), from senior civil servants and forces chiefs, and from members of the public. Sometimes information came in anonymously through the post, but it was always ignored unless it could be checked.[1]

In my book, *Inside Story*, published in 1978, I reported that Wilson's fear about a plot to overthrow him had been well founded because "certain officers inside MI5, assisted by others who had retired from the service, were actually trying to bring the Labour Government down. . . ." This information derived originally from the late Bruce McKenzie, an extraordinarily well-informed Kenyan politician who was a close friend of Sir Maurice Oldfield and a neighbor of mine for much of the year. When I was able to confirm it in conversation with Oldfield himself, I believed it.[2] At the time we discussed the matter, in 1977, Oldfield was most anxious to assure the new Prime Minister, James Callaghan, that his department had not been involved in any nefarious activities, and he was not averse to using nonattributable publicity to make that clear. I was aware of the longstanding rivalry between MI6 and MI5, but Oldfield was a reliable source at the summit of MI6, so I assumed that his information must be based on good intelligence. In fact, as I now know, the basis was totally unreliable. His main source had been Harold Wilson himself, at the time when he was at his most paranoid about plots against him.

In 1975 Oldfield had been called in by Wilson, who was then Prime Minister, to be asked his views about rumors of a plot against him involving MI5. Wilson said that the plot was based on a belief that he and his political secretary, Marcia Williams (now Lady Falkender), were part of a communist cell operating inside Number 10 Downing Street. That was the first that Oldfield had heard of it, but he was soon to hear more from Peter Wright when the two dined together, as Wright revealed in *Spycatcher*. Oldfield raised the subject of the MI5 plot, and Wright told him that some of his colleagues in MI5 were worried about the way Wilson was running the country and suggested that certain entirely uncorroborated allegations about Wilson, indicating that he was a security risk, should somehow be made public.

Oldfield told me that he had followed up Wilson's fear and had confirmed it with "informants in MI5" whom he did not name. He did not suggest that a large number of MI5 officers were involved; in *Spycatcher*, Wright claims that "up to thirty" had given approval to the scheme to discredit Wilson. I find Wright's claim difficult to believe because it would be impossible for so many members of such a small organization—Wright claims it was half the staff—to be involved without the top management's hearing about it.

At the time Wilson called in Oldfield, he also suspected that he was being bugged in Number 10, and presumably he mentioned this, too, because McKenzie, in whom Oldfield had confided, not only told me that Wilson had been bugged but assured me that he knew it to be true when I expressed doubt about it. Once Wilson's fear that he had been bugged had been given publicity by his former press secretary, Joe Haynes, I reported in the *Daily Express* that this fear had been justified.[3]

Like the chief of MI6, an investigative journalist is only as reliable as his sources. Oldfield may have believed what Wilson had told him about MI5 officers spreading rumors, but it is possible that he disbelieved it and passed it on to others, including me, as a deception operation to impugn MI5. In this connection it is significant that Oldfield's closest friend, Anthony Cavendish, a former MI6 officer, has recently stated that Oldfield regarded me as "a contact who could be used to plant leaks."[4]

It so happens that Wilson's story about the communist cell had not originated in MI5 at all but in gossip from Westminster and Fleet Street. I know, because I was the person who had related this gossip, racily as entertainment, at a country-house lunch in 1974, as I confessed in detail in *Inside Story*. My information had quickly reached Wilson by at least two separate channels, and he assumed that I must have acquired it from MI5. One channel was Martin Gilbert, the historian, who had been at the lunch; the other was Lord

Weidenfeld, Wilson's publisher, who had heard a garbled form of my discourse.

Lord Wilson, as he now is, told me personally that Weidenfeld had warned him that certain officers of MI5 considered him to be a security risk and that he had consulted the head of MI5 (at that time, Sir Michael Hanley) about it. He said that Hanley had replied that he believed this to be true but that only a handful of officers were concerned. According to Mrs. Thatcher, Sir Michael Hanley has recently denied making any such reply. [5] It seems likely that Oldfield had warned the MI5 chief about what he had heard and, whether this was done directly or indirectly, they were doing no more than trading gossip.

In short, what had happened was that I had related some Fleet Street gossip, which had reached Wilson, who had passed it on to Oldfield as fact, and eventually Oldfield had passed it back to me as fact backed by the authority of MI6. The Prime Minister, the chief of the Secret Intelligence Service, and I had all been taking in each other's washing!

Wright's alleged claim that MI5 officers had been involved in a plot to topple Wilson, and the Labour government as a whole, was given wide publicity, before the appearance of *Spycatcher*, as a result of leaks from Australia. The basis of this claim, however, could have been nothing stronger than internal MI5 office remarks about the desirability of such action for, whatever a few officers might have said after a good lunch, there is no sound evidence that any of them ever took any illicit action of any kind.

While it is not impossible that some individual MI5 officers may have leaked fabricated stories to journalists, indicating that Wilson and other ministers were involved in various forms of misconduct, the bulk of the relevant gossip that reached Fleet Street undoubtedly came from other sources.

So far as I was concerned, the communist cell story, to which I gave no credence, originated in inquiries I had been making about the financial plight of the widow of Michael

Halls, Wilson's former principal private secretary in Number 10 Downing Street. Mrs. Halls had alleged that there had been problems with MI5 over the security clearance of Marcia Williams. Other former members of Wilson's "kitchen cabinet" had come forward with what they regarded as evidence of pro-Soviet connections—including even Christmas cards from Moscow! I also had information from Lord Wigg, Wilson's former confidant, who had turned against both him and Marcia with considerable venom. The real conspiracy to get rid of Harold Wilson as Prime Minister was, in fact, contrived inside the Labour Party: as early as 1963 a dining club of Labour moderates had been set up to eliminate Wilson as leader and it continued to meet when he was Prime Minister.[6]

Members of the public who disliked Wilson and his "kitchen cabinet" entourage also provided the media with ammunition. That was how Wilson's damaging involvement in what came to be called the "land deals affair" came to my notice.[7]

When I visited Wright in Tasmania in 1980, I took a copy of *Inside Story* with me, and we went through relevant parts of it. Though he was keen to make *Their Trade Is Treachery* as salable as possible, he would not confirm the MI5 "conspiracy," which I had reported, and he insisted that any action contemplated or taken against Wilson and his government had been justified and in line with MI5's duty. He said nothing whatsoever about any group of dissident officers trying to undermine Wilson. John Ware, co-producer of *The Spy Who Never Was*, had a similar experience. Writing in the *Listener* in 1987, he stated, "When I interviewed Wright in January 1984 he refused to talk about Wilson and the events outlined by Pincher."[8]

Before *Spycatcher* emerged in America, the media were claiming that Wright would be describing twenty-three "criminal conspiracies" within MI5. In the ensuing speculation surrounding this apparent leak from *Spycatcher*, Labour MPs have stated as fact, in Parliament, that the "conspiracies" were perpetrated by officers acting illicitly and "out of control." It would, however, be impossible to mount any realistic operation against the Labour Party or any other target without making several departmental heads aware of it. Those in charge of the watchers and technical services, which provide surveillance personnel and equipment, would have to be involved because every action of that nature has to be logged. If politicians or their close friends were to be affected, there can be little doubt that the top management would have to be informed and would have to agree. The widespread allegation attributed to Wright that thirty MI5 officers were involved in an illicit plot against Wilson is totally unrealistic.

There is no doubt whatsoever that MI5 undertook many secret inquiries and some actions against Wilson's friends and associates, but they were officially sponsored and in the line of duty. The reason why the top MI5 management knew nothing about any illicit activities was because they were never undertaken.

To understand the official attitude of the security and intelligence services under successive Labour governments, it is essential to appreciate that their main function from 1946 onward has been to counter Soviet subversion in the United Kingdom, and there has been continuing evidence that the Labour Party and the trade unions associated with it have been prime Soviet targets for infiltration and control. Agents of MI5 were and remain convinced that there were powerful influences bent on turning Britain into a Marxist state. For that professional reason, MI5 has always devoted some of its resources to penetrating the trade unions by means of agents and informers.[9]

All the Parliamentary parties have been regularly penetrated by MI5, in the sense that informers (some of whom are MPs) report on any suspicious activities that might be of security interest, such as close association with Soviet-bloc agents.[10] Numerous MPs are former members of the security and intelligence services and continue to report to their old offices.

The officers responsible for countering communist and pro-Soviet subversion must inevitably suffer from some degree of tunnel vision. Their lives are highly specialized. They see frightening information that is denied to others. They bear heavy responsibility and will always tend to err on what they consider to be the side of national security.

As the judge in the Wright trial pointed out, the members of MI5 were required to observe the law because MI5 had been set up "pursuant to an exercise of the Royal Prerogative," but in practice they had been in the habit of breaking it in the line of duty; and successive governments, including Labour administrations, had been well aware of that. Through the almost total secrecy that, before *Their Trade Is Treachery* was published, had attached to their work, they knew they had a freedom of clandestine action denied to others, including the police. If they were caught in some illegal action in the line of duty, they could be confident that the police would always cover for them, and if the press got wind of such an operation, pressure could usually be brought to bear on editors on the grounds of national security.[11]

The bugging of foreign embassies has long been an accepted practice, as has the bugging of homes and offices belonging to suspected persons. This has continued through all Labour administrations, with their acquiescence. The revulsion expressed by some Labour leaders in response to Wright's widely reported claim that, for years, he and other MI5 officers had "bugged and burgled their way through the Embassies of London" was spurious.

Venues for international meetings, such as Lancaster House in London, were regularly bugged when such meetings held political or security interest. This, too, is a common international practice. Visiting British ministers and officials taking part in meetings in various rooms in Moscow are routinely warned to cover any notes they may write because there are, invariably, spy-holes in the ceilings, with eavesdroppers watching through binoculars.

Deniable operations—surreptitious activities that can be effectively denied if any accusations are ever made—have been a regular fount of intelligence. For example, when it becomes necessary to know whether a suspected spy is operating a radio transmitter and using one-time pads for that purpose, it may become necessary to break into his abode and search it, without making him aware of it. Some MI5 officers are specifically trained for such functions, and one of the main reasons why MI5 has never been formally legalized is to enable its staff to carry out essential operations that might well be impossible under tight legal control. Surreptitious entries have always to be sanctioned by the MI5 senior management; and because substantial resources in personnel, transport, and equipment are needed for such operations, they cannot be staged extramurally by a group of "rogue officers out of control." Wright was at great pains to assure me that, for bugging and telephone surveillance, Home Office warrants always had to be obtained.

Again, governments of all parties have deliberately turned a blind eye to this situation for many years, and Parliament has been party to it through the convention of desisting from raising security and intelligence issues, precisely to avoid revealing MI5's methods.

Over the last thirty years, the Labour Party has made itself a legitimate target of MI5 interest through its penetration by Marxists, communists, and militant extremists. The unions that serve the Labour Party have been similarly penetrated, to the extent that some have been under communist control. A brief chronological survey of events establishes this.

Communist infiltration of Parliament began in earnest in 1945, when at least eight or nine crypto-communists were elected on a Labour ticket.[12] Some ministers in the new Labour government had been associated with communism to an extent that caused deep concern in Washington. Shortly after the end of the war, when Lord Rothschild was in Washington to establish liaison with American scientists about radioactive fallout from atomic weapons, the chairman of the Atomic Energy Commission, Admiral Lewis Strauss, who was a friend, put on a dinner for him. After the meal, Strauss said: "I want to ask you, in front of these other gentlemen, why we should let you have what is secret information when Mr. Strachey, a communist, is War Minister?"

Rothschild was unable to make any sensible comment, except to say that his information would not be going in Strachey's direction. But on his return to London, he sought a meeting with the Prime Minister, Clement Attlee, and told him what Strauss had said, interpreting it as a warning that he was expected to transmit. Attlee merely said, "They would, wouldn't they?" But he got the message, as Lord Longford eventually told me quite independently.

Attlee called in not only Strachey but George Strauss and Lord Longford (then Lord Pakenham), who had also been associated with prewar moves to improve cooperation between the Labour and Communist parties. Attlee told them of the American objection to any association of British ministers with communism, and then he snapped, "That doesn't apply to any of you, does it?" None of them replied. "Right. Then that settles it," Attlee said and dismissed them without further action.

In 1947, the Joint Intelligence Committee produced a paper dealing with techniques for penetrating trade unions that were being used by Moscow-trained agents.[13] Their purpose was not only to cause industrial unrest and disruption but to induce trade union leaders to push the policy of the Labour Party increasingly to the left through their influence at party conferences.

Government papers for 1950, released in January 1981, show that the Labour cabinet feared the outbreak of a series of communist-inspired strikes to disrupt the economy at the time of the Korean War.[14] Reports from MI5 to Attlee were so alarming that he set up a secret committee under Field Marshal Sir Gerald Templer to forecast what British communists would do. The committee questioned many witnesses, and its report (which remains unpublished) concluded that the communists would concentrate on achieving influence and power through three main institutions: the unions, the media, and higher education.[15]

The trade union then known as the Association of Scientific Workers was so heavily penetrated by pro-Soviet communists that, at one stage, of twenty-two members of the union's council, eighteen were active Communist Party members. One of its General Secretaries, Ted Ainley, had been trained at the Lenin School in Moscow and was functioning as a talent-spotter for the KGB.[16]

In 1955, the MI5 operation, Party Piece, described in chapter 11, revealed that the Communist Party's underground membership included thirty-one MPs serving under the guise of Labour Party membership. Several former ministers in Labour governments and senior trade union officials are still regarded by MI5 as having been Soviet agents of influence— some having been rewarded for that service.[17] Understandably, officers felt that they were wasting their time trying to combat possible communist subversion among civil servants if no effective action could be taken against ministers, MPs, and trade union leaders.

In 1961 Hugh Gaitskell, the "moderate" Labour Party leader, and his colleagues, George Brown and Patrick Gordon Walker, established themselves as a committee aimed at exposing communists who were fraudulently posing as socialists and at expelling them publicly from the party. That way, as Brown put it to me, they could go into the next election "clean of crypto-communists." They had a list of about a dozen suspects and thought there were more but could do nothing without hard evidence. They therefore sought the assistance of MI5, believing that the management there would be only too keen to have the more dangerous communists exposed.[18] They were wrong. According to my conversations with Peter Wright, "everybody in MI5 was opposed because it would have blown all their sources inside the Labour Party"—people like Tom Driberg, for example.[19] The Conservative leaders, headed by Harold Macmillan, were also against having MI5 provide any assistance because it suited them to leave the Labour Party encumbered with its problem. The only cleansing that occurred was the exposure of the long-established head of the Labour Party's press department, Arthur Bax, as a paid agent of Czech intelligence. Bax was allowed to resign quietly, claiming ill health. The whole operation by the Labour leadership against its crypto-communists was mounted in great secrecy, and I was required to say nothing about it for many years.

MI5's suspicions of the trade unions were amply confirmed by the public exposure of blatant ballot-rigging in the Electrical Trades Union in June 1961. Frank Chapple (now Lord), a disillusioned Communist Party member, and others invoked the conspiracy laws to show that communists had used fraud to secure the post of General Secretary for a communist and had effectively conspired to hijack the union. The circumstances were so appalling that the TUC expelled the union; to save face, the Communist Party then expelled two of the leading conspirators.[20]

In the following year, the report of the board of inquiry, headed by Lord Radcliffe, to review security procedures—and particularly the report's secret parts—had a profound effect on MI5's attitude toward the unions.[21] It showed that the Civil Service Staff Associations and trade unions had been effectively penetrated by communists, some of whom were holding positions providing access to secret information. As a result, Whitehall departments declined to negotiate with such communists, some of whom were removed.[22]

With the accession of Harold Wilson to the premiership in 1964, MI5 felt it had deep cause for concern. According to

Peter Wright's conversations with me, Wilson's antipathy to MI5 began early in his premiership when he asked it to clear certain friends of his for regular access to Number 10 and they declined. These friends included Rudi Sternberg, who was knighted in 1970 and made a life peer in 1975 as Lord Plurenden. His wealth was based on huge contracts for the export of potash from East Germany, and he also secured business in Rumania. MI5 assumed that he must have had influence in Moscow and wondered why. They believed that leaks of information to Moscow originated from him. Also suspect was the wife of Sir Leslie Plummer, a Labour MP. A close friend of Wilson, Plummer was heavily involved in the East German lobby, and when he died his wife, Beattie, who was of East European origin, carried on his work. Wilson made her a life peeress in 1965. Her home, Berwick Hall, near Halstead in Essex, was something of a left-wing political salon. MI5 was very suspicious of her because, to quote Lady Falkender, "She was always in and out of Number 10." [23]

Wright also told me that MI5's concern about such friends, who were mainly Jewish, led to Wilson's later accusations about "fascists" in MI5. There were strong objections to Wilson's pro-Israeli stance, but these did not come from MI5 but from the Foreign Office, which was markedly pro-Arab, and from Labour politicians such as Wigg, who had connections with Arab states.

In 1965, while Sir Roger Hollis was still Director General of MI5, James Angleton, the CIA counterintelligence chief, told the MI5 representative in Washington that the CIA had evidence from a defector-in-place behind the Iron Curtain that Wilson was "assisting the Soviets." He insisted that, to protect the contact, who was in a most sensitive position, MI5 should take no action without first consulting the CIA. Hollis consulted first the Cabinet Secretary and then Burke Trend, and they decided to take no action. It was not believed or suspected that Wilson was any kind of agent, except possibly an agent of influence. Wilson was asked by MI5 if the KGB had ever "made a pitch" at him and he said, categorically, that it had not.[24]

Later, when Furnival Jones became Director General of MI5, Angleton was approached again about the Wilson allegation, which was code-named Oatsheaf, but he would give no further information—the secrecy surrounding his alleged source being paramount. Under the circumstances, MI5's management would have been derelict in its duty had it not tried to follow up a lead from such a prestigious informer.

In 1966, the National Union of Seamen launched a strike calculated to bring the country's trade to a standstill. The people behind the strike included Bert Ramelson, the "industrial organizer" of the Communist Party, and Wilson soon received indisputable evidence from MI5, obtained surreptitiously, that the strike was politically motivated. Under the threat of exposure, those responsible capitulated.[25] Because of the secrecy demanded by MI5 to cover its sources who had penetrated the union, Parliament and the public could never be given the details of this sordid affair.

First-hand evidence that trade union leaders and Labour MPs had been recruited as Soviet-bloc agents came from Josef Frolik, a Czech intelligence officer who had served in London and defected to the CIA in 1969. He disclosed how he had recruited some of them. Frolik and another Czech defector, Frantisek August, alleged that a Labour minister, John Stonehouse, had been an agent. The allegation was taken most seriously by MI5 because Stonehouse, who had been a minister in the aviation and technology ministries and, later, Postmaster General and Minister of Posts and Telecommunications, had disappeared and was later found to have faked his suicide. The defectors alleged that Stonehouse had been recruited by sexual entrapment and subsequent blackmail threats while visiting Czechoslovakia. He was said to have supplied Soviet-bloc intelligence with aviation secrets and counterintelligence material. MI5 was not permitted to interrogate him save for a limited interview at which Wilson insisted on being present. Wilson announced that there was no evidence to support the allegations, and Stonehouse maintains his innocence.[26]

Frolik identified Tom Driberg, a Labour MP, as a paid Czech intelligence agent known by the code-name "Crocodile." When taxed by MI5, Driberg admitted that, even while he was chairman of the Labour Party, he had continued to give the Czechs information about internal party squabbles and personal scandals concerning who was sleeping with whom and might be blackmailable. While MI5 could do nothing— because the management could not admit that it had itself employed the Labour Party chairman as an agent—the information increased its suspicion of the party as a whole. Though MI5 believed that Driberg was being controlled by the KGB, he continued to provide information even after Harold Wilson elevated him to the peerage as Lord Bradwell.

Later, in the United States, Frolik was to name other Labour MPs as Soviet-bloc agents, while giving evidence to investigative committees; and though these names were expunged from the published reports, they were made available to MI5. Meanwhile MI5 had interrogated Bernard Floud, a Labour MP whom Wilson wished to make a junior minister. MI5 already had evidence that Floud was a crypto-communist and had been a recruiter for the KGB. Following interrogation by Peter Wright, in which he admitted his former communism but denied being a Soviet agent, Floud killed himself.

Niall MacDermot, a junior minister under Wilson who was regarded as having a bright future, was required to resign from the government "on personal grounds" after MI5 received reports that his second wife, who was half-Russian and half-Italian, had been named as a Soviet-bloc agent. He resigned as an MP in 1970. To further the cover-up of his departure, George Brown, then Foreign Secretary, was asked to find him a nongovernmental post, but refused.[27] During the Wright repercussions in 1987, MacDermot, who had worked in MI5, confirmed the circumstances but denied that there had ever been any substance to them. [28] He told the *Observer*, "I decided to resign and later to leave politics when MI5 could not be dissuaded from their unjustified suspicions about my wife." [29]

MI5 had grave suspicions regarding Stephen Swingler, who had been Joint Parliamentary Secretary to the Ministry of Transport since 1964. Swingler was a left-winger whose "dabbling" in Eastern Europe raised the concern of Labour cabinet ministers, as his political chief, Barbara Castle, recorded in her diary. [30] Wilson knew of MI5's suspicions that Swingler had compromised himself with the Soviet bloc but did not remove him. Swingler died suddenly in 1969.

The defection of the Czech, Major General Jan Sejna, provided further evidence of carefully planned penetration of the trade unions for purposes of subversion and sabotage. [31]

Harold Wilson's personal integrity in MI5's eyes was not improved by his decision to make MPs virtually immune to surveillance. In 1966 he told Parliament that, although a Privy Councillors' report on security had recommended that MPs should not be treated differently from anyone else, he had issued a directive to MI5 and to Special Branch forbidding the tapping of telephones belonging to MPs. This ban, which also applied to the Lords, extended to the examination of bank accounts and the opening of mail. It was widely believed in MI5 that Wilson brought in the rule to prevent his own phone from being tapped.

In spite of the restrictions, Will Owen, sixty-eight and the Labour MP for Morpeth, was arrested in 1970 and charged with selling confidential information to Czech intelligence. He had learned the information while serving on Parliament's Estimates Committee. He admitted to having received £2,300 but was acquitted on a technicality. Owen, a miserable and dishonorable creature, had to resign from Parliament, but the impact of the case on MI5 was far greater than was appreciated outside because he confessed to what amounted to treason and to receiving a great deal more money, once he knew that he could not be reconvicted and was safe from imprisonment. [32]

The evidence of the Director General of MI5, Sir Martin Furnival Jones, to the Franks Committee on the Official Secrets Act in 1971 showed that MI5 had evidence that "very many MPs" were in contact with Soviet-bloc intelligence officers.

Oleg Lyalin, the KGB officer who defected in London in 1971, warned MI5 that one of Harold Wilson's close friends, Sir Joseph Kagan (now Lord), was on close terms with the KGB chief in London, Richardas Vaygauskas. Both were Lithuanians. During the six months that Lyalin was under MI5 control before defecting, he reported on the relationship. MI5 was then duty-bound to put Kagan under surveillance, and this meant covering meetings with Wilson when possible. [33] Lord Kagan has admitted his friendship with Vaygauskas, who was expelled along with 104 others in 1971, but he insists that he did not know he was a KGB man and that their common interest was purely social. [34] When Wilson was questioned about Kagan by MI5, he said that he had no idea of his friend's relations with the Russians except through trading. Kagan was elevated to the peerage in Wilson's controversial resignation honors list in 1976.

By 1973, the National Executive of the Labour Party was so heavily infiltrated by left-wing extremists, some of them secret communists, that it was able to induce that year's Labour Party Conference to abandon the list of proscribed organizations that Labour Party members were forbidden to join. [35] Until then, Labour Party members had been forbidden to belong to organizations known to be communist fronts or to give them support. The MI5 management realized that this would intensify the Labour Party's lurch to the left and increase communist influence and opportunity. The decision quickly enabled militants to penetrate the Labour Party in a bid to manipulate it and eventually take it over. In more recent times, the infiltration of the Labour Party by revolutionary militants, several of whom are now in Parliament, is a matter of public knowledge.

In 1975 MI5 infiltrated a secret Soviet-sponsored meeting, in Düsseldorf, of communist trade union leaders from Britain and Europe to discuss tactics for disrupting industry. The results were soon to be seen at various factories, where the use of devious methods by communist shop stewards to gain decisions at mass meetings had long been in evidence.

During Wilson's second term of office, there were rumors inside MI5 concerning the many visits he had paid to Moscow while working as a consultant for a timber firm and suggesting that he had been compromised there. While MI5 had no legitimate suspicion of Wilson, there was concern about three of his junior ministers, and any tapping of his telephone conversations would have been mainly in that connection. Arrangements were made to stop these ministers from seeing especially sensitive papers. MI6 was particularly concerned about intelligence it was supplying to certain government departments about terrorist organizations operating abroad. This information was being supplied by agents who had penetrated various groups of "freedom fighters," and MI6 was deeply worried that some Labour ministers who supported the "freedom fighters" might leak enough information for the agents' identities to be revealed.

The United States government must have been concerned when a former Deputy Director of MI6, George K. Young, wrote to an American security contact that "at one point under Wilson there were five Ministers of the Crown whose membership of the Communist Party is not known to have been renounced and, overlapping with them, other Ministers whose ultimate allegiance is outside Britain."[36]

The reputation of the Wilson government inside MI5 was not enhanced by the appointment of Lord Brayley as Army Minister in 1974. He was a friend of Wilson, who had rewarded him with a life peerage in the previous year. Brayley's brief term of office came to an end with evidence of financial corruption prior to his appointment, and he died in disgrace, facing criminal charges. Sir Eric Miller, another close friend of Wilson's, killed himself when faced with possible charges.

During the last few months of Wilson's tenure at Number 10, he believed he had reason to suspect that microphones had been placed there surreptitiously. According to his press secretary, Joe Haynes, he had even employed a private agency to carry out an electronic sweep of certain rooms, since he did not trust the official agency to do it.[37] My report about the bugging of Wilson was eventually to be denied by his successor, James Callaghan, who instituted an inquiry into the allegation, but journalists were to claim that, in *Spycatcher*, Wright would reveal that MI5 did bug Wilson. There was no such claim in the American edition, and when I questioned Wright about it in 1980, he told me nothing to that effect, merely denying that Number 10 itself had been bugged.

Whatever the truth, Wilson became so excessively suspicious that his judgment was affected and he saw conspiracies that did not exist, as he has since tacitly admitted. During my researches for a book on the extremist infiltration of the Labour Party, both Lord Wilson and Lady Falkender, who was collaborating with me, alleged that there had been attempted burglaries of his papers. Wilson's homes in Lord North Street and Great Missenden were said to have been entered, and he was particularly concerned about break-ins at offices in Buckingham Palace Road, which he used for storing private papers. Lady Falkender told me that papers relating to the history of the Labour Party were kept there. These burglaries were attributed to MI5 without any supporting evidence.[38]

Only two months after his resignation, Wilson felt so strongly about the alleged MI5 conspiracy that he called to his presence two young BBC journalists, Barrie Penrose and Roger Courtier, to tell them, in considerable detail, of his strange experiences. He suggested that they should investigate the forces that were threatening democracy and indicated that some of these forces in MI5 and in MI6 were spreading smears. Later, in 1978, Wilson was to claim that the allegations attributed to him by the two reporters in their consequent book, *The Pencourt File*, were "cock and bull written by two journalists of limited experience and with so little sense of humour that they cannot distinguish between a disclosure and a joke."[39] Both he and Lady Falkender denied to me ever having said anything about MI5 or MI6 to Penrose and Courtier. I have no doubt, however, that the journalists accurately reported what they had been told, because Wilson continued to make the same accusations about MI5 to others.

At a literary lunch in Leeds, in January 1977, Wilson sat next to Professor Hugh Trevor-Roper (now Lord Dacre), and told him that MI5 had been out of control and had "spied on him, plotted against him and tried to secure his downfall."[40]

Ten years later, Lord Wilson now seems convinced that the MI5 "plot" against him was groundless rumor. This also applies to the suspicion he held shortly before his resignation that he and some members of his staff were under surveillance by the CIA.

There is no doubt, however, that the CIA and the U.S. National Security Agency were extremely concerned about the extent of the procommunist penetration of the Wilson administration, as they had been about its predecessors led by Attlee. They were also perturbed by the communist infiltration of the trade unions. The United States has an enormous military investment in Britain, which is the main reinforcement base for American forces attached to NATO in Europe. The CIA has always felt that it has a duty to protect the investment, and therefore it took some action to penetrate trade unions to secure independent information about their activities. Much local labor is employed by the American facilities in Britain, especially by the National Security Agency establishments, and the CIA made efforts to penetrate the unions in order to guard against subversives and saboteurs. They were particularly perturbed about communist trade unionists whose loyalty might be to the Soviet Union in a conflict.[41]

Whether this surveillance extended to independent bugging by the CIA and NSA is unknown, though the CIA has denied it. Under the Anglo-American agreement dating back to 1947, there has long been an exchange of surveillance information, including cable and letter intercepts, but it is not impossible that the American agencies occasionally undertook activities denied, by writ or circumstances, to the British.[42]

In summary of the situation up to 1976, when Wright left MI5, it can fairly be said that the considerable attention paid by MI5 to the Labour Party and leading figures associated with it had generally been in the line of duty as perceived by the MI5 top management. At certain stages, during the leadership of Attlee and Gaitskell especially, its activities were encouraged by Labour leaders who were deeply concerned about pro-Soviet infiltration of their own party and associated trade unions.

Whatever any edition of *Spycatcher* might contain about these causes for concern, it could hardly be detrimental to a Conservative government. On the contrary, exposure of MI5's fears about the Labour Party and trade unions could only be advantageous, especially as the alleged misbehavior occurred mainly when Labour was in office. So allegations in Parliament and the media that the government's main reason for trying to suppress Wright's book has been to prevent his disclosures about MI5 activities against the Labour Party can hardly be true.

There is no good reason why the climate of opinion in MI5 concerning the Labour Party should have changed much since Wright's departure. MI5's worst fears about the Labour Party were realized when Michael Foot, a nuclear disarmer and Committee for Nuclear Disarmament (CND) supporter, became leader and a possible future prime minister in 1980. Far from resisting pressure from left-dominated unions for unilateral nuclear disarmament, he favored it. The possibility of a government that would expel the Americans from their nuclear bases and severely damage, if not terminate, the Anglo-American relationship suddenly became very real.

The succession of Neil Kinnock to the Labour leadership in 1983 did little to diminish security fears because the policy of unilateral nuclear disarmament was continued and presented with even greater determination.[43]

In 1984, the miners' strike organized by Arthur Scargill turned out to be a blatant attempt by revolutionaries to overthrow the government for political motives. Scargill had been trained by Frank Watters, a dedicated communist, who had been sent to Barnsley in October 1953 by the Communist Party as "organizer" (meaning disorganizer) of the Yorkshire coalfields. Scargill, who stood as a communist candidate in a local election in 1960, was his protégé.[44]

In 1985, Oleg Gordievsky, a KGB officer who had been working as a spy for MI6, defected to London and provided a full list of British agents of influence serving the interests of the Soviets. MI5 already knew the names of most of them, but Gordievsky's confirmation and extension underlined the continuing reality of the threat within. Around the same time, there was publicity in Parliament concerning certain Labour MPs and trade union leaders involved with the World Peace Council, which is the major Soviet front organization.[45]

The climate in MI5 was bedeviled in 1985 by what became known as the Massiter affair, which was to be exploited by Wright's defense in the Sydney trial. Two independent television producers prepared a film, entitled *MI5's Official Secrets*, based on interviews with two former MI5 employees: Cathy Massiter, a former intelligence officer; and another who was unnamed and had been a clerk mainly involved in transcribing the tapes of intercepted telephone calls. Ms. Massiter, then thirty-seven and working as a gardener, had joined MI5 in 1970 and spent fourteen years there. She claimed, in some detail, that MI5 regularly broke its own rules by tapping the telephones of peace movement leaders and by falsely listing some of them as subversives to secure permission to do so. She said that MI5 had expanded its surveillance in the 1970s to include journalists and lawyers. She and her unnamed colleague claimed that the home of Ken Gill, the communist General Secretary of the TASS union, was broken into and searched during merger talks with another union. John Cox, a vice-president of CND and a member of the Communist Party's executive committee, was named as a key target for MI5 attention.[46]

Ms. Massiter's criticisms were certain to provoke the sympathy and acclaim of the left and particularly of the ultra-left, as was proved by the reaction of the communist and militant press and hard-left politicians when the program was eventually screened on Channel 4 on March 8, 1985. Left-wing MPs warned of a "McCarthyite-style threat to civil liberties." It was inevitable that the far left would use the alleged disclosures in attempts to undermine the efficiency of MI5 in countering certain forms of subversion that it would like to foster. As regards the general public, a Gallup poll revealed significant support for the monitoring of the activities of communists in trade unions and of political organizations with policies of promoting civil disobedience.[47]

The government maintained the position that MI5 must be able to keep subversives under surveillance, if need be, and that it cannot safely wait until they commit criminal offenses.

When the program was investigated and analyzed in advance by MI5, there was no doubt in the service that Ms. Massiter had breached her security obligations and that if the program were televised it would damage MI5. Nevertheless, no action was taken to restrain the program or even to interview Ms. Massiter, although she had left the service fairly recently. Again, the requirements of secrecy took command, and the MI5 legal advisers decided that, in any action, they would have to make too many damaging admissions. The circumstances surrounding the production of the film were investigated by the Director of Public Prosecutions, but no action was ever taken against anybody. All that occurred was that Lord Bridge, of the Security Commission, was asked to investigate Ms. Massiter's allegations that telephone conversations had been improperly intercepted. Lord Bridge reported to the Prime Minister in March 1985 that, during Ms. Massiter's time in MI5, no warrants had been issued in contravention of the established criteria.

The government's failure to prevent the showing of the film or to take any action against Ms. Massiter and the producers was to be cited by Justice Powell in Sydney as further evidence that the government's insistence that MI5 must be seen to be leakproof was humbug.

In the spring of 1987, following Parliamentary demands for a full-scale inquiry into Wright's allegations, Prime Minister Thatcher announced that an internal investigation had already been carried out by the Director General of MI5, Sir Anthony Duff, and the service had been cleared of involvement in the plot alleged by Wright.[48] She stated:

The Director General of the Security Service has reported to me that, over the last four months, he has conducted a thorough investigation into all these stories, taking account of the earlier allegations and of the other material given recent currency. There has been a comprehensive examination of all the papers relevant to that time, including officers whose names have been made public.

The Director General has advised me that he has found no evidence of any truth in the allegations. He has given me his personal assurance that the stories are false. In particular, he has advised me that all the Security Service officers who have been interviewed have categorically denied that they were involved in, or were aware of, any activities or plans to undermine or discredit Lord Wilson and his Government when he was Prime Minister.

The then Director General [Sir Michael Hanley] has categorically denied the allegation that he confirmed the existence within the Security Service of a disaffected faction with extreme right-wing views. He has further stated that he had no reason to believe that any such faction existed.

No evidence or indication has been found of any plot or conspiracy against Lord Wilson by or within the Security Service; or any misuse of information obtained in the course of their investigations. Further, the Director General has also advised me that Lord Wilson has never been the subject of a Security Service investigation or of any form of electronic or other surveillance by the Security Service.

As David Owen pointed out, Sir Anthony Duff was not a career MI5 man—he had been brought in from the Diplomatic Service to "clean up" MI5—and was, therefore, unlikely to be doing a cover-up job for old colleagues.

What did this comprehensive statement imply for Wright? It meant either that he had told lies in order to increase interest in his book, or that what he had reported as a serious "plot" had been no more than idle office gossip that came to nothing. Such action as had been taken had not been illicit because it had been done in the normal course of MI5's duties, with the agreement of the management.

‖ 16 ‖

The Web of Deceit in Australia

A secret is your slave if you keep it, your master if you lose it.

—Arabian proverb

On August 20, 1985, Australian attorneys acting for the British government wrote to Wright warning him that the Treasury Solicitor knew that Heinemann Australia was planning to publish his memoirs. He was told that, unless he replied within seven days, giving details of what he proposed to do, the government would "protect the interests" of the Crown. The publisher was also warned. Wright and Heinemann did no more than acknowledge the letters.

The government then launched the case in September 1985 by obtaining injunctions and undertakings to prevent publication of the book until the matter had been settled in the Australian court. There were various delays and adjournments until the case of *HM Attorney General* v. *Heinemann (Aus-*

tralia) and Another (Peter Wright) came before Justice Powell on March 24, 1986.

The government's decision to oppose the publication of *Spycatcher* had been made by the Attorney General, acting mainly on the advice of the legal adviser to MI5, whose management ensured that it would not have to supply any witnesses for questioning. There was proper concern that, if Wright was not opposed, other former secret service officers, some of whom had already been refused permission to publish memoirs, might break their bonds. It was a collective ministerial decision, with other ministers, including the Prime Minister, being consulted.

The principle involved was genuinely of the gravest importance to national security, and the stakes were very high. While much of Wright's material was by no means old in intelligence terms, what was far more menacing was the possibility that other, more recently retired, officers with much more sensitive information might be tempted to make their fortunes if resolute efforts were not made to inhibit Wright. Explaining this to me, a senior minister quoted the case of Oleg Gordievsky, the KGB officer who had been run as a penetration agent by MI6 for many years and who was required to defect when the KGB suspected him in 1985. Any officer who knew the astonishing details of the Gordievsky case, including the way he was spirited out of the Soviet Union, and the secret political repercussions, could make millions out of a book published with the credibility of his name and former occupation behind it. The film rights alone would command a huge sum. Disclosure of the details, however, could not only be extremely damaging (by revealing the secret methods of MI6) but might threaten the lives of other agents who had been involved in the long operation and especially in the escape.

The government therefore felt that it had no option but to pursue Wright and his publisher to the limit of the law, depriving him of all his profit, if possible, and making it clear that, whatever the outcome, any further renegade could expect the same relentless treatment.

Seen by the government's law officers, the case was simple because it was only about the obvious fact that no former officer who has signed the Official Secrets Act and is bound by contract and confidentiality has any right to reveal any of the secrets he has learned in the course of his duties. The claim that the government was entitled to restrain publication was not based on the Official Secrets Act but on the terms of employment. It was confidentiality, not secrecy, that was the central issue, as has been the case with many commercial firms and private citizens who have taken court action to protect confidential information that they claimed was their property. Nevertheless, secrecy was to be repeatedly invoked, with parts of the trial being *in camera*.

If Wright had found an American publisher first, the odds are that, apart from expressing its disgust at his behavior, the government would have taken no action. There would have been little chance of legal success against an American publisher in the United States, with Wright resident in Australia and, allegedly, unable to travel long distances on medical grounds. But the government had no sensible option once an Australian company attempted to publish the book in Australia. An action could be brought there on behalf of the Crown and, had the government failed to do so, it would have created a precedent that would have made subsequent actions against similar alleged offenders extremely difficult. Most secret service officers remain in Britain after their retirement and thus remain subject to the Official Secrets Act, but some do not. If Wright's book proved to be a money-maker, others might be induced to emigrate to write their memoirs. The government therefore had no option but to bring the case because, even if it lost, it could make it clear that it had done its proper duty and could repeat the process if necessary, using every legal device open to it.

According to Nicholas Thompson, the managing director

of Heinemann in London, nine senior lawyers were hired and
fired during preparations for the case before they settled on
Malcolm Turnbull, and started again. The nine had advised
that the publisher stood little chance of winning.

Turnbull, who was hired in January 1986, has been described as "chunky, dark-haired, with a falling lock of hair and
the appearance of a young Oscar Wilde." [1] He was only thirty-
two—bright, brash, ebullient, and (like many Australians) ir-
reverent toward authority, especially British authority.

The whole presentation changed after the arrival of Turnbull. He decided to reject the government's case concerning
confidentiality and concentrate on the public's right to know of
the treachery, incompetence, and illegalities in the secret services alleged by Wright. He also decided to concentrate on the
apparent inconsistency between the government's attitude
toward my book, *Their Trade Is Treachery*, and their attitude
toward Wright's; for this reason, the case came to be as much
about my book as about *Spycatcher*.

From the publisher's viewpoint, the tactics were two-
edged. It was hardly good for prospective sales for Turnbull to
keep repeating, as he did, that all the essential material in
Spycatcher had already been published by me. (The government would have been justified in suggesting that Wright's collaboration with me had been partly a deliberate ploy by Wright
to get the information published so that he could then repeat it
under his own name, but it refrained from doing so.)

Turnbull traveled to London to see the Treasury Solicitor,
John Bailey, who was responsible for advising the law officers
—the Attorney General and the Solicitor General. According
to his own account, he was unpleasantly aggressive and took a
bullying line with Bailey, from whom he got little change. [2]
The confrontation had begun with undisguised animosity on
Turnbull's part and would continue in that fashion.

From an early stage and by various stratagems, parts of
Wright's book dealing with contentious matters were leaked to
the British media and to Labour backbenchers, as I have al-

ready described, to establish sympathy for Wright as a crusader trying to expose evil. Backbenchers looking for a new cudgel with which to beat the government were not hard to find. In particular Dale Campbell-Savours, an obscure Labour MP, seized on old allegations of attempts by MI5 to blacken the Wilson government that had been ventilated in the 1970s.

Turnbull is on record as saying that he particularly wanted to "nail Mrs. Thatcher" over her statement to Parliament about Sir Robert Hollis and had wanted Neil Kinnock, the Labour leader, to "get her about that."[3] He eventually expressed disappointment that Kinnock, with whom he had been in personal touch by telephone, had failed him, although the Labour leader had, in fact, been as helpful as he dared.

Turnbull has stated that, in August 1986, he was telephoned by Jonathan Aitken, the Conservative MP, about a business matter, though Aitken has assured Parliament that all the relevant telephone calls were instigated by Turnbull. The Wright case was raised, and Turnbull claims he was told that Aitken had advised the Attorney General, Sir Michael Havers, against proceeding in the Australian court. Aitken agreed to speak to Havers again about a possible deal for settling the case by removing agreed material. Aitken passed on the terms to Havers, and Turnbull sent a copy of Wright's book to the Attorney General with the suggestion that the government should itemize any parts it wished to delete. The book was read by the Attorney General as well as by MI5 officers. There was general surprise and some relief that the book contained so little that I had not already disclosed. There were some further examples of MI5's incompetence and some embarrassing allegations concerning France, Egypt, and Turkey, but the legal adviser to MI5 told the Attorney General that many statements in Wright's book were false.

It was decided that no deal could be made and that the book had to be suppressed in its entirety.[4] This decision frustrated and angered Turnbull, and from that moment, Havers became one of the main targets for his animosity. Some time previously, Havers had told me jokingly that he was hoping for a "closed season" on spies until after the next general election. His hope could hardly have been more forlorn, and nobody was to suffer greater personal and political damage from the Wright affair than he.

The government was so determined to suppress the contents of Wright's book that it secured injunctions in British courts against British newspapers, preventing them from attributing any information to Wright, apart from what I had already published. According to Sir John Donaldson, Master of the Rolls, its main purpose in doing so was to make MI5 appear to be leakproof, because leaks are bad for the exchange of secrets with foreign agencies, such as the CIA, which will not trust it. In making this judgment, Sir John argued, incorrectly, that if the government had known about *Their Trade Is Treachery* in advance, the Crown might have moved swiftly to prevent its publication. In a letter to *The Times*, I pointed out that the Crown had had several weeks during which to obtain injunctions and had failed to do so.[5] The legal argument that MI5 must be seen to be leakproof was unrealistic.

Turnbull hinged his case on the fact that the major statements in Wright's book had already been made in *Their Trade Is Treachery*, five years previously, and that the government had not only failed to prevent its publication but had authorised it. On Wright's instructions, he then went further and put forward the ludicrous theory that my book was the result of a conspiracy involving MI5 and MI6, the government, Lord Rothschild, and me, in which Wright had become entrapped. Its alleged purpose was to expose all the skeletons in the MI5 and MI6 closets, especially the Hollis case, in a way which would enable Mrs. Thatcher to deny them in Parliament and so dispose of them. The book would also provide Wright with enough money in the form of royalties to resolve his financial difficulties and silence him. For good measure, the theory explained Lord Rothschild's involvement as being due to his need to deflect suspicion that he was the fifth man of the Cambridge spy ring, by turning the spotlight on Hollis.

In discussions with me, Turnbull seemed confident that the judge would accept this infantile scenario. He told me that the judge had special qualifications because he had been an intelligence officer, but this turned out to be nothing more impressive than service in the territorials as an Intelligence Corps captain.

The government's response was to deny the theory with derision and to point out that any book by a former MI5 officer would carry greater credibility than a book by me or any other investigative writer. The long legal argument was, inevitably, to plunge me, my publisher, and various friends into the maelstrom of the case.[6]

Before the case began, I was visited by David Hooper, Wright's London-based attorney. I gave him some information but declined to sign any statement that could be used in court. Hooper gave me Turnbull's numbers and suggested that I should call him.

The pretrial hearings and interlocutories took place in August, September, and October, with the trial proper beginning on November 17, 1986. By that time it was clear that, if the government won the case, it would stand accused of suppressing unsavory truths about the secret services for political purposes; if it lost, it would be seen to have spent a great deal of taxpayers' money to small purpose, because Wright's book contained little that I had not already published. This was so much the situation that one minister told me that he wished the action to suppress the book had never been launched, believing that, without the publicity, the book would have had little impact anyway. The government had decided to fight the issue on a major principle, however, and they were stuck with it.

Ministers took considerable comfort from the fact that the Australian government had agreed to intervene on MI5's behalf and tell the court that publication of Wright's book would

seriously damage Australia's intelligence interests; they regarded this undertaking as an "ace-in-the-hole."

It had been decided that the chief government witness
would have to be Sir Robert Armstrong. The Prime Minister
later explained this choice by telling Parliament that Sir Robert was her principal official adviser in relation to matters of
security. Accordingly, he swore the affidavits for the pretrial
interrogatory questions, which formed a significant part of the
evidence.[7] His presence in connection with those affidavits
was therefore essential. Once he had signed them, it followed
automatically that the Australian court would require his presence. Whether he was aware of this when he put his signature
to them is unknown. In the result, it would have been better if
someone more junior had signed them, for the case would not
then have attracted as much publicity as did the spectacle of
the British Cabinet Secretary at bay, being savaged by a belligerent young Australian out to make a reputation.

Sadly, Sir Robert seems to have been in ignorance of important matters when he signed the affidavits, such as the real
reason why my book had not been suppressed, and the role of
the Attorney General in that nonevent. It later emerged that
the answers were compiled by the Treasury Solicitor's department, which may have been in the same degree of ignorance
because of the dictates of secrecy.[8]

Again it is essential to appreciate Sir Robert's professional
position. His daily workload was so great and involved so many
subjects that he could not afford the luxury of concentrating
all his time on any one of them, a fact of administrative life
that also applies to senior ministers and especially to the Prime
Minister. There was no way that he could research the answers
to Turnbull's long list of pretrial questions himself. He had no
option but to sign the affidavits in the belief that they must be
correct and was then burdened with the responsibility for any
inconsistencies. His excessive workload also made inroads into
his memory of certain events that, at the time, were relatively
unimportant and extraneous to his proper function.

Sending such a prestigious establishment figure—Sir Robert had been educated at Eton and Oxford and had held many important positions—served to underline the seriousness with which the government was approaching the case. Only later did it become clear that it would have been pointless to have sent the Attorney General, since he had been deliberately excluded from the decision to avoid suppressing *Their Trade Is Treachery* and knew even less than Sir Robert.

Turnbull told me on the telephone that he intended to take Sir Robert through Wright's book page by page, forcing him to make all manner of admissions. He said that some 250 pages of Wright's book were devoted to proving that there was at least one high-level pro-Soviet spy inside MI5 in the 1950s and 1960s. Turnbull believed that Justice Phillip Powell, fifty-six years old and known to his friends and to the press as "Perc," would be bound to find that Hollis had been a Soviet agent, a matter of deep concern to Australia because Hollis had been involved in setting up the Australian Security and Intelligence Organisation (ASIO).

Nearly 150 sensitive questions for Sir Robert had been prepared by Turnbull, who told me that he intended to "tear him apart." In a bid to prevent this savaging, the British law officers resorted to the established legal device of admitting in advance to the court that everything in the book, including Wright's allegations against Hollis and his claims of criminal activities by MI5, was true. By and large the media assumed that, so far as Hollis was concerned, the government was admitting that he had been a spy but the law officers quickly denied this, saying that their move was purely procedural and had been misunderstood. It is established practice in British cases for one side to accept allegations that it regards as extraneous to the real issue, simply to get them out of the way and save the court's time. Nevertheless, Turnbull told me on the telephone, "We go into the case on the legally admitted basis that Sir Roger Hollis was a spy." This admission applied to all the other allegations in Wright's book. Such a device may be an accepted legal practice, but ordinary people found it difficult to comprehend.

Turnbull also told me that he would be demanding secret documents concerning the discussions about *Their Trade Is Treachery* and about those leading to the Prime Minister's statement to Parliament about the book and especially her references to the Hollis case. I quickly discovered that the government was preparing to fight any court order that it should hand over any secret documents and, in particular, those relating to the Hollis case. I am sure that the government would sooner have abandoned the case than produced the Hollis documents. For some reason there was information in them that could have damaged relations with Australia. The British law officers knew that, if the government were forced to withdraw from the case under such circumstances, few people would ever believe in Hollis's innocence again, because it would raise reasonable suspicion that the evidence on which Mrs. Thatcher's statement had been based had been rigged in his favor.

I formed the opinion from my several talks with Turnbull that he relished the prospect of haranguing Sir Robert Armstrong, to whom he was soon referring outside the court as "Sir Bob" and whom he described as "a meaningless waffler." This was a monstrous misrepresentation of a very distinguished public servant by a young lawyer who was then of little consequence but saw an opportunity for international publicity, which he was to achieve spectacularly.

I had good reason for my suspicions about how Sir Robert would be treated in an Australian court and went on record deploring his position as a straw man in the nine days he was to spend in the witness box. [9] Some years previously my wife and I had been dining with Australian friends in London when we were joined by the Australian Labour government's attorney general, Mr. Lionel Murphy, who eventually became a judge. Murphy was in London to discuss Australia's withdrawal from any legal control by HM Privy Council and that day had been to see British government ministers, including Lord Home, about it. Asked by one of my friends how he had fared, Murphy replied, "I told Home to stick the Privy Council up his fucking arse." The encounter did not engender much respect for Australian law or Australian lawyers. [10]

Before the trial opened, Wright made a sworn affidavit in which he gave many false statements, as I describe in detail in the next chapter. They were clearly designed to win the sympathy of the court for a frail old patriot who was being harried by the British government when all he wanted to do was to expose treachery and incompetence, with money being of minor importance. Whether through frailty of memory or design, Wright effectively entangled himself in his own web of deceit before the trial.

Shortly before the trial proper began, Turnbull telephoned me to ask how the government had acquired the typescript of *Their Trade Is Treachery*. I did not enlighten him, and he concluded by warning me that Labour MPs would be calling for the prosecution of me and Lord Rothschild for "corrupting Peter Wright." I pointed out that it was Wright who had approached me and that if anyone had been corrupted it was I. Nevertheless, he insisted that the demand would be made in the British Parliament.

From my earliest conversation with Turnbull, he clearly thought that he would begin the case in court with the judge "sympathetic." He told me that Justice Powell had stated, as an aside during one of the pretrial hearings, "Speaking emotionally, and not legally, it sticks in my craw that, if Hollis was a Russian spy, the Australian public cannot be told about it."

Justice Powell turned out to be a Rumpolish figure, with a mustache and horn-rimmed glasses, regarded in Sydney as a "fair-dinkum bloke" and a "jowker," given to making what he considered amusing comments in the court. He also made remarks that would have been regarded as outrageous in a British court. When the government's chief counsel was winding up his case, the judge intervened to remark about Sir Robert, "He would not stoop to a lie when a half-truth would do." [11]

He referred to the affidavit of the Australian Cabinet Secretary, which represented the view of the Australian government, as "baloney" with no credibility.

Before the trial opened in the Sydney court on Monday, November 17, I wrote a front-page article in the *Sunday Express* predicting that the government was headed for failure in the case and that Sir Robert Armstrong would be savaged by Turnbull. It was to prove more prophetic than I had thought.

To Australianize his image and draw attention to himself, Wright wore his interpretation of a drover's hat with a chin strap and only the pendant antifly corks missing. This was ridiculous headgear in sophisticated Sydney, but it became a trademark for Wright and for *Spycatcher* so that only a silhouette of him in his hat needed to be flashed onto the television screen for him to be immediately recognized. The hat was also worn by promoters of the book, supporting the probability that it was a sales gimmick thought up by his publishers. Journalists were told that the handle of Wright's walking stick contained a small flask of whisky from which he could refresh himself.

Probably the most outrageous aspect of the whole case was the presence in court of Paul Greengrass, Wright's collaborator, in an official position as an assistant to Turnbull. The judge allowed it on the grounds that he was "an expert on spy books." The Attorney General regarded Greengrass's position as "highly irregular," but the judge refused to allow Wright to be cross-examined as to whether anyone had given him assistance in writing *Spycatcher*. As a result, a working journalist, who had assisted Wright on a financial basis and whose name was to appear on later editions of the book, was allowed to sit through even the secret sessions as part of the defense team and to assist Turnbull in many ways.

At one stage Turnbull tried to draw Sir Robert into making a statement about the KGB defector, Oleg Gordievsky, apparently believing that he had produced proof of Hollis's guilt. Armstrong insisted on going into secret session on such a sensitive issue, and what he told the court remains secret, but Greengrass was permitted to hear it. I know from other sources that Gordievsky told his debriefers that he had been given no information about the Hollis case by the KGB Center and had not been aware that the KGB had ever had a British source at such a high level. Again, the secrecy cult prevented Armstrong from stating this in open court, although it might have appeared to favor Hollis's innocence; in fact, professional intelligence officers have assured me that it is unlikely that Gordievsky would have been told anything substantial about the Hollis case, since he had no need to know of it. According to a CIA source, Gordievsky was asked by MI6 to make a search of KGB records in Moscow for any evidence regarding Hollis. It is doubtful that such a valuable penetration agent as Gordievsky would be exposed to such a risky undertaking, and it is even less likely that any available records would contain anything about Hollis, because secrets about such a high-level agent would be very tightly held.

The government was represented by Australian QCs led by Theo Simos, an experienced but unimpressive equity lawyer. A team of British civil servants, including the Treasury Solicitor, John Bailey (now Sir), sat in as observers. No proper reconnaissance of the Australian court procedures had been made by the British law officers; the government (and Sir Robert, in particular) thought the experience would be similar to that in a British court. Nothing could have been further from the truth. Turnbull was permitted to deflect the case from its true purpose—whether or not Wright was in breach of the confidentiality he owed to the Crown—and was allowed to take other liberties that would have been quickly curtailed by a British judge. Remarks like Sir Robert's now famous explanation that it was sometimes necessary for a civil servant to be "economical with the truth" would have been acceptable in a British court but alienated the court in Sydney.

Turnbull was permitted to make the wildest accusations and inaccurate suggestions, without reasonable intervention from the judge, in his verbal assassination of Sir Robert, Sir Michael Havers, and, when the opportunity occurred, Mrs. Thatcher. He claimed that Sir Robert had been sent "to lie for his country," and was a man "determined to say whatever he felt would advance the government's cause regardless of its truth or falsity." He accused Havers of "being guilty of the worst form of dishonesty: he allowed another man to lie on his behalf and did nothing to correct it." [12] This was relished not only by the Australian press but by certain sections of the British media, the tone of the proceedings being brilliantly captured in a reconstruction of the case staged by Channel 4 television.

Although I cannot say whether "Perc" Powell enjoyed what seemed to be an orgy of "Pom-bashing," or not, he certainly appeared to and lost few opportunities to encourage Turnbull and to make "jowks" at the British expense. There was little that was good-natured about it. As the Australian writer Robert Hughes is reported to have commented, "all the early Australian settlers could be heard rattling their chains."

With biting invective, Turnbull repeatedly bulldozed Sir Robert into making admissions which were false. While insisting that his memory was hazy, Sir Robert confirmed my 1983 lunch with Sir Arthur Franks, which had never occurred; he said that Franks and I "meet from time to time," when we do not; he agreed that Jonathan Aitken had intelligence experience, which is untrue. These false confirmations were valuable assets for Turnbull, "the wily colonial boy."

To some extent, Sir Robert had brought the ordeal on himself through his advice to the Prime Minister in 1984 concerning the lack of response to Wright's "dossier" on the Soviet assault on the British secret services. A promise of some kind of inquiry and some Parliamentary publicity would have seriously weakened Wright's case for publication of his memoirs. If the Prime Minister had been advised in 1981 to tell Parliament that the case against Hollis was unproved either way and remained open, instead of appearing to clear him, Wright would have been hard-pressed to find an excuse for publishing his book.

In spite of the government's gambit in admitting the truth of Wright's allegations, Turnbull was able to ask Sir Robert so many questions that he was unable to answer that the judge remarked that he could not understand why the government had sent him. Turnbull and the judge would clearly have preferred the Attorney General to be present. With his court experience Havers would have been better prepared to deal with Turnbull's gratuitous insults but, as a minister responsible for legal decisions in many fields, he could not be spared for several weeks, his presence being needed in connection with inquiries into City frauds that the Prime Minister regarded as more pressing. [13]

Among the information leaked to the media in Australia and to the Labour opposition in London were extracts of some of the confidential letters I had written to Wright. The first released letter, which contained gossip about Sir Michael Havers, was passed to Campbell-Savours who read it out in Parliament on November 20, 1986. [14] A report about it appeared in the *Observer* on November 23, 1986. The purpose was to show the Attorney General as being personally friendly with me—support for the mythical conspiracy with the government put forward by Turnbull—and as being a high-level leak-source. The truth was that Havers and I, who are keen pheasant shots, met occasionally when we were both guests at organized shoots. At one of these, during a morning break, I took the opportunity to mention the current case in which the then-prospective Tory MP, Rupert Allason, who writes under the name Nigel West, had been subjected to an injunction concerning a new book he was trying to publish. It was stated in the Australian trial that West had been supplied with information and documents by the MI5 officer, Arthur Martin. Martin's concern at finding himself in a security problem had led to a plea for help from MI5, and the injunction had been the result. Havers had done no more than confirm what I already knew.

I have two sound reasons for knowing that the leak of the letter had been organized. A few days before Campbell-Savours read it to Parliament, I was telephoned by Paul Lashmar, a reporter for the *Observer* newspaper. He said that the letter had been acquired by his colleague, David Leigh, who was covering the case in Sydney, and that it would shortly be in the hands of Labour MPs.

In his sworn affidavit Wright, then seventy, was to claim that he had forgotten where the letters were, giving the impression that they had been missing a long time and had come to light again the day after the trial began. Greengrass told me in 1985, however, that he had seen the letters, and he questioned me about certain aspects of them. Their discovery was decidedly opportune, in view of what was quickly done with them.

Early in our correspondence, I had told Wright that I was destroying all his letters after reading them and digesting their contents. Many things in them were inimical to Wright's case and were hard, documentary evidence of his breach of confidentiality and of the Official Secrets Act. They showed, for example, that his claim that he was not interested in money was quite false, as he was regularly wondering how to make more. I appreciated that, when Wright realized that I had no damaging letters to release in response, more of mine would be made available to the media and Parliament if they suited his case. I therefore secured a statement in *The Times* to the effect that not all Wright's letters had been destroyed. The gambit seemed to work but all I had, in fact, were two letters of little consequence and fragments of three of my own letters to him.

When Turnbull made his next unsolicited telephone call to my home, I remonstrated with him for releasing my private correspondence. He did not deny that he had done so and tried to justify his action by saying, "Your government is playing this so dirty that we are playing dirty, too." When I asked him if he did not mind whose reputation was damaged in the process he replied, "No. We have got to win this case."[15]

Turnbull had telephoned me to repeat that I would be accused of corrupting Peter Wright by offering him money, and I sensed that he was hoping to create a court sensation. Before Wright gave evidence, which he was due to do, the fact that he had received half the net profits from *Their Trade Is Treachery* was secret. A statement in the court could be made to suggest that I had paid the money to Wright personally, with the obvious innuendo of bribery. In such circumstances, I am always reminded of the notice above the cage of a zoo animal: "This animal is dangerous. When he is attacked he defends himself." I therefore decided to deprive Wright of this particular dirty trick and called in Michael Evans, a former journalist colleague, and gave him the true story, which was printed in *The Times* the next day, revealing that Wright had received many thousands of pounds but only in monies paid by the publisher.

Turnbull was furious. With his assistance, Wright staged a media conference on November 25 in which he claimed— quite falsely—that the information had been leaked by the government as a smear to discredit him in advance. Turnbull even referred to a mythical Whitehall "briefing" when, in fact, I had been entirely responsible.[16] Wright told the media that the royalties he received were a "helpful incidental benefit." The truth is very different. Though Wright's original motive may have been to put the Hollis affair and other issues on record, his imminent bankruptcy and desperate need of £5,000 had motivated him in his search for an author in 1980.

Wright's main purpose at this press conference was to support Turnbull's claim that *Their Trade Is Treachery* was an officially authorised operation orchestrated by Lord Rothschild. He said that when he met me at Cambridge, he had sensed he was "being drawn into an authorised but deniable operation which would enable the Hollis affair and other MI5 scandals to be placed in the public domain as the result of an apparently inspired leak."[17] Wright defined a deniable operation as one that the authorities who mounted it could deny if anything went wrong. He said, "All I know about Lord Rothschild and the ease with which *Their Trade Is Treachery* was published leads me to the inescapable conclusion that the powers that be approved of the book." Yet he had never expressed any such view to me either when we met or in our long correspondence. On the contrary, he was always most concerned that MI5 should never be able to prove that he had been a source, however much he might be suspected. Why would he do this if he really believed that MI5 already knew and approved of it? The measures he suggested and took to preserve secrecy are proof enough, in my view, that he believed that MI5 had been totally unaware of the situation and that he was most anxious that it should remain so. In a statement to the same media conference he said, "I was terrified of getting into trouble," but later he attempted to withdraw this in court.[18] In fact, he had remained deeply concerned that MI5 should not learn of our relationship, which surely makes nonsense of any suggestion that Wright believed MI5 was privy to the whole arrangement.

It should be evident from my record that MI5 would never have approached me to take deliberate part in such a major operation. In the past, when I worked for a large-circulation newspaper, MI5 had used me to publicize a few specific matters it wished to release for counterintelligence purposes, but the MI5 management knew that, whenever I had helped them, I had invariably revealed the details at some later stage—as my book, *Inside Story*, clearly shows. Indeed, Wright was to tell me that MI5 had considered trying to recruit me as a paid subagent but decided against it because they knew that I would be "uncontrollable." While I had remained friendly with individual officers, I was abhorred by MI5 as a whole and was, perhaps, the last person it would have chosen for such an operation.

In the darkness of the night, the truth suddenly became

manifest to Judge Powell. At one stage during the trial, he told
the court how, while lying in his bed, a theory had presented
itself that made more sense of the facts than any other he had
yet heard: someone representing the publisher of *Their Trade Is
Treachery* had passed the synopsis to Sir Arthur Franks saying,
"We would like to publish the book but we would not do so if
there were strong pressure from on top and, in particular, we
would not enter into a contract binding ourselves to pay the
author a lot of money until we got a clearance in advance.
Will you pass it up the line and tell us what you think?" This
really was what had happened, but Turnbull dismissed it,
being committed, with Wright, to his great conspiracy theory.

It was at his media conference that Wright stated that he
had brought a "paper" on the Hollis affair with him when he
had gone to see Rothschild and that he had asked him to put it
before the Prime Minister. Neither Lord Rothschild nor I can
remember any such paper, and he never showed me any document about Hollis when we met in Tasmania. I do not believe
any such document existed.

From the start, there were serious weaknesses in the government's case. Not the least of these was its stance that MI5
must be seen as leakproof, when there was a mass of published
evidence showing that it had not been. No organization, not
even the KGB, is leakproof. There was also the complication
that Sir Robert Armstrong, who had been sent to tell the whole
truth and nothing but the truth, knew too many of the relevant
secrets and yet not all of them.

I knew at an early stage that the Australian government
had promised to assist the British case by submitting an affidavit stating that publication of Wright's book would damage
Australian security and intelligence interests. The affidavit was
entered by Mr. Michael Codd, secretary to the department of
the Australian Prime Minister and to the cabinet. The eight-
page statement, given under oath, authorized by the federal
government in Canberra, and developed with advice from the
Australian security services, was based on the fact that Aus-

tralian intelligence agencies have liaison relationships with similar agencies of allied countries; therefore, a loss of confidence in MI5 could decrease the quality of the information available to Australia. The affidavit also argued that publication of Wright's book would encourage similar books by Australian agents.[19]

"Perc" Powell was unimpressed and rejected the affidavit with derision. He could not resist calling Codd's evidence "codswallop," stating that Mr. Codd espoused views entirely without foundation. "I find it very hard to give any weight to Codd's evidence at all," he said. Codd's statement was also attacked by the former Australian Prime Minister Gough Whitlam, who has no love for the United Kingdom. The cavalier dismissal of evidence from such a prestigious figure was extraordinary, to say the least.

The folly of excessive secrecy was to make Sir Robert look ridiculous. Pursuing the traditional line, he declined to admit the existence of MI6, the Secret Intelligence Service, which has been the subject of numerous documentaries and novels. Under cross-examination, he had to admit that his letter to my publisher asking for copies of *Their Trade Is Treachery*, when he had been in possession of the text for weeks, had "misrepresented the facts" and that in the interests of security it was sometimes necessary for a person in his position to be a party to such a deception. This led to his damaging statement about "being economical with the truth."

The government's worst experience, however, was to arise from Sir Robert's recall of the events surrounding the publication of *Their Trade Is Treachery*, which he admitted had been a "bombshell." During the first few days of the case he had assured the court that the decision that no action could be taken to prevent publication of it had been made by the Attorney General, Sir Michael Havers. Sir Robert had wrongly assumed that the MI5 and MI6 legal advisers had been in touch with the Attorney General and had secured his agreement when, in fact, they had not. This misbelief led Sir Robert to swear under oath several times in the Sydney court that the Attorney General had taken the responsibility for not proceeding against my book. For several days, the Attorney General took the severe Parliamentary criticisms for this action on the chin, as ministers are supposed to do, but when they became insupportable he demanded that Sir Robert tell the court that he had not been responsible. Sir Robert did so on November 28, apologizing for having unwittingly misled the court, as his memory was at fault and there had been no documents to consult because of the extreme secrecy requirements. This admission inevitably cast doubt on the veracity of all his evidence and he was not spared by Turnbull. From that moment on, the case seemed lost.

Why was Armstrong not told right away by the Attorney General that he was misleading the court? Instead, several days elapsed, making the situation much worse. The Attorney General has given me two reasons for the delay. First, he told me that it was not permissible for him to intrude while Armstrong was giving evidence, and that may have been legally correct. But the main reason seems to have been his requirement to make absolutely sure, by consulting former officials, including those of MI5, that he had not, in fact, been informed or consulted in any way in 1981—six years previously. The memories of these officials proved to be as uncertain as his own, and it was some days before he could be absolutely positive that he had not been involved in any way. A great deal, of much more importance, had happened in the busy Attorney General's department in the interim, and nobody felt like relying on personal powers of recall concerning what was to be such a crucial correction. Did the Prime Minister know that Armstrong was misleading the court, or was she so busy with other affairs that she was unaware of it? Of course, she, too, may have assumed in 1981 that the legal advisers of MI5 and MI6 had consulted the Attorney General.

What would the judge have said had he known that *Their Trade Is Treachery* could have been suppressed by a simple request made on the telephone? He might well have stopped the case, for I greatly doubt that he would have countenanced the extraordinary, but actual, situation that Armstrong had not known the truth.

In my opinion and that of Lord Rothschild, the government's lawyers made a cardinal blunder in failing to cross-examine Wright and question his veracity, especially about his story that he had been "drawn into" a conspiracy by Rothschild and me. The judge seemed to appreciate that Wright was vulnerable, which he undoubtedly was, as the next chapter will show. On being told by the government's QC, Simos, that he did not wish to reexamine Wright, the judge said to Wright, "Run like blazes before they change their minds." It was excellent advice. A great deal of the evidence he had given about me and Lord Rothschild in his sworn affidavit was seriously flawed or patently false, as I shall show. By failing even to try to demolish it, the government's lawyers deserved to lose.

In his final submission, Turnbull reiterated his great conspiracy theory and other fictions, while Simos stuck essentially to the issue of Wright's breach of confidentiality, with which the judge had never expressed much sympathy.

The judge's problem in reaching a verdict, apart from having to digest a cartload of spy books that Turnbull had submitted as evidence, was that the truth had not been told. The government's lawyers and witnesses had been fumbling in the fog of secrecy and presented a case that was visibly flawed. The defense team had utilized their ignorance to fabricate a myth that some elements of the media were prepared to believe, if only because it made good copy.

On January 12, 1986, Sir Michael Havers told Parliament that the Wright case had cost £170,000 to date from public funds. It did wonders, however, for the sales of the paperback edition of *Their Trade Is Treachery*, which was reprinted several times, five years after its first appearance—something of a record for a documentary.

|| 17 ||

A Statement under Oath

> Res ipsa loquitur—*The facts speak for themselves.*
>
> —Legal axiom

Malcolm Turnbull claimed that his client was so ill that he might die in the witness box if subjected to stress, so Wright was allowed to make a long written statement as a sworn affidavit and to have it by his side when he appeared. It is necessary to consider this sworn statement in detail because it is illuminating regarding Wright's credibility and because it led to serious repercussions in Britain involving the law officers and the police. Although doing so entails some repetition, the relevant facts must be restated in rebuttal of Wright's allegations. The process will also serve to draw together the threads of the complex story.

In a statement to Parliament on February 6, 1987, the Solicitor General said that "most, if not all" of the allegations against Lord Rothschild and me, which were then being investigated by Scotland Yard, formed part of the evidence given by Wright in the proceedings in Sydney. I therefore had cause to examine all the allegations relating to me in Wright's sworn affidavit, except for those given *in camera*.[1] My findings may help those who are interested in understanding why the Director of Public Prosecutions and the Attorney General decided that there was no evidence to sustain any action against Lord Rothschild or me.

I should point out that it is not in my professional interest to discredit Wright as a witness. Widespread publication of his book would obviously give greater credibility to *Their Trade Is Treachery* and my later books. There is little that is more undignified than two former associates slinging mud at each other, but Wright discredited himself with many statements that were clearly intended to damage my credibility in order to improve his own.

Wright's affidavit proved to contain material that was patently false or contrived and could not, in charity, be entirely attributed to failure of memory by Wright, infirm though he seemed to be. His whole statement was calculated to project himself as an injured innocent—a poor and sickly man who was corrupted by two conspirators (Lord Rothschild and me)— and to support the contention that he had been drawn into a deniable operation masterminded by MI5.

From evidence I have already adduced, it should be apparent that, contrary to assertions made by Wright, I was no conscious part of any "deniable operation" masterminded by MI5. Over the years, I sometimes wondered whether I had been drawn into such an operation by Lord Rothschild, especially when MI5 knew that I and other journalists were interested in the Hollis case as far back as July 1980, but it made no sense when Lord Rothschild himself was subjected to police inquiries that were personally distressing, physically injurious to a sick and elderly man, and damaging to his great reputation. Any suggestion that it would have been his duty to grin and bear it makes no sense, because he could simply have referred the police to MI5 without explanation. The crackpot concept put forward by Wright and his lawyer—that Wright

had been trapped into an MI5 operation to expose all the skeletons in MI5's closet and in that way to get rid of them—was
dismissed by Justice Powell, in his judgment, as incredible.[2]

In his affidavit Wright told of beginning to write a "dossier," and he kept using that word. At no time when we spoke,
briefly in Cambridge and then at length in Tasmania, did he
use the word *dossier*; he always spoke of a book. In 1976,
Wright indicated to Lord Rothschild that he was writing a
"book," and Lord Rothschild warned the Director General of
MI5 about it. In a letter to Rothschild dated June 12, 1980,
Wright stated, "I am writing a book whose tentative title is *The
Cancer in Our Midst*. It is about the penetration of our society
by the Russians and how the Soviets have used it to manipulate us to achieve their ends." That letter, of which the government's counsel was unaware, is crucial documentary evidence
that Wright misled the court on a major issue—who suggested
the book that became *Their Trade Is Treachery*. In his affidavit,
Wright volunteered the statement, "I did not suggest the idea
of a book."

In Cambridge, Wright specifically told me that he had
written about ten chapters of a book that he could not complete. He invited me to complete the work as a book under my
name. He would not have asked me to complete a "dossier,"
which really means a collection of separate papers relating to a
person or event.

Wright stated in his affidavit that he brought the ten chapters of his "dossier" to show to Lord Rothschild in the hope
that he would pass them on to Mrs. Thatcher so that she
would institute an inquiry into his suspicions concerning Hollis. This made no sense. I saw the chapters when I visited
Wright in Australia and made notes from them because Wright
insisted on retaining them. They contained nothing whatsoever about the Hollis case, the Mitchell case, or anything else
that would have had any impact on the Prime Minister.

The chapters, which were very disappointing, dealt with
generalities and old history, ending, I believe, with aspects of

Blunt's wartime treachery. Wright told me that he had not done any further work on them since visiting Cambridge.[3]

It is difficult to avoid the conclusion that, in his affidavit, a "book" had been transformed into a "dossier" to support the pretense that the idea of doing a book at all was suggested by Lord Rothschild, and that the mythical Hollis material was introduced to support the claim that he had brought the material only to have it passed on to Mrs. Thatcher. Wright made no mention to me of passing anything directly to Mrs. Thatcher or to anybody else, although he did believe that a book revealing what he called "security scandals" might force the politicians into establishing a further inquiry into the Hollis case. What Wright had brought over comprised ten chapters of a *book*, which he had carried with him in the hope of finding a writer to take it over and finish it.

While Wright specifically claimed that he did not suggest the idea of a book, I can testify that he did so. I do not know what had happened between Wright and Lord Rothschild before I arrived in Cambridge, but the invitation to write a book came from Wright.

In his affidavit, Wright was so keen to limit his contribution to *Their Trade Is Treachery* that he not only denied that he had suggested a book but insisted that I had already known most of the material and that he had no part in the planning or the writing.

At the media conference called by Malcolm Turnbull in Sydney on November 25, 1986, Wright claimed that he had begun a "paper" on the Hollis case and asked Lord Rothschild to give it to Mrs. Thatcher.[4] I do not believe that any such paper existed. Time was short when we were in Tasmania together, and if Wright had had anything on paper about Hollis he would, assuredly, have let me see it. In fact he said he had nothing on paper, and everything he divulged to me about the Hollis case was given verbally.

In Tasmania, Wright told me that he had no notes whatsoever regarding his MI5 activities, having left them all with

MI5, as the Official Secrets Act required. When specifically asked during the Sydney trial, "Did you take any material with you from the British Security Service when you left?" Wright said that he had not. Yet it later emerged that on November 3, 1976, Wright had written to Lord Rothschild about Anthony Blunt, stating, "I have still got all my notes of my talks with him." The precise dates and details of certain events related in *Spycatcher* also strongly suggest that he could not be relying entirely on unaided memory, although he assured the court that he was.

Despite statements by Wright in court that he was the one at risk if Lord Rothschild should let him down, he was at no risk at all so long as he remained in Australia, as he did. I and my publisher were the ones who were mainly at risk.

In his affidavit, Wright repaid Lord Rothschild's friendship by suggesting to the court that his old friend had breached his confidentiality to the Crown by briefing me about the Hollis case before I met Wright. Lord Rothschild told me nothing about Hollis. My material had been obtained from Jonathan Aitken, the MP who had warned the Prime Minister about the Hollis affair in January 1980. Wright knew this because I had disclosed the details in *Their Trade Is Treachery*.

Wright was also at pains to implicate Lord Rothschild by suggesting that he had been involved in an incident I had recorded in *Inside Story* in 1978. A peer and former politician of great distinction, who was then an important figure in the City, told me how he had been approached to find a position for a dissident MI5 officer who was prepared to expose two Labour ministers as subversives, and how he had been unable to find such a position. In his affidavit, Wright identified himself as the officer and suggested that Lord Rothschild had put him in touch with the City man. The way Wright described this incident in *Spycatcher*, however, proves that he was referring to a totally different episode. His description of the businessman who interviewed him could not possibly fit the City man I knew. Wright and I had discussed the incident in which

I was involved when we went through parts of *Inside Story* in Tasmania, and he had denied all knowledge of it.

I had never heard of Wright before my chance meeting with him at Lord Rothschild's house in September 1980, yet he told the court that we had met previously. I have no recollection of any such meeting. As a trained observer, I would not have forgotten Wright's face or his speech impediment. Wright did not remind me that we had met during any discussion at Cambridge (where he continued with the "Philip" deception) or in Tasmania. Nor, as he admits, did he tell Lord Rothschild that he knew me, which surely he would have done. Wright's purpose in saying he had met me may have been to suggest that I had a close relationship with MI5.

When Wright gave me the names of certain journalists who, he said, were paid MI5 agents, I asked him why no attempt had been made to recruit me. He replied that this had been considered but had been rejected because I would have been uncontrollable. Yet Turnbull told the court in his summing up that I was "a British agent" and a "double agent."[5] Wright may have alleged this to support the thesis that I was part of an MI5 plot to trick him into collaborating in the writing of *Their Trade Is Treachery* and to support his contention that I was knowingly a part of a "deniable operation." The occasional services I did for MI5 and the Defence Ministry in my journalistic capacity, receiving scoops in return, were revealed fully in *Inside Story*; there is no mystery about them.

During the Australian trial, Wright claimed to have become opposed to any surreptitious acts by MI5 not authorized by warrant; but during my conversations with him in Tasmania he showed no such scruples. On the contrary, he tended to revel in his involvement in placing bugs and in making surreptitious entries, projecting himself as a great expert. At no time did he express any regret at having taken part in such operations, and clearly he regarded them as justified and necessary to counter an adversary that would stoop to anything. Nor did he suggest to me that any of the operations had been performed outside the limits within which MI5 had always operated. I understood that warrants or some other forms of government agreement were necessary and had been obtained. His recent conversion and his crusade against alleged illegalities may have been genuine, but it was also conveniently in accord with his attempt to portray himself as an admirable patriot and to secure the sympathy of the court.

In his affidavit, Wright insisted that he was not motivated by financial gain. I have no doubt that Wright's original motive, in the late 1970s, in deciding to write a book was to expose what he regarded as a dangerous cover-up of Soviet penetration in MI5 and MI6. By 1980, however, his financial and medical situations had deteriorated, and he became greatly concerned about leaving his wife in penury. From the start of our conversation in Cambridge, Wright had made his bleak financial situation very clear. He complained about his pension and told me about the incipient bankruptcy of his small stud farm, which could only be staved off by some other source of income. I believe that Wright's statement that he would not have collaborated with me if Rothschild had agreed to pass the "dossier" to Mrs. Thatcher is patently untrue.

When I decided to write *Their Trade Is Treachery*, it was entirely as a means of placing on public record old history that I considered to be in the national interest. It was not because I felt sorry for Wright and wanted to assist him. As a professional author, I was, of course, interested in the financial reward myself, but that was definitely secondary in my case because I was financially well placed (having just sold my big house), did not need the money, and never expected such a windfall. The initial attraction of the project for me was essentially journalistic.

As I have described in chapters 1 and 3, the question of payment had been raised at the outset by Wright, and there would have been no book without it. Wright's affidavit statement that the banking arrangements made by Lord Rothschild were designed to protect the identity of the person sending him the money—i.e., Rothschild or me—could just be an expression of a devious mind, or it could be support for Turnbull's claim that we had "corrupted" Wright by offering him money. The arrangements were made solely to protect the confidentiality of Wright himself. Sidgwick and Jackson would have had no objection whatsoever to sending the royalties directly to Wright, and Lord Rothschild's involvement in the banking arrangements would then have been unnecessary. Wright had insisted that I should not give his name to any publisher, and an intermediary was therefore required.

In retrospect, I am convinced there was a strong element of resentment against MI5 and the British establishment generally in Wright's motivation for promoting a book. This resulted from his treatment by MI5 and the Treasury in relation to his meager pension. He also seemed resentful that his achievements for MI5 had not been fully appreciated by his colleagues. In that context, I should point out that one of the most disturbing discoveries of my extensive inquiries into the secret services is the extent to which former officers criticize and censure each other and the service itself once they are out of it and free to talk.

In his affidavit and public statements, Wright repeated that money had never been a major incentive; but from the moment I secured a contract, Wright began pestering me to expedite his payments. No money was ever paid to Wright by me or by my company. Although Wright received £31,827.69 as his share of net proceeds—far in excess of his expectations—he continued to plead poverty with complaints about his income tax and the poor Australian exchange rate.

In April 1987, Wright's London lawyer began a series of demands for more money from the early sales of *Their Trade Is Treachery*, which Wright claimed (wrongly) had been owed to him for several years. He even claimed to be entitled to 50 percent of my journalistic earnings concerning anything I wrote about the book. Why had he waited so long, when royalty payments on sales of the hardcover edition to him had ceased at the end of 1982? If he really had believed that MI5

had masterminded the book as a means of providing him with
extra money to shut him up, why did he not act sooner? The
answer, surely, is that MI5 had done no such thing, and
Wright knew it. He still wanted to avoid admitting his involvement because, although the MI5 managers were aware that he
had leaked massively to me, they could not prove it. Once his
exposure became essential to his bid to publish *Spycatcher*, he
had nothing more to lose.

Spitefully, Wright suggested in his affidavit that I misled
him over my later book, *Too Secret Too Long*, to deprive him of
further royalties. There is no truth in that. The material that
had previously appeared in *Their Trade Is Treachery* was public
property, and Wright had no claim to further payment for it.
Indeed, various authors had drawn heavily from it. This would
seem to throw further doubt on Wright's claim that his financial interest was incidental—especially as he had even suggested providing material for newspaper articles on a sharing
basis to make some quick money.

Wright's claim that money was of secondary interest in his
bid to see *Spycatcher* published makes no sense in view of
Turnbull's repeated statement that the material that Wright
wished to publish was already in the public domain through
my books and others. When accused in July 1987 on television of betraying secrets for money, Wright demolished any
argument that he was putting them on record as a public service by claiming that they were secrets no longer.

In his affidavit, Wright claimed to have been very disappointed with *Their Trade Is Treachery* because it did not demand an inquiry, yet at no time did Wright ever express any
disappointment to me while we corresponded over a period of
two years. Indeed, he seemed pleased with the book, especially
the paperback. Would he have been so keen for me to write a
second book in collaboration with him had he been as disappointed as he alleged? *Their Trade Is Treachery* did in fact produce the first independent inquiry in twenty years into the
efficiency of the existing precautions against Soviet-bloc pen-

etration of the secret departments of state. Wright was disappointed, as I was, that the inquiry did not backtrack into the Hollis affair but that was the Prime Minister's decision and not the fault of my book.

In a tear-jerking finale to his evidence, Wright indicated that because of his patriotic disclosures he was being forced to die in exile. When I visited him in Tasmania, he told me that he had emigrated to Australia to be near his married daughter who lived close to Cygnet, because he believed living there would be cheaper, and because the climate would suit his failing health and his Arabian horse stud farm. At no time did he say that he considered himself to be "in exile." Indeed, the purpose of maintaining his confidentiality was to enable him to visit Britain, although he said he had no intention of returning to live there.

He also told me that he had no intention of taking Australian citizenship, and the date when he did take it might be significant. Clearly, to be an Australian citizen would be helpful to his defense in an Australian court. His medical condition almost certainly made any journey to Britain impracticable by the time he and his publishers decided to fight the case.

In addition to the various false statements made about me, Wright also made statements in his sworn affidavit about his relationship with Lord Rothschild that Rothschild has shown to be untrue. He alleged that Rothschild had sent him a first-class return ticket to Britain and that, as he could not travel safely alone, he had exchanged it for two economy tickets so that he could take his wife, too. When the police made inquiries about this at the agency Rothschild had used to provide the ticket, they were shown a document proving that Wright had been sent one economy-class ticket. Why should Wright make up such a story? Whatever the reason, it suited his case to appear in court as a man so poor that he could not afford to buy a ticket for his wife.

Wright alleged that Rothschild told him that Mrs.

Thatcher had visited his London flat, with the implication that they may have discussed intelligence matters. A check with Number 10 Downing Street, where the Prime Minister's movements are recorded in detail, showed that she had never paid such a visit. Some time earlier in 1980, when she had been visiting Cambridge on business, the Rothschilds had invited her to stop in for tea. She did so, accompanied by her husband, Denis, and her political aide, Ian Gow. No opportunity for the discussion of intelligence issues arose. She had not been there before and has not been there since.

In his affidavit, Wright alleged that Rothschild had introduced him to Roy Jenkins when the latter was Home Secretary. Neither has any recollection of this supposed event.

Wright claimed that Rothschild had been involved in the plot to overthrow Muhammad Mussadegh, the Iranian Prime Minister, but this was an MI6 operation. Rothschild assured the police that he had had nothing whatsoever to do with it.

At the end of the trial, on December 17, 1986, Wright's sister, Elizabeth, sixty-eight years old, branded Wright a liar and a vindictive mischief-maker prepared to betray secrets for money. Her husband, Robert Sutton, a retired scientist who had served in the admiralty with distinction, joined her in condemning Wright, stating: "He was so unreliable you could not believe a word he said. He lived in a fantasy world. Once I accused him of telling lies and he said to me, 'Bob, I know I tell lies but I just cannot help it. Can you help me stop it?'" Both claimed that they would never speak to Wright again for betraying secrets and taking money.[6] Understandably, the comments were rebutted by Wright's children, but they justified my exhaustive efforts to check everything that Wright told me in Tasmania before publishing it.

In view of the Prime Minister's statement to Parliament that Wright's alleged account of the MI5 "plot" to unseat Wilson is false, it follows that those of his old colleagues who had been consulted consider him either to be a liar or to be deluded. Without exception, those to whom I have spoken despise him for what he has done to his old service.

The apparent strength of Turnbull's case lay in the charge that Sir Robert Armstrong had knowingly lied in the witness box, but the man who had supplied the court with the most false information—having had plenty of time to consider its implications—was his own client.

|| 18 ||

Echoes in Parliament

Let echo, too, perform her part
Prolonging every note with art.

—Addison

On November 20, 1986, two days after Turnbull had telephoned me as described in chapter 16, the Labour backbencher Dale Campbell-Savours—a strange, astringent character who seemed to want to prosecute anybody—called for the prosecution of five named people and for inquiries into eighteen former members of MI5 and MI6 who had been named as sources in various books.[1] Later, in Parliament, he admitted that his overriding objective was to destroy the case in the Australian courts—which, of course, was also Turnbull's purpose.[2]

Previously, in July, Campbell-Savours had unwittingly assisted Turnbull's cause by using his Parliamentary privilege to reveal claims allegedly in Wright's book that MI5 had carried out certain illegal operations in Britain. That way, he was able to accuse the Attorney General of trying to suppress Wright's book to cover up MI5's illegalities.[3]

On November 25, Campbell-Savours fulfilled Turnbull's prediction to me on the telephone by asking the Attorney General, in a written question, if he would prosecute Lord Rothschild under Section 7 of the Official Secrets Act for soliciting Peter Wright, by means of an offer of money, to pass documents known or believed to contain official secrets relating to the security services to Chapman Pincher.[4] In fact, Rothschild had made no offer of money. Three days later it was stated in a written Parliamentary answer that the Attorney General and the Director of Public Prosecutions were considering the allegations against Rothschild.

In the following week, Campbell-Savours specifically asked the Prime Minister if she would prosecute me under Section 7 of the Official Secrets Act for inducing Peter Wright to break his duty of confidentiality on security matters to the Crown by being party to the offer of payments by Summerpage Ltd. of monies in respect of information to be included in my book, *Their Trade Is Treachery*.[5] The Prime Minister pointed out that she was not responsible for prosecutions, as Campbell-Savours must have known. In fact I did not induce Wright to do anything; he volunteered it. No payments were ever made to Wright by my company. Summerpage, as the police were eventually able to establish beyond doubt.

On December 8, Campbell-Savours put the same question to the Attorney General, and it was reinforced by a similar question from the Labour MP John Morris. Havers replied that he was considering the allegations that Wright had made with the Director of Public Prosecutions.[6] The media treated this as an "announcement." Like MPs, the media should have exulted in a government that had not been prepared to prosecute an investigative journalist. Surely it was tribute to the government's attitude to press freedom that it had not stifled my book. But some newspapers, such as the *Observer*, which supported Wright, used that decision to attack the Prime Minister and the Attorney General. Few had done more than I had, over so many years, to break down the barriers of secrecy in the interest of freedom of information. Yet I detected that some journalists—and not only those of the left wing—would have been quite pleased to see me in the dock.

In a debate initiated by Campbell-Savours on December 15, 1986, he again called for my prosecution and that of others, being supported in this by some of his Labour colleagues. How consistent is a party whose members campaign for freedom of information and for the prosecution of those who provide it at considerable personal risk? They exulted when the civil servant, Clive Ponting, was acquitted after providing confidential information to MPs. It was no coincidence that Rothschild was a rich establishment figure and that I had been referred to by Campbell-Savours as a prominent Conservative when in fact I have never been a member of any political party.

Previously, on November 27, the Labour Party leader Neil Kinnock had made party political use of *Their Trade Is Treachery* by asking the Prime Minister if the decision not to impede its publication had been taken by Sir Michael Havers. When she declined to answer, Kinnock asked if the Attorney General had been "a fool or a fall-guy." [7] Kinnock's attempt to make party political capital out of the case rebounded, however, when it was discovered that he had been in personal communication with Turnbull by telephone. This was learned by accident during attempts by the Chief Whip, John Wakeham, to protect the Prime Minister from excessive harassment, but Labour MPs were soon claiming, no doubt with MI5 in mind, that Kinnock's telephone might have been tapped.

The Prime Minister and many MPs regarded it as unworthy that the leader of the opposition should consort in any way with a lawyer opposing the Crown in a foreign court on an issue of national security. Kinnock replied, lamely, by claiming to support the government's case in principle on the grounds that Wright was in breach of his undertakings under the Official Secrets Act. The government was in little doubt, however, that Kinnock continued to encourage Campbell-Savours in his role as hatchetman.

The maverick Labour MP Tam Dalyell was to stage a short adjournment debate on prosecution policy, accusing the government of inconsistency. It was aimed at the Conservative law officers and at Sir Michael Havers in particular. In fact, Labour backbenchers were inconsistent. While calling for police action against me, they condemned the recent police action against Duncan Campbell, the left-wing journalist, even though Kinnock himself admitted that there had been a serious breach of security.[8]

On a social occasion following the Campbell-Savours demand, Havers warned me that he was considering some action. On December 17, after consultations with the Director of Public Prosecutions, the metropolitan police force was asked to begin inquiries into Wright's allegations about Lord Rothschild and me.

The assault on the reputation of Havers that Turnbull originated in Sydney was continued by him. On New Year's Day, Turnbull telephoned my home and asked for Mr. Greengrass. When he heard me on the line, he claimed that he had confused the numbers, but nevertheless he kept me in conversation for about twenty minutes. He asked if I had given copies of the synopsis and page proofs of my book to Lord Rothschild, and when I told him that I had not, he tried to question me about possible alternative sources. His main theme, however, was his insistence that Havers was the "most dishonorable Attorney General of this century," a grossly untrue description that he had used in Australia to the Attorney General's great personal distress. He said that Kinnock would be gunning for Havers when Parliament reassembled, the charge being that he had allowed Sir Robert Armstrong to lie to the Sydney court for several days about his alleged involvement in clearing *Their Trade Is Treachery*. Turnbull argued that the only alternative explanation was that Havers had quickly complained to the Prime Minister about Armstrong's misinformation and that she had then permitted him to go on misleading the court. Either way, Turnbull believed, Kinnock would be able to score valuable points and to call for resignations.[9]

Long after the Sydney trial had been concluded, Campbell-Savours and other Labour backbenchers continued their harassment by latching onto various decisions taken by the law officers against newspapers. Though the Attorney General repeatedly pointed out that he was acting for the Crown, in furtherance of respect for the law, the critics did not desist from their campaign to attribute the decisions to the government, and to Mrs. Thatcher in particular.

After many years of observing the behavior of MPs when they are in opposition, I am convinced that they are more often motivated by the political advantage of inflicting damage on their opponents than by a sincere quest for the truth in the public interest. It is sad, in a proud democracy, that Parliament can be used in this way to foist misinformation on the public through the media that report its activities. The behavior of the Labour Party in the Wright affair to date has been something of a long-running deception exercise in itself.

19

The Vindication of
Lord Rothschild

Falsehood has a perennial spring.
—Edmund Burke

Following the disclosure in the Sydney court
that Lord Rothschild had been involved with Peter Wright, he
was besieged by reporters and photographers at his homes and
at Rothschild's bank in the City. Any Rothschild is likely to
attract media attention—particularly the head of the British
branch of that illustrious family—and the connection with
Wright had raised the hoary rumor that Victor might have
been the so-called "fifth man" of the old Cambridge spy ring.
On November 27, 1986, a headline in the *Daily Express* had
asked, "Rothschild: Was He the Fifth Man? Labour MPs Demand an Answer." There were disgraceful melees with press
photographers, in one of which, at the age of seventy-six, Lord
Rothschild was knocked down. At his Cambridge home,
bribes were offered to tradesmen in efforts to secure close-up
photographs. After enduring this for many days, Rothschild

wanted an end to the harassment and to ludicrous speculation concerning his loyalty, which was hardly good for the reputation of the family bank in which he was an active and senior figure.

There was no prospect that MI5 might take the initiative and provide the Prime Minister with the evidence on which to clear his name. That had become apparent in 1980, when Rothschild had been driven to ask Wright to visit him, as described in chapter 1. To maintain their fog of secrecy, both MI5 and MI6 always remain remote and totally unprepared to assist when their former servants are in difficulties. They abandon them to the wolves, even when no security is involved. Sir Dick White, former head of both MI5 and MI6, has complained about this.

While Wright made it clear in the Australian court that Lord Rothschild could not possibly have been a pro-Soviet spy, Rothschild was, understandably, concerned about statements he might make in *Spycatcher*, in view of the false statements he had made in his affidavit. This fear was, in part, responsible for driving Lord Rothschild to demand public vindication, an act that was out of character for such a private person.

There was a further reason why he felt he had to move without delay. An essential component of Turnbull's ludicrous conspiracy story was a claim that Lord Rothschild had induced me and Wright to publish the book so that the disclosure that Hollis was the fifth man would divert attention from the rumor that the fifth man was Rothschild. The government was alleged to have favored this ploy for the purpose of protecting Rothschild!

The suggestion was palpable nonsense. Hollis could never have been the fifth man because the term referred to the fifth person recruited to the Cambridge spy ring in the 1930s; Hollis had been at Oxford in the 1920s. The entire Cambridge ring had been recruited by what became known as the KGB. If Hollis was a spy, all the evidence suggests that he was not recruited by the KGB but by Soviet military intelligence, the

GRU, then a completely separate organization. So any disclosures about Hollis could not have affected arguments about the identity of the fifth man. Wright was fully aware that Turnbull's fifth-man thesis was poppycock.

Their Trade Is Treachery put forward another Cambridge contemporary, Alister Watson, as the likeliest candidate for fifth man, a view with which Wright fully agreed. It may be thought that Wright could have suggested to Rothschild that the disclosures about Watson and another fifth-man contender, John Cairncross, might switch the spotlight away from him. In that case, however, Lord Rothschild would surely have asked to see that part of the book in advance, but he took no interest in it whatsoever. In the result, the disclosures, although supported by detailed evidence and widely read, had no impact on the rumors about Lord Rothschild.

On Wednesday, December 3, Max Hastings, editor of the *Daily Telegraph*, visited Rothschild's office with a view to receiving a statement for publication. Lord Rothschild chose the *Daily Telegraph* because he knew Hastings and was confident that he would print the statement on the front page and without qualifying frills.[1] It appeared in the form of a brief letter to "The Editor and Readers," accompanied by a splash front-page "story" on Thursday, December 4. The letter stated:

> Since at least 1980 up to the present time there have been innuendoes in the Press to the effect that I am "the 5th man," in other words a Soviet agent. The Director General of MI5 should state publicly that it has unequivocal, repeat unequivocal, evidence that I am not, and never have been, a Soviet agent.

Thursday happened to be the usual day for Prime Minister's questions in Parliament and it was inevitable that she would be asked about the letter. Had Mrs. Thatcher had more notice and time to consult MI5, she would have been able to answer without delay, and the fact that she did not do so fueled speculation that she was unable to clear Lord Rothschild or did not wish to. I have been told that she was annoyed that Lord Rothschild had not first cleared the issue with Number 10, but this would have been an error on Lord Rothschild's part because Mrs. Thatcher would, almost certainly, have tried to persuade him to postpone any action until after the completion of the Wright case, which then seemed likely to drag on into the autumn of 1987.

Eventually, on December 6, Mrs. Thatcher issued a statement, in the form of a press notice, that read:

> I have now considered more fully Lord Rothschild's letter in the *Daily Telegraph* yesterday, in which he referred to innuendoes that he had been a Soviet agent. I consider it important to maintain the practice of successive governments of not commenting on security matters. But I am willing to make an exception on the matter raised in Lord Rothschild's letter. I am advised that we have no evidence that he was ever a Soviet agent.

The advice had come from MI5 and the legal adviser had insisted that it should be as short and curt as possible.

Lord Rothschild's friends regarded this response as negative, grudging, and possibly damaging. There seemed to be no good reason against some mention of his positive work for MI5—the unequivocal evidence to which he had alluded in his letter.

Lord Rothschild's intervention had been well timed, because Turnbull specifically raised the conspiracy theory involving him as the fifth man in the Sydney Court of Appeal on December 4.[2] Fortuitously, the clearance also prevented any fifth-man speculation later, when Lord Rothschild was being questioned by the police about Wright's "conspiracy allegations."

Many of Rothschild's friends considered that Mrs. Thatcher's refusal to confirm immediately that he has never been a Soviet spy did him a grave injustice. However, those of us who know how the Whitehall cogs grind were not surprised that a twenty-four-hour delay, at least, would be necessary before the MI5 management could bring itself to produce the evidence, which inevitably had to be kept secret.

As a friend and admirer of Victor Rothschild for many years, I know a great deal about his contributions and have information from MI5 sources. The rumors and smears he suffered in silence for so long originated from the accident that he was at Cambridge University with several undergraduates who became proven traitors and was friendly with some of them—Blunt and Burgess in particular. He was also a friend of Michael Straight, the rich American who was recruited by Blunt for the Soviets but recanted and eventually exposed Blunt to the FBI and to MI5.

Far from being the elusive fifth man, Rothschild had given the first lead to Alister Watson, the confessed secret communist now believed by MI5 to have been the real fifth man recruited to the Cambridge spy ring.[3] He had also been instrumental in proving the treachery of the "first man"—Philby. When Donald Maclean became suspect as a Soviet agent in 1950, eight others were put under some degree of surveillance by MI5, as I have recorded elsewhere.[4] Rothschild was not one of them.

Lord Rothschild joined MI5 in 1939, remaining in it for the duration of the war. His service was outstanding in many directions and so brave that he was awarded the George Medal, while his courageous assistant, Tess Mayor, who later became his second wife, received the military MBE. In a book published in 1977, he was given permission to reproduce his chilling telephone talk-back to base in 1944 as he dismantled a crate of onions that had been dropped by the Luftwaffe and was a vicious booby-trap containing slabs of TNT.[5]

Among other exploits that can be safely mentioned are Rothschild's secret investigation of the Liberator aircraft crash in Gibraltar, in which the Polish general Sikorski died and sabotage was suspected. Rothschild was also a skilled interrogator who was chosen to break down particularly tough targets such as the Nazi parachutist commander, Otto Skorzeny, the man who had rescued Mussolini.

Like many other officers of MI5, Lord Rothschild retained connections with "The Firm" after the war, and his help and advice was sought repeatedly, especially by Peter Wright. After Blunt confessed to being a traitor in 1964, Lord Rothschild not only gave Wright the names of distinguished people who could be helpful in subsequent inquiries but induced some of them to talk when they had previously declined.

In 1962 Rothschild was instrumental in exposing Philby, who had been wrongly cleared in Parliament by Harold Macmillan. While visiting the Weizmann Institute in Israel, he overheard an Englishwoman, Flora Solomon, declare that she had known for years that Philby was a communist and a Soviet agent. When they were both back in London he induced her to repeat this to Sir Dick White, then head of MI6, who was and remains a close friend of the Rothschilds. White sent the MI5 counterespionage specialist, Arthur Martin, to interview Mrs. Solomon, and she confessed to having kept quiet about Philby's treachery until he began attacking Israel in newspaper articles. It was on her evidence that Philby was confronted in Beirut and made a limited confession to having been a spy. The fact that Philby quickly defected to Moscow was no fault of Rothschild's. The tip to Philby had come from a source almost certainly still in MI5.

Lord Rothschild has put on record his astonishment and despair at Blunt's exposure as a spy; but in common with all Blunt's friends, he was interviewed by MI5 officers and cleared of any suspicion arising out of their long association.[6] Some ten years previously, Rothschild had urged MI5 to examine the career of Alister Watson, a close communist friend of Blunt and Burgess, who had become an admiralty scientist. Rothschild recalled that Burgess had always tried to recruit people whom he admired and that he had admired Watson very much. Watson was eventually interviewed by Wright and admitted to being a secret communist, which he had denied when being positively reviewed; he was quietly transferred to nonsecret work.

I revealed some of these episodes in *Their Trade Is Treachery*, without naming Lord Rothschild, in deference to his general objection to any publicity about his secret service work. If the book had been produced with his interests in mind, I would surely have given him the credit as evidence that he could not possibly have been a Soviet agent.

During my conversations with Wright, he assured me that Rothschild's file in the MI5 registry contained only material to his credit. Allegations that he was responsible for introducing Blunt to MI5 are untrue.[7]

Because of his intellectual brilliance and flair for original thought, Rothschild was appointed head of the government's think tank in Downing Street by Edward Heath in 1971, with Sir Robert Armstrong as his principal private secretary. He underwent stringent positive vetting for the post, which would give him access to many secrets, with no difficulties whatsoever. MI5's own list of his contributions to the security of the nation was considered to be a sufficient guarantee of his loyalty in itself. But later, when he was under public attack, MI5 was not prepared to state this in his defense, even through the Prime Minister.

Lord Rothschild's reputation has suffered severely from his old friendship with the MI5 spy, Anthony Blunt, but his association with the MI5 "spycatcher," Peter Wright, has been even more damaging.

‖20‖

The Charmed Life of
Arthur Martin

> *As a Whitehall caste, officers of MI5 and MI6 are, in general, the Untouchables.*
>
> —Confidential source

On November 28, 1986, Campbell-Savours asked the Attorney General to explain why Arthur Martin, the former MI5 officer, had not been prosecuted for breaching confidence on security matters to Rupert Allason ("Nigel West"). Havers replied that he reached his decision not to prosecute Martin for supplying information to Allason—thereby confirming that Martin had done so—because he was "satisfied that it would not be in the public interest to prosecute." [1]

Sir Robert Armstrong had already been forced to admit in the Sydney court that he had not managed to stop Arthur Martin from leaking information, adding that the only action taken against him had been to remind him of his obligation to confidentiality. This admission seriously weakened the govern-

ment's case for preventing further leaks by Wright, and Turnbull exploited it to great advantage. In his judgment, Justice
Powell pointed to the fact that Martin had confessed that he
had supplied information to Allason and that no charges had
been laid against him.

Martin had been questioned by MI5 as far back as 1980,
when he had been the chief informant for Jonathan Aitken in
a series of secret meetings that had culminated in Aitken's letter to the Prime Minister, as described in chapter 2. Aitken
had been careful not to name Martin as a source but, shortly
after *Their Trade Is Treachery* appeared in March 1981, Martin
was questioned about it by MI5. He rightly denied having
given me any information but volunteered that he had been
Aitken's source and that the sequence of events had been initiated by James Angleton of the CIA.

Remarking that much of the information in *Their Trade Is
Treachery* seemed to be "straight out of the files," Martin told
the MI5 man that he suspected that the book had been organized by high security officials with government approval, a
theory that was later to surface in the Sydney court. He
thought that, after the Prime Minister had received Aitken's
letter about Hollis, there had been a "strategic" decision to
find a reliable outlet for publication of the information, and
that I had been chosen for the task. The MI5 man made no
comment, but the theory was groundless.

In his letters, Wright told me that he was in occasional
touch with Martin, with whom he had been particularly
friendly while in MI5. If Martin ever discussed his theory with
him, Wright never mentioned it to me.

The fact that Aitken was an MP ruled out any action
against him or his informant. Though the MI5 management
was not happy about the relationship, Martin was not told to
desist from seeing Aitken, and he continued to do so.

To understand MI5's attitude and why Martin's name was
mentioned repeatedly in the Wright trial, it is necessary to

know something about his career, which was to give him the reputation of being one of the best counterespionage officers in the West.

His first major success was as case officer in the investigation of Klaus Fuchs. He was also in charge of the Maclean case, in which his spade work in identifying Maclean as the KGB spy with the code-name "Homer" was regarded as brilliant. He built up the case against Philby and prepared the brief for his interrogation by Helenus Milmo in 1951, sitting in on it. He interviewed John Cairncross in 1952 and, though unable to induce him to confess, was convinced of his guilt, which was later confirmed. In 1953, he became the security liaison officer in Malaya, remaining there until 1957, when he returned to London headquarters to take over the Czech desk. He handled the successful case against the British traitor Brian Linney, who was working for the Czechs. In 1960, he became head of Russian counterintelligence and ran the case that ended in the arrest of the Soviet agent who called himself Gordon Lonsdale, the naval spies Houghton and Gee, and the Krogers, who were illegal radio operators and paymasters. Martin also controlled the MI5 end of the case against George Blake, who was a KGB spy deep inside MI6.

It was Martin who went to the United States in April 1962 to debrief the KGB defector Golitsin. In 1962, he was also in charge of the inquiries into John Vassall, the admiralty spy, and interviewed Flora Solomon about her relationship with Philby. In 1963, he developed and improved Movements Analysis, the system that Canadian security men had invented for checking the movements of Soviet officials who might be professional intelligence officers.[2]

Martin handled the Blunt case until fired from it by Hollis and was a founding member of the Fluency Committee charged with investigating Mitchell and Hollis. It was Martin who dealt with Leo Long, the Soviet agent run by Blunt.

This impressive list made Martin a most valuable source

for Allason, and serious consideration was undoubtedly given to the possible prosecution of them both. The confidential letter that I wrote to Wright about their relationship in 1983 makes this very clear. Details were revealed by Sir Robert Armstrong under cross-questioning in the Sydney court case in 1986. It was admitted that Martin had supplied Allason with information and some documents in 1981 and 1982 for use in preparing a book. It was also stated that, when Martin had seen what Allason proposed to publish, he was so horrified that he took the text to MI5 and asked to be extricated from his difficulty. As a result, an injunction was issued against the book, and the direct references to Martin and other matters were deleted before publication.[3] As I understand it, the issue was resolved on advice from the legal advisers to MI5, who pointed out that the requirements of secrecy and the reputation of the service made it impracticable for such a distinguished ex-officer as Martin to appear in any court, either as a witness or as a defendant. In any cross-examination by the defense, the prosecution would have to make too many damaging admissions.

Privately, the law officers also took comfort in the view that Martin's offense was in a different category from Wright's. His name did not appear in West's book as a quoted source, whereas Wright's was presented boldly in *Spycatcher* as the author, giving the whole book credibility, whether its contents were true or not. This argument was seriously weakened, however, when Martin was widely quoted in a later book by two other authors in 1986, and still no action was taken against him—as Turnbull was quick to detect.[4]

This raises the issue of what would really happen to Peter Wright if he ever returned to Britain. The enormous publicity given to his activities and the hostile reaction to them might make his arrest and prosecution unavoidable but it would certainly be unwelcome to MI5. So much so, that I suspect that the leaked statement that he would be prosecuted was calculated to deter him from coming. In 1956, when it seemed remotely possible that Guy Burgess might return to Britain, a warrant was issued for his arrest. There can be no doubt, in retrospect, that the purpose was to deter the traitor from subjecting the authorities to the embarrassment of an arrest and trial.

‖21‖

Enter the Police

Investigative journalism is a high-risk business.

—Duncan Campbell

As the Solicitor General, Sir Patrick Mayhew, told Parliament in the course of an adjournment debate on February 6, 1987, the metropolitan police had been asked to undertake inquiries into Peter Wright's allegations against Lord Rothschild and me on December 17, 1986, and they were still continuing. They were carried out by a detective chief superintendent of the serious crimes squad (CID), the implication being that the police were pursuing the allegations of conspiracy against the state and of the corruption of Wright. While the inquiries continued, as they did over a period of seven months, Rothschild and I were enmeshed in the web of secrecy that we had helped to weave.

The investigation was an affront to Lord Rothschild, but the Attorney General (then, Sir Michael Havers) had been put in a Parliamentary position where he decided that it had to be done, though the spiteful backbencher who initiated it, Dale Campbell-Savours, could have been told that such an inquiry would be a waste of public money. There was never any possibility that MI5 or the government would countenance the appearance in the dock or the witness box of a former officer who knew as much as Lord Rothschild. The same applied to Sir Arthur Franks, the former MI6 chief, who would have been an essential witness. And for reasons already stated, no legal action with any hope of success was possible against me. The whole inquiry was nonsense from the start because there could be no case without cross-examination of the main witness—Wright—and he could not appear in a British court without the certainty of prosecution.

While politics are not supposed to affect such legal issues, no government in its right mind would have taken steps that would have meant reopening the highly damaging Wright case in London. Had such a case been possible, it would have been one of the most widely covered of the century, if only because of the eminence of the witnesses that both I and Rothschild would have called. As with the D-Notice affair, the prosecution of an investigative writer would have alienated the media. In any prosecution concerning *Their Trade Is Treachery*, the publishers would necessarily have been involved, and this would have meant not only Sidgwick and Jackson but the *Daily Mail* and *The Times*, since they were the *first* publishers through their serializations.

Shortly before Christmas, the police approached Lord Rothschild to interview him concerning statements made by Wright in his sworn affidavit. He was seen by the Scotland Yard's chief superintendent, with his lawyer present. The first interview took about four hours, with Rothschild's answers being taken down by a metropolitan police inspector in longhand. The details have been reported to me.

Lord Rothschild had a copy of the parts of Wright's sworn affidavit that were read in open court but the police were soon asking him questions about statements made by Wright *in camera*, which puzzled him. They questioned him about Peter Kapitza, the Russian scientist who had been at Cambridge in the 1930s, and about a former friend and confidant of the late Shah of Iran, Sir Shapoor Reporter. Reporter had been involved in the restoration of the Shah, in 1953. At that time, he was working in collaboration with MI6 but may also have had some connection with MI5. It would seem that Wright had tried to involve Rothschild with Reporter in the overthrow of the Iranian Prime Minister, Mussadegh, but Rothschild told the police that he had no involvement in it whatsoever.

The police saw Lord Rothschild three times for a total of about ten hours, taking him through each of Wright's allegations. He gave them proof that Wright was wrong about the first-class ticket, which he could not have exchanged for two economy tickets as he claimed. Rothschild had the receipt from the agency that handles his travel arrangements, showing that Lord Rothschild had sent Wright one economy-class ticket. The police confirmed this with the agency, so Wright was presumed to have bought his wife's ticket. Wright's affidavit claim that Lord Rothschild had sent out a courier to recover one of his letters was also discounted.

Wright had stated in his *in camera* evidence that Rothschild had introduced him to Roy Jenkins, but neither could recall any such meeting.

Lord Rothschild was asked how we had first met. He thought we had been introduced by Lord Sieff, then the chairman of the famous chain-store, Marks & Spencer, which I had already confirmed with the latter. I am confident that this occurred at a dinner at the Sieffs' London flat and that a few other people had been present, including Lady Rothschild.

Lord Rothschild told the police that he had asked Wright if he was interested in meeting me and that I had been his guest for a night but insisted that he had not mentioned the idea of a book to Wright. It has always been my recollection that the concept of a book came solely from Wright. Lord Rothschild was able to show the police letters from Wright proving that Wright was working on a book, and even had a title for it, three months before he had been invited to Britain.

He told them that he thought that, if Wright was put in touch with me, he would not think it worthwhile to write a book on his own because I already knew so much about the Hollis affair and other issues.

The chief superintendent asked why, if everything was aboveboard, there had been so much secrecy about the banking arrangements. Rothschild replied that it was normal banking practice and that Wright had requested confidentiality. Rothschild had consulted a colleague, who had said that there was nothing illegal about it, and the colleague had made the arrangements. It was inconceivable that an organization with a reputation like that of Rothschild's bank would do anything that was illegal. The police were able to confirm that, indeed, nothing illegal in this respect had occurred.

These visits by the police would seem to be proof enough that Lord Rothschild was no conscious part of any MI5 setup. He was deeply upset by the ordeal; he was not well, and police inquiries—however reasonably conducted, as they certainly were—were undignified to one of his eminence and were potentially damaging to the name of a great family and to the banking concern of which he had been chairman. Had Rothschild been party to an MI5 conspiracy, he could simply have referred the police to MI5 and declined to see them again, knowing that no action would be taken against him.

On Thursday, February 12, I was telephoned by the chief superintendent, who said that he would like to interview me. He took the opportunity of saying that it was in connection with the Official Secrets Act and was therefore "serious." He thought that he might be able to complete his questioning in one day, but I preferred to split it into sessions as I knew that it would probably take longer than he anticipated and would be exhausting. He agreed and we fixed an interview for the afternoon of Wednesday, February 18. He said he would be accompanied by an inspector who would be taking longhand notes.

I decided to make a preemptive strike by preparing a substantial advance statement for him.

The police officers proved to be pleasant, highly professional, and determined to pursue their task. Suggestions that they were simply going through motions to pacify Parliament quickly proved to be groundless.

The chief superintendent began by assuring me that I was not under arrest and that I did not have to tell him anything if I did not wish to do so, although if I did, it could be used in evidence. He observed that various MPs were "after my blood"; I gathered this was purely from his reading of *Hansard* (the official report of the proceedings of Parliament), which probably impressed him more than it did me. There have been few Labour backbenchers for whom I have had any respect. The officers also seemed unduly impressed by the fact that the inquiries were being made in connection with the Official Secrets act, for which I have long had justifiable disrespect.

I declared that I would cooperate because I had nothing to hide. I pointed out that, as the truth unfolded, the chief superintendent would appreciate that it would be in my interest for the facts to be fully exposed, but that others, some of whom were friends, could be embarrassed. I made it clear, however, that, while I did not want to harm the government or expose my friends, there was a limit to the extent to which I was prepared to be harassed at the age of seventy-three to satisfy the whim of a Labour backbencher.

At one stage the chief superintendent said to me, "You hold the reins in this affair." He was right. I could have blown the whole thing sky-high by going public on television, which I was repeatedly invited to do. I could, in fact, have made £20,000 at any time simply by lifting the telephone and telling a national newspaper the inside story of the clearance of *Their Trade Is Treachery*. The chief superintendent said that Lord Rothschild and I were exposed "like being alone in the middle of a parade ground" and that nobody was coming to our rescue. I certainly needed nobody to come to mine. He then began to ask me questions that were routine, except for one arising out of a statement by Wright *in camera* that I was not only an agent of MI5 but a double agent and a misinformation agent. I riddled that with a factual account of the few services I had done for MI5, none of them for payment.

The interview lasted three hours. During it, I convinced them that my information about Hollis had not come from Lord Rothschild, as Wright had suggested, but from Jonathan Aitken; as proof, I gave them a copy of Jonathan Aitken's letter to the Prime Minister dated January 31, 1980, knowing that this had been made available to Turnbull.

I told them that a distinguished figure had, effectively, handed in the book for vetting on behalf of Sidgwick and Jackson and that the book could have been stopped simply by a telephone call to him. The chief superintendent, quite properly, tried hard to induce me to name him in a written statement but I declined and suggested that they should direct their inquiries at William Armstrong of Sidgwick and Jackson, who had been responsible once I had delivered the typescript to him. If he cared to assist them, they could then take it from there. They were going to see Armstrong anyway to question him about the contract for *Their Trade Is Treachery.*

I had already advised the police that as their inquiries progressed, they might find themselves entangled in politics and problems involved with the operations of the secret services.

A further meeting with the police of at least three hours' duration was fixed for Tuesday, February 24. I therefore prepared a full written analysis of Wright's affidavit, demonstrating through documents and witnesses that it was packed with false statements and misinformation. No difficult questions arose at that meeting.

The police officers called again on February 27, by appointment, and again we talked for about three hours, which ended the main questioning. The only "fast ball" was a statement that clearly originated in Wright's *in camera* evidence and was, presumably, what he was referring to when he told

the media that he would prove that I had sent him money.[1]
The chief superintendent asked me to explain a quote from
one of my letters to Wright: "5 is on its way to you through
V-Channel." The explanation could not have been more
straightforward. When the contract for *Their Trade Is Treachery*
was signed, £10,000 of the advance became payable by Sidgwick and Jackson. I received my share—£5,000—within a
couple of weeks or so and assumed that Wright would do the
same, which he did. The V-Channel was simply Overbridge,
the offshore company handling Wright's account, and I had no
hand whatsoever in the payment.

On the morning of March 3, the police called to see William Armstrong at his office. They asked for and received a
copy of Sir Robert Armstrong's letter, though I had already
given them one, and a copy of the contract for *Their Trade Is
Treachery*. William Armstrong then made a statement in the
form of a narrative regarding what had happened between us.
The police told me that it corresponded with what I had told
them. In particular, the chief superintendent was to tell me
later, when I questioned him, that he was satisfied that at no
time had I or Summerpage paid any money to Wright and that
all he had received were net profits from Sidgwick and
Jackson.

The police were astonished to learn that William
Armstrong had known nothing about Lord Rothschild's involvement until that became public during the Sydney trial.[2]
There was no reason why he should have known. After the
book was submitted, most of our communication was by letter
or telephone, and Armstrong never asked any questions. Once
he had the address for the royalties, the rest was carried out by
the contracts department, and he lost interest in that side of
the business. The police were equally surprised to discover
that William Armstrong had known nothing about the involvement of Peter Wright before the Sydney trial.[3] I had
never told him about it because Wright had insisted on ano-

nymity and Armstrong had never asked about the "consultants" mentioned in the contract. If he had questioned me about their identities, I would have declined to answer.

William Armstrong later described his position as follows:

> I have never published a book that has produced so many after-publication surprises. I had no idea that Peter Wright was a prime source for I have never questioned Chapman Pincher about his sources, which have always proved impeccable. I did not know that Lord Rothschild was in any way involved. Nor did I suspect that when Sir Robert Armstrong telephoned me to ask for a copy of the book, he already had the manuscript of it in his possession. Right up to the moment when I received his letter, three days before publication day, I was most uncomfortably convinced of the real risk of our being prevented from publishing.
>
> It was not until some considerable time after publication that I learned that the typescript had been shown in advance to the authorities. I was in turn astonished, irritated, highly amused and, after reflection, relieved, as the consequences could have been so very unpleasant if the Government had decided to go for us: this they probably would have done if the "Arbiter" had not taken things into his own hands and obtained for us some form of immunity.

Armstrong was asked who had received a synopsis of *Their Trade Is Treachery* and said that one had gone to the Arbiter, whom—in the serious circumstances, and being assured of confidentiality—he felt he was required to name. He was then asked if the Arbiter had requested a typescript and was told that he had. The chief superintendent made it clear that he believed that the Arbiter had passed both of them on to the security services but Armstrong declined to speculate about that.[4]

On March 4, the police officers arrived at my home for a two-hour signing session, in which the questions and answers I had given were signed after a few very small corrections. (By that time, I do not think that the more observant of my neighbors were slow to identify two fairly obvious "coppers" wearing identical blue raincoats and knocking on my door precisely at 1:30 P.M.) At the conclusion of the signing, the chief superintendent then asked to see my personal files, still believing, for some reason beyond me, that I had Wright's nine chapters tucked away when, in fact, I had never possessed them. It was clearly in my interest to show them the chapters, if I really had them, because they would prove my crucial point that Wright's story about bringing them to Britain to be passed on to Mrs. Thatcher was bogus. When I said that there was nothing of consequence relevant to his inquiries in the files, he produced a search warrant signed by a judge on February 16, two days before he had first visited me.

I affected to show annoyance at this intrusion, as did my wife, but the police insisted; and while they restricted their search to my large study, I thought at one point that they were going to take away every folder and box-file. They settled, however, for about ten folders dealing with individuals, including Sir Arthur Franks, Sir Michael Havers, and Margaret Thatcher, and two box-files labeled "Hollis" plus folders on the Official Secrets Act, Intelligence, and Espionage. I agreed that they should take them away rather than sit reading them for hours in my home. I told them that they were unlikely to find anything of consequence regarding the case. I had, regrettably, destroyed almost all Wright's correspondence as it arrived, and if I had still had anything at all incriminating, it would not have been in my house during police inquiries.

The police said that they would let me have the documents back in about a fortnight. The warrant permitted only one search within a month, but as that month would soon be over, I realized that they could be back with a further warrant. I therefore removed any potentially embarrassing documents from my files so that no more of my friends could be involved in what might become a general "fishing expedition."

Early on the morning of March 17, the Arbiter called me to tell me that he had been telephoned by the police, who wished him to assist them concerning *Their Trade Is Treachery*. He sounded very relaxed and had agreed to see them, having nothing whatsoever to hide. I told him that it was greatly in my interest and in William Armstrong's for the police to know, without any doubt, that the book had been submitted to the proper authorities and that he had secured a tacit understanding that neither I nor Sidgwick and Jackson would be prosecuted. After making private inquiries he decided to tell them exactly what had happened.

Regrettably, the police inquiries were ended before the Arbiter had the opportunity to make a signed statement, presumably because there was already enough evidence to satisfy the Director of Public Prosecutions and the Attorney General that Wright's allegations were unfounded. To have secured more might have required the questioning of Sir Arthur Franks and Sir Robert Armstrong, and that would have meant exceeding the police brief. The police were disappointed that they had not been allowed to complete their investigations.

On March 20, I telephoned the chief superintendent, seeking information about the return of my papers. He rang me back at 9:30 P.M., when he was still working in his office, and said that he would return the papers in one or two weeks. Later the inspector telephoned to make an appointment to return my documents, which he did on April 13, 1987.

The chief superintendent submitted an interim report on Lord Rothschild to the Director of Public Prosecutions on April 24, after his return from an overseas assignment. I do not know if he also submitted an interim report on me, but presumably he did so. Neither of us was told, and Rothschild did not know until Sir Michael Havers answered a Parliamentary question by Tam Dalyell on May 7. Havers revealed that the Director of Public Prosecutions was considering the report and that it might be necessary to ask the police to make further inquiries before a decision could be made. [5]

Lord Rothschild's lawyers then telephoned the chief superintendent to ask if he wished to see their client, who had given the police another good reason for seeing him by informing them that he could offer some further relevant documentary evidence about Peter Wright. This was a letter from Wright dated November 3, 1976, in which he had stated that he still had his notes of his talks with Blunt, in contradiction to what he had told the court in Sydney. It was an offense to retain such notes, and Wright's reference to them implied that very quickly after his arrival in Australia he was thinking about writing a book. The police did not avail themselves of the opportunity to see Lord Rothschild again, but they received the letter.

It seemed that any decision about us would be delayed until after the general election, perhaps to avoid any hustings jibe, in the event of Lord Rothschild's clearance, that the rich and powerful always get away with their misdeeds. I also have reason to believe that Sir Michael Havers was anxious to avoid having to announce the decision because of his known friendship with me. He was leaving the Commons, and a new Attorney General would be better placed. I have established, however, that the final police report was with Havers in plenty of time for him to read it while he was still in office during the election.

The failure to reach a decision before the new Parliament posed some danger for both Lord Rothschild and me in the event of the return of a Labour government and a Labour Attorney General.

Nothing further was heard by me or Rothschild until July 8, 1987. I suspected that the government was hoping to have to say nothing before Parliament went into summer recess on July 24, which would have meant silence until late October at the earliest. I attributed this to the government's difficulty in saying anything that impinged on the Wright case before the appeal proceedings in Australia had been exhausted, any detailed explanation being impossible while the case remained *sub judice*. Once those legal barriers were removed, the Attorney General could not only clear Rothschild and me but might feel able to tell Parliament in an oral statement that Wright's sworn allegations had proved to be false.

Earlier in July, however, Robert Rhodes James, the Tory MP for Cambridge, let it be known that his distinguished constituent Lord Rothschild and his family were suffering intolerable distress because of the continuing uncertainty. It would not seem to be a coincidence that this was followed by a statement from the Attorney General in the form of a brief written Parliamentary answer on July 8. It read:

> Allegations made against Lord Rothschild and also against Mr. Chapman Pincher have been investigated by the police. The Director of Public Prosecutions has now decided that the investigation has not disclosed evidence justifying the bringing of proceedings against either Lord Rothschild or Mr. Chapman Pincher. The Director has consulted me and I have agreed with his decision.[6]

The media showed scant interest in this negative result and did not appear to appreciate what it meant for Wright. The allegations that the police had been asked to investigate were those that had been made under oath by Wright to the Sydney court. They had been investigated by the police in depth, with collateral inquiries wherever possible. Their rejection by the police and by the law officers could only be interpreted as implying that much of Wright's evidence to the court had been unreliable.

I was gratified to have been cleared but felt that it had been ludicrous for exceptionally able officers of the serious crimes squad to spend several months talking to me and others

simply to pacify one or two mischievous backbenchers seeking
to make political capital and to support Wright. They had been
required to chase the fantasies of Peter Wright and Campbell-
Savours, and much public money, apart from their time, had
been wasted in the sterile process.

While I had known from the start that a prosecution was a
legal impossibility, I genuinely welcomed the prospect of a
court action in principle. All my professional life I had cru-
saded for press freedom, and a court action over the Wright
affair, which would have revealed so much of the truth about
it, would have offered me a splendid platform in the closing
years of my career. I would not have been averse, even at seventy-three, to a contest in which I had to defend the journalist's right to acquire knowledge in a free society. A
succession of governments have known over the course of forty
years that I have constantly been making inquiries about officially secret affairs, and they have never taken any action
against me. If I had been prosecuted for being in possession of
secret information, I would have to ask for 10,000 previous
offenses to be taken into consideration.

As had happened with the D-Notice affair in 1967, most
of the media would have been likely to rally in support of a
journalist and writer being prosecuted for pursuing his calling.

I had courted prosecution when *Inside Story* was published in 1978. Three Labour backbenchers had risen to the
bait by demanding my prosecution under the Official Secrets
Act for securing information from MI5 and MI6 sources. The
Attorney General, Sam Silkin, had instigated inquiries and,
after a decent interval, announced that he had decided that
there were no grounds for prosecution. It was a pity because in
the privilege of the court I could have revealed quite a lot
about covert communists in the Labour government, past and
present.

In the unlikely event of an action in 1986, I had decided I
would conduct my own defense for two reasons. First, the case
would be complex, and no counsel, however talented, could

possibly learn the facts of the case as I knew them. Second, the court costs could be high, and conducting my own defense would help to preserve the modest inheritance that my wife and family could expect—though I might, of course, have more than recouped my costs from a book about the case.

Any prosecution of me and Rothschild in our seventies, when it had been declined when we were seven years younger, would have looked obscene, and we could have made much of that. Further, because of the nature of the evidence, no case could have been heard before the completion of the appeal proceedings in Australia, and by then we would have been at least a year older still.

A thorough cross-examination of Wright would have been essential, but the Attorney General had let it be known that he would be prosecuted if he set foot in Britain, and it would have been politically unacceptable for Wright to receive immunity to appear as a witness. Without Wright in the witness box, I do not see how either I or Rothschild could have been given a fair trial on any of the possible legal issues.

The sequence of witnesses I would have been required to call would have been like the procession of peers in *Iolanthe*. I should certainly have wanted to subpoena the Prime Minister, Sir Robert Armstrong, Sir Arthur Franks, and, above all, Havers, by then the Lord Chancellor.

In the middle of the police inquiries, on April 19, 1987, I had perhaps complicated my position with the government— and the Prime Minister, in particular—by disclosing that Sir Maurice Oldfield, the former Chief of MI6, had been a secret homosexual and, as a result, had been driven to conceal his problem by falsifying his positive vetting statements over many years. From prime sources I knew how this had come to the notice of the security authorities in 1979 and 1980, when Oldfield had retired from MI6 but was serving as Co-ordinator of Intelligence in Northern Ireland, which gave him continued access to highly secret information. I also knew how, after confessing to the security authorities, he had been confronted by the Attorney General, Sir Michael Havers, and had given a solemn promise to curb his behavior while he finished his time in Northern Ireland.

Some of Oldfield's friends immediately assumed that this disclosure was the result of yet another MI5 conspiracy to blacken the reputation of MI6, and that the information had been leaked to me for that purpose.[7] In fact, MI5 had not been involved in any way, and I had been sitting on the information for two years. It emerged only because, having decided to write a book on the various motivations for treachery, I felt it would have been dishonest to withhold the Oldfield case from the chapter on the factor of homosexuality.[8] It was perhaps unfortunate that the disclosure, which caused a media sensation, should have appeared just prior to the general election, but that was entirely due to the fact that the *Mail on Sunday,* which had bought the serial rights from the publisher, chose to print the installments then.[9]

Whatever the Prime Minister's private reaction to this additional embarrassment about the secret services—Oldfield had been a personal friend—she was typically robust in answering a Parliamentary question about it. On April 23, in a carefully worded written answer, Mrs. Thatcher confirmed that in March 1980 Oldfield had admitted that, from time to time, he had engaged in homosexual activities and revealed that, as a result, his positive vetting clearance had been withdrawn. She added that after a lengthy and thorough investigation, it had been concluded that, while his conduct had been a security risk, there was no evidence to suggest that security had ever been compromised.

Oldfield's friends were greatly dismayed by the official confirmation, and some (including some former members of MI6) continued to see a mythical MI5 conspiracy behind the incident.

The chief superintendent telephoned me on his return from a holiday to inform me personally of my clearance, as a matter of courtesy. To mark the occasion and their professional intrusion into the secret world, I sent him and his colleague inscribed copies of my recent book, *Traitors: The Anatomy of Treason*. They had behaved with admirable professionalism throughout, and I would have had to admit that even if their report had gone against me.

I told the police that I believed that Wright had made false statements to the court and that this could have been proved, had he been cross-examined more effectively. Instead, whatever the motivations of Wright, the judge had been effectively deceived.

‖22‖

Judgment and Appeals

> *Till from its summit,*
> *Judgement drops her damning plummet.*
> —Browning

Shortly before Justice Powell's verdict was due to be announced, the law officers learned, from me, that the serial rights of *Spycatcher* were being hawked at American newspapers. It seemed obvious that, if the verdict went against the government, an American newspaper could start serialization, and the government would be powerless to stop it. This could make an appeal in the Australian court seem so pointless that the government might be unable to pursue it.

The American publisher of *Spycatcher* proved to be the Viking Press, a subsidiary of a British conglomerate. There appeared to be no immediate takers for the serialization, but in May 1987 excerpts were printed by the *Washington Post* and were copied by hundreds of newspapers across the United States.

On Friday, March 13, twelve weeks after the Sydney trial had ended, Justice Powell issued his judgment, a 286-page document which found totally in favor of Heinemann and Wright and was savagely critical of the government and Sir Robert Armstrong.[1] The defendants were given their full costs, and Wright, who was back in the hospital in Hobart being treated for temporary problems caused by his blood pressure and diabetes, was given permission to sue for damages.

The judge did not accept that Wright was tied to MI5 by any contract but agreed that he had an obligation of confidentiality. He argued, however, that this obligation should continue only so long as the information that Wright had discovered during his service remained confidential. The judge ruled that the British government's argument had failed with him because the information in Wright's book was no longer confidential as it had been dealt with extensively by me in *Their Trade Is Treachery*, the publication of which had been unimpeded by the government. He concluded that the government had forfeited its right to suppress Wright's book because it had not prevented the publication of previous books like mine. As regards *Their Trade Is Treachery*, the judge ruled that the British government had to be regarded as "having abandoned any claim to confidentiality in respect of any confidential information contained in it." The judge believed that the failure to restrain its publication was tantamount to acquiescence: "It is clear that the British Government authorised, or at least acquiesced in, the publication of *Their Trade Is Treachery*." He repeated a statement he had made in court that for years MI5 had "leaked like a sieve."

The judge was, of course, unaware of the peculiar secrecy requirement that had made ministers decide that it was impossible to suppress my book. The fog of secrecy that had enveloped them had also enshrouded the judge.

He was highly critical of the way the government's case had been conducted. He accused the government of perpetually changing its ground in search of tactical advantage.

He expressed "reserve" about the credibility of Sir Robert Armstrong, while dismissing Turnbull's wild claim that he had been sent to Australia to "lie for his country." He argued that any past iniquitous conduct by MI5, as alleged by Wright in *Spycatcher*, should be brought to light. He also favored the exposure of more information about Sir Roger Hollis, especially since Hollis had been involved in setting up the Australian Security Intelligence Organisation.

He dismissed Turnbull's outrageous scenario claiming that *Their Trade Is Treachery* was the result of a conspiracy between Lord Rothschild, the government, and me, saying, "It seems fanciful to talk of a conspiracy, if only because one would have thought that the publishers would necessarily have been a part."

He thought that the government had failed to show that it would suffer detriment from Wright's book. Powell said, "it is not the law, as was once thought, that those responsible for national security must be the sole judges of what the national security requires." He argued that it is for the courts to determine the validity of such claims.

The only benefit the government secured was twenty-eight days in which to lodge an appeal in the New South Wales Appeal Court in Sydney. Any appeal would have to be heard on the evidence of the original case—new evidence, such as doubts about Wright's veracity, being inadmissible. I felt that the government's case had been badly served by the failure to cross-examine Wright effectively and to show him to be a most unreliable witness. In view of Wright's sustained effort to incriminate Lord Rothschild and me, I told the Attorney General I would be prepared to offer evidence in that respect by affidavit, but he said it would be inadmissible.

The process of appeal, which could be repeated as a last-ditch effort in the High Court in Canberra, if necessary, meant that the case would remain *sub judice* for several more months and that little could be said about it in Parliament.

The Times described Powell's handling of the case as eccentric and bizarre, and a *Times* editorial regarded the judgment as "very questionable" because it had not adequately differentiated between a book like mine and the manuscript written by Wright. The editorial pointed out that there was a world of difference between any work by an investigative journalist, however skilled, and one by a man like Peter Wright, whose knowledge and experience of Whitehall were so intimate and far-reaching. It advised the government to appeal.[2]

The judge's verdict was, unquestionably, based on misleading evidence. It was crucial to an understanding of the case that the judge should know the truth about the way the book had been dealt with by the security authorities. He did not know the truth because, as I have explained, Sir Robert Armstrong, the chief witness, did not know it. There was the additional fact that much of Wright's evidence had been untrue, as the police inquiries had established.

After the Sydney verdict, the government felt it might be on a wild-goose chase, but still it had to go through all the motions it could to show its total disapproval of Wright's behavior. Ministers knew they would incur the anger of much of the media but felt—rightly, I believe—that public opinion would, generally, be on their side. On March 16, Sir Michael Havers announced in Parliament that the government had decided to appeal against the judgment and felt that it had a better than 50 percent chance of winning. On March 31, the appeal was filed in the Court of Appeal of New South Wales. This bound Wright and Heinemann not to divulge the contents of the book before the case was settled. Havers insisted that a major issue of principle was at stake and that the judge had been mistaken because Wright owed a lifelong duty of confidentiality to his employers and only the British government had the power to release him from it; the fact that "outsiders" had already disclosed Wright's information was asserted to be irrelevant.

The appeal would be based on submissions that Justice Powell misinterpreted English law in finding that there was no contract between Wright and the Crown. Powell's conduct of the case was criticized as "idiosyncratic to the point of being perverse." The law officers also realized that Justice Powell might be held to be at fault for his cavalier dismissal of the Australian Cabinet Secretary's evidence concerning the potential damage Wright's book posed for Australia.

Turnbull, who was in London, reacted by stating that the appeal would be vigorously defended. It was later announced that Turnbull would not be representing Wright during the appeal, as he was going into an investment bank venture in partnership with the son of Gough Whitlam, the former Australian Prime Minister who had appeared for him in the Sydney case as a valuable witness. Later it was stated that he would be acting as instructing solicitor, while the case would be argued by his father-in-law, Tom Hughes QC, a leading Australian lawyer. In the event, as will be seen, Turnbull did appear at the appeal.

Announcement of the appeal was well received by the Conservatives but, inevitably, the Labour opposition tried to make party capital out of it, claiming that it was a device to keep the Wright case *sub judice* until after the general election. In fact, publication of the book before the election would not have been in Labour's interest, in view of its focus on secret communists and suspect Soviet agents in the Labour Party.

In mid-May 1987, Viking let it be known that it intended to publish *Spycatcher* in its entirety in America in June or July—before the hearing of any appeal in Sydney, although this date seems to have been delayed by a month or so.[3] Making the announcement, its publicity director stated that the previous part-serialization in the *Washington Post* and the government's failure to win the case in Sydney justified the decision. The temptation to expedite publication had been intensified by the public interest in the alleged bugging of the American embassy in Moscow and the arrest of a Marine embassy guard who had been "honey-trapped" by a woman working for the KGB.[4] This decision must have horrified the Attorney General, who, many months previously, had taken the considered view that the government could never contest publication in the United States because it would have no chance of success. This was also the view of Viking's lawyers, who were prepared for possible intervention.[5] While the Australian appellate judges would be required to consider only the evidence that had been available to the Sydney court, could they bring in a judgment that prevented the Australian people from reading a book that had already been published in America?

There would be a new Attorney General in the government following the election, since Havers was retiring from the Commons. It did not seem likely that he would want to inherit the problem; and a quiet withdrawal from the appeal, on the grounds that the American publication had unexpectedly undermined the government's case, would have been understandable. Instead, however, the new Attorney General, Sir Patrick Mayhew, told Parliament that the appeal in the Sydney court, scheduled to begin on July 27, would go ahead as planned by his predecessor.[6] Sir Patrick explained, "The Government is seeking to uphold the principle that those who have served in the security services in this country owe a lifelong duty to the Crown to preserve confidentiality on any material which came to their knowledge by reason of their employment."

The long-term purpose was to prevent others from following Wright's example, but there was a more immediate fear that, if the government withdrew and thereby acquiesced in the publication of *Spycatcher*, Wright might then be free to tell or allege whatever he wished in expanded editions of *Spycatcher* or further books.

Labour MPs deplored the decision as a continued interference with press freedom. Some Conservative MPs thought that the Attorney General was throwing good money after bad; but many, probably most, admired his resolve.

Meanwhile, the Prime Minister had delivered her opinion of the various strictures on Sir Michael Havers by appointing him Lord Chancellor, as Baron Havers. It was a telling kick in the teeth for Turnbull and his supporters on the Labour side, who had questioned Havers's integrity and Mrs. Thatcher's confidence in him. Later, she recorded her confidence in Sir Robert Armstrong and her appreciation of his services by listing him in the 1988 New Year's Honours as a life peer.

Wright's American publisher finally decided to issue the U.S. edition of his book in mid-July—very shortly before the hearing in the Sydney appellate court. The *Sunday Times*, operating in great secrecy, secured the serial rights for Britain and published four pages of *Spycatcher* extracts on July 12— again in advance of the appeal in Sydney. Extreme precautions were taken to ensure that the government had no advance knowledge of the serialization. The material was even withheld from the first edition of the newspaper so that the government would not be alerted in time to secure an injunction preventing further publication. This was clearly a deliberate attempt to undermine the government's position, and especially that of the law officers, and the *Sunday Times* exulted in its initial success in a two-page account of the secret operation, which even had a code-name, "Eagle."[7]

The timing of the whole American–British enterprise was widely interpreted as being deliberately calculated to destroy the government's case in the imminent appeal proceedings in Australia and to secure quick, worldwide publication of Wright's book. It was no surprise, therefore, when the Attorney General announced that proceedings for criminal contempt would be taken against the *Sunday Times*.[8]

In the media, the editor of the *Sunday Times*, Andrew Neil, explained his action as being in defense of press freedom—to give the British public the same right to read the book as the American public had. In the later *Sunday Times* account of the secret operation, however, he made it clear that a major motive had been to defeat other newspapers that had been competing for the serial rights, believing that the material would boost circulation. Neil claimed that the newspaper had been advised by legal counsel that, as the law currently stood, the newspaper could not be in contempt. The Attorney General thought differently.

Sir Patrick Mayhew stressed that he was acting as a law officer for the Crown and not on behalf of the government, but the government's anger at what it regarded as the *Sunday Times*'s surreptitious and underhanded action was not in doubt.

According to *The Times*, government sources let it be known that, if the appeal in Australia succeeded, it intended to "seek sanction from the court to force Wright or his publishers to pay back any money made from writing *Spycatcher*," including that from the American edition and its serialization.[9] Such action could be based on Wright's breach of confidentiality in selling secret information he had gained through his paid employment by the Crown. Wright's position was regarded as being comparable to that of an employee of a manufacturing firm who moves abroad and sells his former employer's commercial secrets. Nobody would doubt the justice of a claim that such a man and the firm paying him could be sued.

The writer, Paul Johnson, expressed the government's feelings and those of many of its supporters when he wrote: "Rogue agents must be made to understand that the Crown will never allow them to profit from their treachery with impunity. It will use every legal means open to it to frustrate their cupidity. It will hound them to their dying day and wherever they may be."[10] At that time, and since, Wright has been widely described as "treacherous," a renegade, and even "a squalid traitor," as he has admitted himself on television, with disagreement and some disgust.

The action by the *Sunday Times* had coincided with the reopening, in the Court of Appeal, of legal arguments against the dismissal of the contempt case previously brought by the Attorney General against the *Independent*, *London Evening Standard*, and *London Daily News*. The appellate judges, led by Sir John Donaldson, Master of the Rolls, ruled that the publishing of confidential information that is the subject of a court order can, indeed, be contempt of court. The newspapers were told that what was at issue was the administration of justice itself, which depends on respect for the courts.[11] The judgment stated, "The law of contempt is based upon the broadest of principles, namely, that the courts could not and would not permit interference with the due administration of justice."[12] The ruling gave the Attorney General freedom to pursue proceedings for criminal contempt against the newspapers. No action has yet been taken due to pending appeals on previous proceedings against several British newspapers.

The *Sunday Times* announced that it would "fight on" for press freedom, but other newspapers regarded this as grandiose, sanctimonious, and somewhat specious, especially when it announced that it might sue the law officers for damages if the delay imposed on the serialization of Wright's memoirs caused financial losses because the expected increase in circulation had not been achieved.

On July 22, in a separate action, the High Court lifted the injunctions banning newspapers from publishing extracts from *Spycatcher*, but the Attorney General immediately appealed against the ruling.[13] Two days later, appellate judges, again headed by Sir John Donaldson, restored the ban but agreed that the original injunctions had been too wide. They modified them to permit the newspapers to report Wright's allegations in a general way, stating that their purpose was not to stifle the allegations but to prevent Wright or anyone else making a profit out of what he was doing. The judgment stated, "The purpose which their Lordships sought to achieve was to enable the media to report on Wright material as legitimate news but not to act as his publisher or publicist."[14]

The judgment left Wright and his publishers in no doubt that, in the judges' eyes, he was guilty of a breach of confidentiality, whatever the Australian courts might decide. "Any information acquired by Mr. Wright as a servant of the security service was impressed with the seal of confidentiality and he was not entitled to place that information in the public domain." "The publications by Mr. Wright and derived from him were tainted by his breach of duty of confidentiality. . . ." "To restrain publication would prevent Mr. Wright from profiting from his wrong-doing. . . ."[15]

The editor of the *Sunday Times* condemned the decision and sought to have the ruling overturned by the House of Lords. Meanwhile, the Attorney General had indicated that, if his bid to maintain the injunctions failed, he would consider applying for an injunction against the *Sunday Times* for breach of confidence. This presumably implied that the newspaper might be regarded as an accessory to Wright's breach.

Lords Bridge, Ackner, Brandon, Templeman, and Oliver considered the issue for three days, during which Lord Templeman asked, rhetorically, why nobody from MI5 had come forward to give evidence about the importance of confidentiality to their work. "They are so obsessed with secrecy they won't even come and tell us about it," he said, adding that they could present themselves masked if they wished. It was a fair comment.[16] Again, secrecy was dictating the terms of a hearing even in the highest court of the land.

The government's failure to act against Wright and Granada television, when he appeared in *World in Action* in 1984, came back to haunt the judgment. The law lords wondered why no action was taken, when Granada was probably watched by 8 million people and the *Sunday Times* was read by far fewer.

On July 30, they announced their judgments. By a majority of three to two, it was decided that the original ban on the publication of allegations in Wright's book should be reimposed until the conclusion of a full trial against the *Guardian* and *Observer*, which was scheduled for the autumn of 1987.[17]

Further, the lords ruled that the ban should be extended to cover any of Wright's allegations that might be repeated in the appeals court in Australia. Some of the judges astutely appreciated that long extracts might deliberately be read out in the appeal court by Turnbull so that the *Sunday Times* could repeat them, claiming court privilege.[18] The extension therefore seemed sensible to legal minds because otherwise the ban might be rendered futile. The media, however, and many members of the legal profession and the public regarded it as a gross infringement of media freedom, even though the court case in Australia had only one more day to run.

Lord Bridge dissented on the grounds that freedom of the media was more important than an attempt to preserve confidentiality when Wright's disclosures had already been widely circulated. He believed that maintaining the ban would make the government look increasingly ridiculous. The judges who opposed that view argued that, if the ban were removed before the full trial, the Attorney General would be denied justice because his case would be demolished in advance. They pointed out that the injunction was only temporary, until the cases against the newspapers came up for full trial. Save for the *Sunday Times*'s pressing need to recoup its investment in the Wright serialization, there was no urgency because it had been stated repeatedly in Wright's defense that all his material was old and was already on public record. They also believed that Lord Bridge was paying insufficient attention to the need to prevent other secret service officers from behaving in the same way as Wright, which was described as "unlawful" and "treacherous." Lord Ackner warned of the danger of establishing a "Charter for Traitors."

All the law lords accepted that Wright owed an obligation of lifelong confidence to the Crown, which he had flagrantly breached. They deplored any situation in which he could profit from the sale of secrets and pointed out that the Crown could sue to recover his profits.[19]

The lords' ruling was regarded as a victory for the Attorney General, who considered it a vindication of the principle that members of the secret services must not reveal their secret knowledge. But the extension to the Australian court proceedings, for which he had not asked, brought the media to an unprecedented state of concerted revolt. Rarely do newspapers collaborate, competition being the name of their game, but editors put their heads together to devise ways of defeating the ban, amid cries of "Soviet-style censorship." Even those who believed that Wright should be pursued, describing him as "a money-grubbing old man lining his pockets," joined forces in condemning the law lords as fools who had brought the law into disrepute. [20]

The *Sunday Times*, which was forbidden to continue its expensive serialization of Wright's book, responded by publishing a full-page account of the investigation into Hollis, using information in *Spycatcher, Their Trade Is Treachery*, and Wright's Granada interview. [21] The *Observer* reproduced what it called a key page from *Spycatcher*, with areas blanked out to indicate South African–style censorship. [22] The strongly anti-government *News on Sunday* put its head on the block by blatantly printing uncensored extracts. [23] The Attorney General decided to proceed against *News on Sunday* for criminal contempt of court. [24] He secured an injunction to block publication of excerpts in New Zealand. [25] Editors announced that the case would be taken to the European Commission of Human Rights in Strasbourg, and the *Sunday Times* quickly lodged a complaint there.

The editorial writers were virulent against the three law lords who were responsible for the ban, accusing them of making an ass of the law. The highest court in the land was accused of being a bigger menace to press freedom than the government—a hysterical assertion. [26] The law lords had acted totally independently of the government, as was shown by the fact that the senior judge, Lord Bridge, who had been a member of the Security Commission, dissented so forcefully. Nevertheless, Labour MPs joined in the attack, hoping to direct some of it toward the government and the Attorney General. The ubiquitous Campbell-Savours challenged the Attorney General to prosecute him by reading out in public allegations in Wright's book, which he had previously stated under the privilege of Parliament.[27] Anthony Wedgwood Benn also vainly courted prosecution by reading extracts from *Spycatcher* at Speakers' Corner in Hyde Park. It was claimed that the whole object of the bans was to prevent Wright's disclosure of the MI5 plot against the Wilson government, which any discerning reader of *Spycatcher* would dismiss as dubious.

While the *Sunday Times* editor, Andrew Neil, was vociferous in his condemnation of the law lords, their decision may have saved him from considerable danger. The Attorney General had hinted that, if the appeal to the House of Lords failed, alternative action was in prospect. This could have been prosecution under the Official Secrets Act. Publishing extracts from *Spycatcher* under Wright's name meant that the former MI5 officer had published official secrets in Britain and had, therefore, committed an offense under the Official Secrets Act to which he was, unquestionably, bound and which still applies in Britain. A warrant for Wright's arrest might therefore have been issued and, though he could not have been touched while he remained in Australia, he would have become a fugitive from British justice. This might have made the editor of the *Sunday Times* chargeable as an accessory to the offense.

Meanwhile, the appeal in Australia had opened on July 27 in the New South Wales Court of Appeal in Sydney, before Sir Laurence Street (the New South Wales Chief Justice), Justice Michael Kirby, and Justice Michael McHugh. Sir Laurence pointedly stated that the British law lords' decision did not advantage either party, being a "two-edged sword." Again, the government's case was presented by Theo Simos QC, who had not distinguished himself in the previous hearing. He based the appeal on the claim that Justice Powell had erred in finding that Wright was not bound by contract to the government and in finding that his disclosures had lost the quality of confidentiality because of prior publication. He quickly raised the issue of Wright's profits, claiming that it was an important element in retaining the confidence of friendly governments that he should be deprived of them. Later it was indicated to the court that these should include money he had made from *Their Trade Is Treachery.* Simos's main argument was that Wright and his publisher had to be made to understand that they could not be released from their obligations because the book had been published in the United States.

The evidence of the federal Cabinet Secretary of Australia, Michael Codd, that publication of Wright's book could damage Australian intelligence interests, which had been dismissed by Justice Powell with contempt, was given serious attention, especially when the judges learned that Codd had discussed the issue with five senior Australian cabinet ministers before submitting his affidavit. The judges seemed to be impressed by the fact that the Australian government's position, as expressed by Mr. Codd, was firmly that former intelligence officers should not publish books without their employer's consent. As the *Sydney Morning Herald* put it, Wright could not win if the Court of Appeal accepted that his memoirs could damage Australian national security.[28]

Malcolm Turnbull decided to present the case for Wright and Heinemann after all, developing the theme that the secrets that Wright wished to reveal were no longer secret. He did not raise the point that the reason many of them were not secret was because Wright had originally leaked them to me and received royalties for doing so. His opponent might have argued that Wright's part in *Their Trade Is Treachery* was a longterm device to secure publication of *Spycatcher,* although I do not believe that Wright was that farsighted.

Daringly reporting the last day of the appeal (July 31) in detail, the *Guardian* stated that Turnbull had told the court that Wright's revelations would show that some of MI5's activities, even against friendly nations, had been criminal. He argued that Mrs. Thatcher's clearance of Hollis had been falsely based. The *Guardian's* report indicated that Turnbull might have had some success with his theory that I had been involved in an MI5 plot to secure the publication of "skeletons in MI5's cupboard" when Justice Kirby remarked that "Mr. Pincher was very much an insider-outsider."

The court reserved its judgment, meanwhile leaving the ban on publication of Wright's book in place until the judgment could be given.

In the interim, the legal steamroller moved inexorably on with an injunction against publication of *Spycatcher* extracts being obtained in Hong Kong.[29] In Britain, even the *Sunday Telegraph*, which had supported the government's action against Wright, found itself subjected to legal action by the Attorney General for criminal contempt relating to reports alleged to have repeated material from *Spycatcher*.

More litigation seemed inevitable as moves were made to publish the book in Ireland and the Netherlands. With book sales in North America exceeding 250,000, Wright seemed set to become a dollar millionaire, provided that the government failed in its determination to sequester his earnings.

The New South Wales Court of Appeal issued its judgments on September 24—after deliberations lasting almost eight weeks.[30] They illustrated the legal complexity of the case in Australian law because the three appeal judges concentrated on entirely different issues. The judgment of the President of the Court, Justice Michael Kirby, was based on his belief that no foreign country, such as the United Kingdom, can use the courts of another independent country to enforce its penal laws. He rejected the fact that the original case had been a civil action brought on the grounds of breach of confidentiality and claimed that it was really an attempt to apply what, in Britain, would have been the Official Secrets Act, had the case been tried there. This view owed nothing to the defense mounted by Turnbull.

Justice Michael McHugh took the view that the action had been contrary to Australia's national interest. He suggested that the original court should not have entertained the British claim of breach of confidence against Wright in the first place. He declined to accept the view of the Australian government that publication of Wright's book was detrimental to Australian interests.

The Chief Justice, Sir Laurence Street, disagreed with both of his colleagues. He accepted the evidence of Sir Robert Armstrong that publication would damage Britain's security and intelligence interests and rejected Turnbull's submission that he had set out to mislead the court. He also accepted the belief of the Australian government, presented by Michael Codd, that Australian interests could be injured. He judged that, for both reasons, the ban on the book in Australia should continue.

The government lost the appeal by a majority of two to one but, in view of the widely differing opinions, quickly decided to appeal again to the High Court in Canberra, its last resort. From the beginning of the case, the law officers had believed that their best chance of winning lay in Canberra.

The newspapers, especially those anxious to print Wright's material, criticized the government for what appeared to have become an obsession. To others, however, it seemed reasonable to make the final appeal, especially as Turnbull had made it plain that Wright would have done so if the verdict had gone against him.

In interviews, Wright claimed not to be bitter about the length of the court battles but his description of the government as "those bastards" and Mrs. Thatcher as "that bitch" suggested otherwise.[31] He admitted that he was making money by selling secrets but explained that this was because of his poor pension situation. Claiming that the British public misunderstood his purpose, he challenged the government to prove that he had been treacherous. The government's view was that it would have no difficulty in doing so if he would oblige by returning to British jurisdiction.

In Australia, however, the government received an unexpected legal jolt when a judge in the New South Wales court refused to extend the ban on the publication of *Spycatcher* until the appeal in Canberra was decided. The government had regarded the extension as a formality but the judge, Sir William Deane, ruled that it would be "unrealistic" because so much of the book was already common knowledge. Again, the government had not appreciated how Australian judges would react. Clearly shocked, it responded by attempting to appeal against the decision which it regarded as unfair. To do so it required the services of three New South Wales judges in a hurry. The law officers were not surprised when it proved impossible to find three judges with time to spare.

The jubilant publisher immediately announced that 50,000 copies of *Spycatcher* would be printed and put on sale within three weeks and, probably, before the government had time to appeal against Sir William Deane's decision. To establish the *fait accompli*, *The Australian* newspaper decided to serialize the book without delay.

Spycatcher was eventually published on October 13, 1987, and became an immediate best-seller with an unprecedented print run of 70,000. The case to prevent publication was totally lost, with Turnbull headlined as "The Aussie Who Took on the British Government—and Won" and seen by many in Britain as a worthy winner. As for Wright, his position as an Australian folk hero seemed established.

Stubbornly, the government decided to press ahead anyway, in the hope of proving its principle that Wright had broken his bond and to sequester his earnings and possibly those of his publisher. The Canberra High Court heard the appeal, and a verdict is expected in July of 1988, when the government hopes to secure a court order to seize all profits from the Australian sales. Sir William Deane offered some recompense by instructing Heinemann to keep a careful record of its profits.

It looked increasingly unlikely that the book would ever be published in Britain, at least in hardback. So many copies of the American edition were seeping into Britain that it seemed that the market would be saturated. This was bad news for Heinemann, which had looked on Britain as its main market because it derived little in the way of income from the American publishing house. The government had looked silly in failing to block imports of the book, which was a practical impossibility, but it was wreaking some revenge, even if inadvertently, on the publisher that had initiated the problem by approaching Wright.

In November 1987, Sir Robert Armstrong appeared as a witness in the High Court in London in the main case brought by the Attorney General to secure permanent injunctions against the *Observer* and *Guardian* newspapers. *The Spycatcher Affair* (published in Britain as *A Web of Deception*) was already on general sale, and when questioned about its contents under oath, Sir Robert confirmed the major disclosures that I had made in it.

Under cross-examination by counsel and by the judge, Justice Scott, Sir Robert confirmed that, before the publication of *Their Trade Is Treachery* in 1981, Sidgwick and Jackson had made contact with an intermediary (the person whom I have called the Arbiter) who, in turn, approached a government representative, who was "a member of the security or intelligence services." This representative's name was carefully withheld from the court but the evidence clearly indicated that it was Sir Arthur Franks. (For example, Sir Robert confirmed that the person he had been referring to had been invited to give evidence to the court, and that person was named as Franks in the newspapers, having been unsuccessfully subpoenaed.)

Sir Robert went on to say that the intermediary told his contact (Franks) that, in the event that a clear indication was given by the government that it objected to publication of the book, he was in a position to ensure that publication would not occur. He stated that the intermediary's conversations (with Franks) took place on the understanding that his identity would not be disclosed to anyone and that he (Sir Robert) had not been told it at the time. That understanding was arrived at solely between the two, nobody else being involved.

The possibility that the intermediary could have been asked to tell Sidgwick and Jackson that there were security objections to publications was, therefore, not known to Sir Robert at the time. Consequently, though it was not so stated in court, the Prime Minister could not have been told either, because Sir Robert was her conduit for such information. It is inconceivable that she might have been told of the circumstances by another person, such as Franks himself, and then have failed to tell Sir Robert. The fact that she took no action herself, when a telephone call to the Arbiter would have been sufficient to suppress the book, speaks for itself.

According to Sir Robert's evidence, the overture (to Franks) was not from Sidgwick and Jackson but was a personal approach by the intermediary, taken without the agreement or knowledge of me or the publisher. He confirmed that the authorities had not been able to state their security objections to Sidgwick and Jackson directly because that would have revealed that they had the text and would have prejudiced the source.

He agreed that the statement eventually made by the security and intelligence authorities to the intermediary (the Arbiter) was to the effect that "they were not asking him to take any action to prevent publication or suggest any modifications or deletions."

Sir Robert then testified that, when he was sent to Australia in 1985, he was still totally unaware of the offer that the intermediary had made to suppress the book if there were objections to it; all he knew was that the text had been acquired from a source under conditions of confidentiality. He had not known the identity of the source "which we were not prepared to compromise."

He said that the existence of the offer and the part played

by the intermediary (the Arbiter) were not known to him until
the Treasury Solicitor obtained an advance copy of the text of
The Spycatcher Affair in the autumn of 1987 and showed it to
him: "I knew before I gave evidence in Sydney that the source
had handed the text over to a certain person. What I did not
know until I saw the advance text of *The Spycatcher Affair* was
that the source, at the time of handing over the text [of *Their
Trade Is Treachery*], had indicated an offer . . . that publication
by Sidgwick and Jackson could be prevented. . . ." This igno-
minious situation for Sir Robert—and for the Prime Minister—was emphasized in Parliament in a speech by Dr. David
Owen, a former Foreign Secretary.

Sir Robert indicated that he had recently learned the
name of the source but did not feel at liberty to disclose it to
the court because the promise of confidentiality still stood. (I
have reason to believe that Sir Robert learned the source's
identity only when shown an early draft of the typescript of
The Spycatcher Affair, which contained the name of the Arbiter, later removed at the Arbiter's request.) Sir Robert also
said that he knew the identity of the person to whom the "offer" was made (i.e., Franks), but he did not reveal whether or
not he knew it in 1981.

In answer to questions, Sir Robert agreed that the court in
Australia had not been given "the full picture" of the circumstances surrounding the publication of *Their Trade Is Treachery.* "The court in Australia was not told about the offer to
prevent publication of the book because I did not know of it,"
he explained. He also agreed that, while he was giving evidence in Australia, nobody from the security and intelligence
services (including Franks) had contacted him, the Attorney
General's office, or anyone else to say that Sidgwick and Jackson had been told that there had been no objections to publication. He went on to say that he did not think that this
omission affected the judgment "at the end of the day."

Sir Robert was asked why nobody from the security and
intelligence services (including Franks) had taken direct action

with the intermediary and asked him to suppress *Their Trade Is Treachery* in their interests. He replied that he supposed that the reason was that it was believed that I would take the book to another publisher.

Armstrong said that the intermediary (the Arbiter) had stressed that, if Sidgwick and Jackson were not allowed to publish, I would be likely to go elsewhere and would have little difficulty in finding another publisher. This implied that, while government ministers or officials could have stopped publication by Sidgwick and Jackson, had they been aware of the special circumstances, action was likely to be frustrated "in the ultimate" because I would have secured another publisher. It may be that the Arbiter pointed out this possibility to Franks with some force, but—as the court was told—it did not really explain why advantage had not been taken at least to delay publication by silencing Sidgwick and Jackson. That, surely, would have been done had the Prime Minister or the Attorney General known about the situation. It would have given the authorities a breathing space of several months during which they could have discovered any new prospective publisher and dealt with it or with me without any further confidentiality complication. The stress placed by Sir Robert on the danger that I might secure a different publisher savors of an excuse to save the face of the security and intelligence authorities.

I expected that efforts would be made to induce me to give evidence and perhaps to require me to reveal the identity of the Arbiter, but I was left in peace. Presumably, lawyers for the newspapers considered that Sir Robert Armstrong had made the necessary admissions.

Justice Scott delivered his lengthy judgment on December 21, 1987. He found in favor of the newspapers and against the government, mainly on the grounds that *Spycatcher* had been so widely published that the government could not effectively argue that newspaper extracts from the book could damage British security any further. Moreover, all the more important allegations had already been made in

Their Trade Is Treachery, which the government could have suppressed but failed to do for reasons which, to the judge, were shallow and unconvincing.

Though Sir Robert convinced the judge that he had not been informed of the offer to stifle *Their Trade Is Treachery* made by the intermediary, Justice Scott seemed unable to appreciate that this automatically meant that nobody else could be informed. He repeatedly stated in his judgment that "the Government had it in its power to prevent publication of *Their Trade Is Treachery*," but the only person who had this power was Sir Arthur Franks who did not use it, and he could hardly be described as "the Government." If the judge had assimilated the text of *The Spycatcher Affair*, with which he was provided, he should have appreciated that its main thrust was to the effect that the government—meaning ministers and senior civil servants, such as Sir Robert—did *not* know of the intermediary's offer.

Regarding Peter Wright, the judge stated that in publishing his memoirs he was "in clear and flagrant breach of the duty of confidence he owed to the Crown." He conceded that the spectacle of Wright making money would be offensive and an affront to most decent people. Nevertheless, it was one of the bulwarks of a democratic society that newspapers should be allowed to report allegations of scandals in government, whether these were true or not. "If the price that has to be paid is the exposure of the government of the day to pressure of embarrassment when mischievous or false allegations are made then, in my opinion, that price must be paid."

The judge commented, "I found myself unable to escape the reflection that the absolute protection of the security service, that Sir Robert was contending for, could not be achieved this side of the Iron Curtain."

The government was ordered to pay the costs of the *Observer* and the *Guardian*. Nevertheless, it was the judge's view that permanent injunctions would be granted against Wright if he were sued in Britain, so Heinemann would still not be free to publish *Spycatcher* there. Further, Wright's breach of duty made him accountable for any profit—an indication to the government that they might sue him in the courts for all the money he has made.

The government immediately appealed against the verdict, and the injunctions against the newspapers were extended to January 18, 1988, when the appeal was due to be heard; the Prime Minister indicated that, if necessary, the government would take the issue to the House of Lords.

While I agreed with the judge's verdict, I remained of the opinion that the government had no alternative but to continue with the various legal processes once these had been set in motion. There was much at stake, and any court action is a lottery that either side can win.

Judgment on the appeal in the *Observer–Guardian* case was delivered on February 11, 1988, and again was generally in favor of the newspapers and against the government. A permanent injunction against publication of material from *Spycatcher* was denied on the commonsense grounds that it was now so widespread throughout the world that an injunction would be silly. The judges, once again headed by Sir John Donaldson, Master of the Rolls, agreed that Wright was in gross breach of his confidentiality to the Crown and that there was "very great public interest" in discouraging other officers from doing the same. The government interpreted the judgment as indicating that it would be justified in seeking to sequester the profits that Wright and his publishers had made from *Spycatcher*. It immediately lodged a final appeal with the House of Lords, the supreme British court of law.

Meanwhile American and Canadian sales of Wright's book were said to have soared to 750,000, making Wright a pound millionaire. The *Daily Telegraph* raised the question of Wright's pension, pointing out that there will be many people "who will consider it grotesque if the public purse continues to pay it."[32] The question of Wright's CBE, awarded to him in 1972, was also raised in Whitehall.[33] Though Anthony Blunt was never prosecuted, his honors were removed. While MI5 managers felt that Wright should be officially disgraced for his grave disservice, some mandarins were counseling against goading him into taking further revenge by publishing still more secrets. With the commercial success of *Spycatcher*, however, pressure on Wright and his ghostwriter Greengrass to produce *Spycatcher 2* seems inevitable.

‖ 23 ‖

Damage Assessment

| *A wounded reputation is seldom cured.* |
| —H. G. Bohn |

Whether the publication of the facts and allegations in *Spycatcher* did real damage to British security is a matter for argument among those who are professionally qualified to make a judgment. As I have learned from long experience, the obvious is often untrue in the intelligence world; and as an example, I would point to the release of information about the wartime triumph in decoding German radio messages, now well known by the name "Ultra." It seemed ludicrous to me that the security authorities should seek to suppress information about an operation that was almost thirty years old—until I learned the secret reason. The operation had centered on a code-producing machine called "Enigma," which the Germans had believed to be inviolable. Many third-world countries, some of which were hostile to Britain, were using that same machine, and British intelligence was regularly decoding their messages—until the first publicity, in 1974, put an end to that advantage.

Most British and American intelligence officers who have been consulted by me and by others are of the opinion that some of the technical details revealed in *Spycatcher* have damaged the Allied interest. There is particular concern about the extent to which Wright included details of trade craft and operational procedures in the field of radio surveillance.

The fact that Wright put his name to his claims has undoubtedly damaged the relationship between the British secret services and their allies because it has always been mutually accepted that professional officers of any of the services could be trusted to maintain their secrecy. Without confidence in that understanding, no interchange of secret information between allied agencies can be regarded as safe. There had been several instances in various services—British and foreign—in which officers had turned out to be spies, but Wright set a new example for agents who might eschew straightforward treachery but might, conveniently, convince themselves that they "owed it to society" to reveal secrets they had learned during their duties. Wright's action must, inevitably, have raised doubts about the extent to which the British secret services could be trusted to preserve secrets passed to them by allied services, the American ones in particular.

According to the British appeals judgment of July 25, 1987, Wright's allegations had also damaged the morale of the secret services, and my own information would support this. The events in Australia and the publication of *Spycatcher* brought the whole Hollis story back to prominence at a time when the government (and the Prime Minister, in particular) thought it had been buried. The paperback edition of *Their Trade Is Treachery*, which was five years old, was reprinted and sold in thousands. The book cover appeared night after night for weeks on television and, with the consequent newspaper publicity, made it possibly the most publicized nonfiction work of the century—until *Spycatcher* appeared.

While Wright tries to maintain his stance as a patriot, his reputation has been irreparably damaged by his activities from the time that he first contacted me in 1980. The retired secret service officers whom I and my friends have consulted are appalled that one of their number should have betrayed his trust—both in briefing me and in determining to publish *Spycatcher.* They include some of those who support Wright's contentions about Hollis and other moles. They consider that his behavior reflects on them all, has irreparably tarnished the image of MI5, and has set a disgraceful example to those still serving and especially to the younger members of the services. In the instructional lectures to new recruits to both MI5 and MI6, the results of his actions are already being presented as every bit as damaging as those inflicted by proved traitors, and some officers rank him among them.

Wright has been branded a traitor in Parliament and has been publicly accused of behaving feloniously and treacherously. Sir Edward Gardner QC told Parliament, "I can see no difference between a member of the Security Service who breaks his oath and sells his secrets to a publisher and a member of the Security Service who sells his secrets to the Russians."[1] The editor of the *Today* newspaper, David Montgomery, expressed the view of many other journalists when he said the real issue was that "a treacherous old man had taken a trip down memory lane to make money." Lord Annan has compared him with Philip Agee, the renegade CIA officer who left his native country to secure the freedom to blacken his old service.[2]

The Wright affair has certainly inflicted damage on the reputations of others. Sir Robert Armstrong, a most distinguished public servant, has been ridiculed and branded a liar. He wanted to become provost of Eton but, as one of the Eton masters remarked to me, his half-jocular remark about being "economical with the truth" could have ruled him out because pupils would recall it.

Sir Michael Havers was branded as the most dishonorable Attorney General of this century, a totally unfounded assertion that was widely publicized. It hurt him deeply and might have

cost him the promotion to Lord Chancellor to which he as-
pired. Fortunately the Prime Minister demonstrated her loyalty to Havers and her contempt for his critics by appointing
him to the post immediately after her general election victory
in 1987.

Malcolm Turnbull did his best to besmirch the integrity
of Mrs. Thatcher, although the effect was like that of a gadfly
trying to kick an elephant. But the evidence, as revealed by Sir
Robert, did not help the Prime Minister, for it showed that she
had been overborne by lesser officials who seemed to be pursuing sectarian interests.

Lord Rothschild's reputation was certainly damaged by
Wright's false assertions and the use made of them by Turnbull
in the Australian court. So was mine, although I have always
maintained that those of us who dish it out must be prepared
to take it. Had we been successfully prosecuted, as some virulent Labor backbenchers demanded, we might have been
gravely damaged.

The most immediate damage was not to me but to investigative journalism as a whole. When the names of various
people who had allegedly given secret information to writers
were raised by Turnbull, it meant that no such sources were
likely to be available again for many months, if ever. All have
been warned individually by letter of the dangers of speaking
about officially secret affairs and, whether the government
ever really intended to make an example of anyone or not,
there was always the risk that it might feel compelled to do so.

My conversations with the Treasury Solicitor over the
present book, *The Spycatcher Affair*, prior to its publication
revealed an astonishing legal situation of which many journalists may still be unaware. The various hearings in the British courts consequent to the *Spycatcher* affair have made it
very clear that the government is determined to prevent any
other secret service officers from committing breaches of
confidentiality by publishing information they have learned
during the course of their careers. Anyone who attempts to do

so or succeeds in doing so is in danger of being pursued in the civil courts for breach of his contractual undertaking. What surprised me was the Treasury Solicitor's insistence that any writer who publishes information obtained from such a source can also be held to be in breach of confidentiality, even though he may never have been in government employment, and can also be pursued through the civil courts. My publisher's lawyer confirmed that, as of the autumn of 1987, this was the legal situation; as a result, various attributions had to be removed from the text of this book.

During an interview with David Frost on TV-am on March 29, 1987, Turnbull made two statements that were extremely damaging to me, in view of the fact that police inquiries into such matters were then still in train. First, Turnbull said that I had received a check for the advance on *Their Trade Is Treachery* and had sent half of it on to Wright. As the police had established, this was quite untrue. No such check ever came to me or to my company. All monies to Wright were paid directly by Sidgwick and Jackson, notwithstanding that Turnbull had done his best to convince the Sydney court that I had forwarded the payments to Wright, in support of his false claim that Wright had been "corrupted."[3] In the context of the police inquiries into possible bribery, this was extremely damaging, and I wrote to Scotland Yard about it right away.[4] I also ensured that the information reached the law officers.[5] Turnbull went on to allege that I was holding much more money for Wright and had failed to pass it on, which again was untrue. As a result, I issued a writ for libel, it being served just before Turnbull returned to Australia. The case is proceeding as of this writing.

Respect for the law was undoubtedly damaged as a result of the newspapers' reaction to various court rulings that did not suit them, and this is always serious for a true democracy. Some of the judges suffered, too, and while the hostility was directed mainly at those who had supported the Attorney General, the most self-damaging remark was made by Lord Bridge, who suggested that the temporary injunction was a step down the road to a totalitarian state. Such a gross exaggeration does not engender confidence in a man in such a powerful judicial position.

The anger and resentment of the media was probably more damaging still to the government. Recent history both in Britain and America shows that alienation of the media—and the newspapers, in particular—can have serious consequences for a political party and especially for its leader. The only comparable British event of recent times was the D-Notice affair of 1967, which centered on my disclosure that the British security authorities were in the habit of examining private cables. The national press closed ranks when Harold Wilson refused to accept the ruling of an independent tribunal that absolved me and my editor from any security breach and instead passed his personal censure on a newspaper and its journalists. Wilson never retrieved his former good relationship with the press, and he later described his action as his worst self-inflicted wound. Mrs. Thatcher still had nearly five years to run in office after *Spycatcher* emerged, but newspaper editors have long memories that could be activated in the event of some future problem, as President Nixon discovered when involved in the Watergate affair.

In my opinion, the actual damage to press freedom inflicted by the Wright affair was slight and temporary. The injunction imposed by the law lords was only an interim ruling, and the Attorney General kept the prosecutions of newspapers to a minimum, conditioned upon the circumstances created by their action. No law officer and no government wants to prosecute a newspaper if it can avoid doing so, but they are sometimes placed in positions where they have no option but to proceed, if they are to maintain credibility.

In the eyes of many people, to judge from letters to newspapers and comments by friends, the media suffered damage from their own behavior. When writers are prevented from publishing, we all tend to scream like stuck pigs, but the reaction to the government's determined efforts against Wright's book was so excessive that, to many detached observers, the media seemed hypocritical humbugs. Frustrated in their efforts to improve their circulations, they were seen as trying to prove that an injunction imposed by the highest courts can be rendered void simply by defying it.

Cries of censorship were so exaggerated—one *Sunday Times* cartoon showed Mrs. Thatcher burning a book entitled *Freedom of Speech*—that some newspapers could legitimately have been accused of pursuing a deception exercise against their readers.

‖24‖

Lessons to Be Learned

> *Nothing is secret, that shall not be made manifest.*
> —New Testament: Luke, viii, 17

There are many lessons to be learned from what may probably be referred to in legal and Parliamentary history as "The Wright Affair." Surely the most important is that unnecessary secrecy is not only nonsensical but potentially highly dangerous to all involved in it. The experience of Sir Robert Armstrong, in particular, should be noted by all civil servants when they blithely involve themselves in secrecy without ensuring that it is absolutely essential: it can have a backlash effect. It should also be apparent—even to those blinkered by the cult of secrecy—that, in free societies with media that are determined to preserve their freedom, the truth will always emerge eventually, and the timing may not be of the choosing of those who have attempted to conceal it. Those who have been no more than "economical with the truth"—a practice that has been standard in Whitehall and Westminster for decades—may find themselves branded as devious or worse.

The circumstances of the Wright affair offer some of the best evidence to date of the need for some degree of external supervision of the secret services—what has become known as oversight. Oversight, such as exists in the United States, would seem to be perhaps the only safeguard against unnecessary secrecy. It could be a built-in deterrent to the preparation of misleading briefs for ministers, such as the one foisted on the Prime Minister when she made her statement on the Hollis case in March 1981, which will come back to embarrass her if Wright's original version of *Spycatcher* is ever published. As was stated in the Sydney court, that book contains many pages that effectively contradict Mrs. Thatcher's statement, which was prepared by MI5, but they are omitted in the American edition.

Perhaps more importantly, the existence of oversight would gradually curb the influence that MI5 and MI6 can exert over government because of the mystique attaching to them. It was fatuous that the legal adviser to MI5, a person of no great seniority or ability, should have been able to override the judgment of the Prime Minister and other eminent politicians and public servants as described in chapter 5. The secret services are servants of the state, and they should not be permitted to make an excuse of secrecy to avoid explaining their actions or inactions. As James Callaghan stated in the debate on the Blunt case, "Secrecy allows incompetence and corruption to thrive," treachery being the form of corruption he had in mind.

Oversight would regenerate American trust in British security, which has been undermined by the Wright affair. Senators and congressmen who have been involved with the oversight of the U.S. secret services are convinced that it has substantially improved the services' effectiveness and would do the same for the British counterparts.

If Wright's disclosures and the more serious allegations attributed to him really indicate that there have been any excesses of behavior on the part of the secret services, that would be further evidence of the requirement for independent oversight. There is a pressing need to restore public confidence and trust in both MI5 and MI6. The statement made by Merlyn Rees that MI5 should be brought "within the ambit of the law" is compelling evidence that it is currently outside the law.[1] Mr. Rees is a former Home Secretary of admirable integrity who took a special interest in MI5, for which he had high regard. In view of the furor over the recent allegations, however, no chief of MI5 or MI6 is likely to risk his job and reputation by allowing his officers to act like buccaneers, whatever may or may not have happened in the past. Nor are prime ministers ever likely to distance themselves from the operations of the secret services, as they did in relatively recent years; political control is now certainly tighter than it has ever been.

How oversight should be accomplished is a matter for Parliament to decide, but it would seem certain that the Wright affair will be used as a lever by the growing body of MPs intent on securing it.

The government should certainly consider the possible virtue of introducing the American system of having a publications review board to which former officers can submit their writings. This already operates here to some extent in that officers can and do submit prospective articles and books to their former offices or to the Treasury Solicitor, but those authorities tend to be severe, always erring on the side of extreme caution. It is unlikely, however, that Wright's book could ever have qualified for publication, being far too revealing of operational matters, as Wright well knew when his lawyer submitted the draft to the Attorney General.

While he was Attorney General, Lord Havers repeatedly stated to me that the difference between Wright and me was that I had not signed the Official Secrets Act, implying that he was not prepared to prosecute investigative "historians," as he called me, unless it became unavoidable. The implication was that the onus is on those who have signed the Official Secrets

Act to keep their mouths shut. The airing that the Wright case has given to such books will, I hope, establish that investigative writers have the legal right to *acquire* official secrets, although technically it is an offense simply to be in possession of them. The government must either accept this or decree that investigations into the secrets world by "outsiders" are totally banned—an impossible proposition, since it would also rule out inquiries into whole areas of defense and foreign affairs. If writers are to be punished simply for acquiring such information, as some Labour backbenchers suggested, to their everlasting shame, then unnecessary secrecy and the cover-up of security scandals and administrative embarrassments will continue. The legal right to acquire information could be established by modifications of the Official Secrets Act, which have been repeatedly promised and always shelved.

I endured a tough seven months when the police inquiries were under way, but they will have been worth it if my account of the experience and the events leading up to it helps to give the *coup de grâce* to Section 2 of the Official Secrets Act. Successive governments have agreed that Section 2 is urgently in need of replacement, but none has taken any effective action, largely due to objections from the secret services and Whitehall mandarins.

In 1987—fifteen years after the completion of the Franks inquiry into the Official Secrets Act—the Home Secretary, Douglas Hurd, indicated that the government intends to reform Section 2. This seems more likely to tighten restrictions on the publication of information about the secret services than to relax them.

The Wright case is unlikely to have much influence on the campaign for a freedom-of-information act. Even in countries that possess one, such as the United States and Australia, really secret matters remain excluded. There is little point in securing documents in which all the really interesting material is blacked out.

The issue of *publishing* an investigative writer's findings is different, and any responsible person must accept that some matters should not be published and may attract a penalty. Nobody of goodwill is suggesting a publishing free-for-all in the world of secrets but following the Parliamentary reaction to the Wright affair, the Treasury Solicitor apparently feels duty-bound to intrude whenever a book involving the secret services is being prepared. An announcement about my last book, *Traitors: The Anatomy of Treason*, was made in the trade press in February 1987; yet two months later the Treasury Solicitor wrote to my publisher, requesting a copy of the proofs of the book before any part of it was serialized or otherwise published. The letter arrived when the managing director and the rest of the staff had left for the Easter holiday, and he could not reply to it until he returned on April 22. By that time serialization of the book had begun in the *Mail on Sunday*. Shortly afterward, the Prime Minister confirmed to Parliament the major disclosure in the book—that Sir Maurice Oldfield, the former chief of MI6, had been a practicing homosexual and had lied to conceal the fact.

A bound copy of the book was then provided, and the Treasury Solicitor went through it looking for security breaches. The only one he found was in a source note. I had recorded that Oldfield had been suspicious of a certain MI6 officer, and the footnote gave the source of this, correctly, as Anthony Cavendish, who had worked for MI6 long ago and had been a friend of Oldfield's. Cavendish was immediately contacted and denied giving me the information. As a result Armstrong received a letter dated April 28, stating that, because Cavendish had made his denial, the Crown did not intend to institute proceedings against us! When the Treasury Solicitor was made aware of the imminent publication of *The Spycatcher Affair*, he immediately requested a copy of that, too, and eventually required the removal of certain paragraphs under threat of advising the Attorney General to injoin publication of the book. The authorities would deny that such action constitutes censorship, but its effects are the same.

Clearly the repercussions of the Wright affair have made life more difficult, and perhaps more dangerous, for writers, since, contrary to what might have been expected, it has probably increased restrictions on the reporting of secret matters. This may not necessarily be beneficial for security. We "outsiders" can generate some improvements, as *Their Trade Is Treachery* demonstrated. The inquiry by the Security Commission, set up entirely because of that book, produced many important changes in security practice. This book, *The Spycatcher Affair*, told the Cabinet Secretary and the Prime Minister so much about the *Spycatcher* affair that had been withheld from them by the secret services that they were able to take steps to decrease the possibility of such an embarrassing eventuality in future.

The government's decision to appoint an ombudsman, to whom secret service officers with grave misgivings about the nature of their work or the behavior of their colleagues could complain, derives from a letter which I wrote to *The Times* suggesting such a step and resulting in Parliamentary pressure.[2] The improvements made to the organization and practices of MI5 by Sir Anthony Duff following the public uproar over the Bettaney case owed something to the long campaign waged by writers and the media.[3]

I have always appreciated that investigative writing is a dangerous profession. My experience in the Wright affair shows that prosecution for reporting the truth is a possibility six years after the event and that, in this apparently free society, a writer's home can be searched and his private correspondence taken away at the whim of the Attorney General. When this was done to me, there were no doubts in anybody's mind that my general motives were patriotic, in that I had always sought to secure improvements to the efficiency of the secret services by exposing their weaknesses. Nevertheless I received the kind of treatment that is meted out to suspected criminals.

The unfortunate disclosures during the Wright trial, and following it, must have raised doubts in the minds of politi-

cians, civil servants, and former secret service employees of
the wisdom of associating with investigative writers. Wright's
unforgivable behavior in making my confidential letters to him
available to the media was damaging to Sir Michael Havers
and to Sir Arthur Franks. Sadly, the embarrassment did not
end there. Not long after the letters had been aired in Parliament, I was interviewing the former spy, John Vassall, in the
grill room of the Café Royal in London. Purely by a fluke,
Havers was lunching at the far end of the room with two
friends of mine. The *Evening Standard* eventually discovered
the facts and printed a gossip item entitled "Spy in My Soup"
calculated to embarrass Havers and, quite monstrously, revealing Vassall's new name and details of his employment. [4]

Conversely, investigative writers would be wise to appreciate that association with secret service officers can have its
dangers, with prosecution always a possibility. Nor is the information provided by such people always to be believed. Sir
Maurice Oldfield's acceptance of the MI5 plot against
Wilson—if his belief in it was genuine—showed a degree
of gullibility of which I did not think he was capable. The
Sydney trial showed that even the most prestigious sources
may have unreliable memories and that they may also be
misinformed.

While some aggrieved newspapers howled for changes in
the law concerning the impact of contempt of court on freedom to publish, nothing is likely to happen in that regard.
Such impact is rare, and respect for the courts of law should
rank higher as a feature of a civilized community than avoid-
ance of occasional intrusions into press freedom, provided that
the intrusions are not imposed by government. I am in no
doubt that the Attorney General and the judges were acting
quite independently of government ministers when they were
involved in actions against the media. Most newspapers that
suffered as a result of legal action did so through their own
folly. They put their heads on blocks and challenged the law to

sever them. The art of fighting intrusions into press freedom is to do it without being sacrificial.

Arguments will continue about the government's wisdom in bringing the action against Wright in Australia when it was already conceded by the law officers that the book could be published in the United States without hindrance. My own view, as a citizen and taxpayer, is that the government had no alternative and that it would have happened even if Labour had been in office at the relevant time. The principle of confidentiality could hardly be more important—not just in regard to secret service officers but to all former servants of the Crown who have had access to secret matters. A former Cabinet Secretary, for example, or a senior Foreign Office official could reveal information that might inflict enormous damage on international relations.

Using hindsight, others argue that perhaps all that was needed was a Parliamentary statement that Wright was committing a serious offense and would be prosecuted if he ever set foot in Britain and that injunctions would be taken out to prevent the sale of his book in Britain—its main market. Such a statement could have pointed out that similar treatment would be meted out to others who behaved likewise. The claim that failing to prosecute Wright in the Australian court would open the floodgates was arguable, since most retired secret service officers live in Britain and remain covered by the Official Secrets Act. Those who live in places with no Crown relationships, such as in the United States and France, can do what they like anyway. This argument was vitiated to some extent, however, by Wright's apparent financial success. If he or his family manages to hold onto a large fortune, then other, more recently retired, officers with sensational stories they could tell might be tempted to emigrate to a foreign country for that purpose.

In any future instance where the British authorities need to operate in a foreign court, they would do well to study the local environment, which they singularly failed to do in the Wright case. Two of the appeal judges in Sydney ruled that the case was not really permissible in an Australian court, though that view could be challenged.

There was clearly legal doubt about whether Wright owed a contractual obligation to MI5 once he had left it, because of lack of binding documentation, though his moral obligation was glaringly obvious. There may, therefore, be some need to reword and clarify existing and future contracts, if this has not already been effected. The inclusion of a copyright clause in the contracts of recruits to the secret services, stating that all information that they receive during their service remains the property of the Crown, might strengthen the government's legal position. It might also be made retrospective for those officers and former officers prepared to sign it. In *Spycatcher,* the copyright is claimed in Wright's name. During its various appeals in the British High Court, the government was at some pains to stress that it was not pursuing its case under the copyright laws, so perhaps they are fraught with too much difficulty. It might be impossible to prove copyright concerning information as opposed to written statements.

In return, the managements of the secret services should reconsider their practice of maintaining silence when their old servants are being savaged, as Lord Rothschild was by Wright, Parliament, and the media. To continue with the principle that making any statement would provide proof of the existence of the secret services is ludicrous when they have been subjected to such publicity. Leaving their former officers to the wolves simply to maintain the fog of secrecy is cowardice.

The case presented by Wright and Turnbull could have been greatly weakened if an authoritative MI5 officer had been permitted to give evidence disproving the suggestion that *Their Trade Is Treachery* was the result of a conspiracy involving MI5.

While some people saw Wright as a courageous lone crusader taking on the British establishment, his actions surely indicate that he was not a fit person to have been entrusted with secrets for, however he may try to explain his motives, he imparted secrets for financial gain. This happened with *Their Trade Is Treachery* and, even more so, with *Spycatcher*, which has been a straightforward commercial venture. There may have been an error of judgment when he was first recruited to MI5, but after a sojourn in Tasmania he decided to break his bond of confidentiality and was in grave breach of it when he gave secret information to me. The deep resentment he felt toward MI5 and the British government because of his poor pension position was a potent factor, and it seems stupid to allow any former officer with such a load of salable secrets to go into retirement abroad on an inadequate pension. This was especially so in Wright's case because the danger was pointed out to the authorities at an early stage by Lord Rothschild. Pensions, of course, are linked to pay, and the pay scales of those who carry such a load of responsibility may need review.

A further sensible safeguard would be legislation to terminate the pension rights of anyone who misbehaves in such a manner. Under the existing rules, an officer's pension can be ended only if he is prosecuted and convicted, which means that the pension of somebody like Wright who is outside the jurisdiction of the British courts cannot be touched, whatever he does short of physical defection.

Parliament's own part in the Wright affair should give it cause for reflection. The manner in which a matter of serious security principle was exploited for party political gain was unattractive, to say the least. While doing everything they could to promote Wright's cause, believing that his victory would embarrass the government, Labour backbenchers who usually champion press freedom were calling for the criminal prosecution of other writers and their sources, without demur from their leaders. Many of those sent to Westminster to help make good laws displayed more interest in electoral gain than in upholding justice.

Should I have any personal regrets about my association

with the Wright affair? If I were to have any, I would have to regret the whole of my journalistic career, which has been directed toward similar efforts. In spite of some apprehensive moments, I would not have missed it. *Their Trade Is Treachery* was the investigative scoop of the century; there has been nothing like it before or since. It placed much old history on public record and led, directly or indirectly, to many improvements in the security of the secret services. It has now enabled me to demonstrate the perils of the fetish of secrecy.

Bureaucratic secrecy is more than a sacred cow. It is a golden calf worshiped for its own sake in temples called MI5, MI6, GCHQ, the Foreign Office, and the Cabinet Office.

‖ Appendices ‖

Appendices

Appendix A

Letter to the Prime Minister from Jonathan Aitken, MP, reproduced with his permission after it had been made available to the Sydney court.

HOUSE OF COMMONS
LONDON SW1A OAA

Ref: JWPA/ay

31st January 1980
STRICTLY PRIVATE AND CONFIDENTIAL

The Rt. Hon. Margaret Thatcher, MP
Prime Minister
10 Downing Street
London SW1

Dear Prime Minister,

I am writing to you in your capacity as Head of the Security Services to alert you to certain developments and possible new disclosures arising out of the Blunt affair.

As you are aware, a great deal of information on this subject is still circulating among journalists on both sides of the Atlantic. Some of it has already been published, but the most dramatic disclosures of all may yet be forthcoming. My purpose in writing to you is first to forewarn you about some of the facts and allegations which could see the light of day. Secondly, to suggest that you should brief yourself fully on all aspects of this material in order to be able to make an immediate and appropriate response should the need for public comment arise. Thirdly, to suggest certain actions which you may like to consider taking either in advance of, or as a result of, the possible publication of the information concerned.

Perhaps I should first attempt to summarise from American and British sources the broad headings which the new material covers. This states or alleges:

a) That our Security Services were penetrated by Soviet agents at a far more senior level than that at which Philby, Burgess, Maclean, and Blunt were operating.

b) That the principal Soviet agents were Sir Roger Hollis, the Director General of MI5 from 1955–1964, and his immediate deputy, Mr. Graham Mitchell.

c) That the damaging activities of Hollis that have so far been alleged included:

   (i) warning Philby in 1963 of his imminent arrest.

   (ii) thwarting the investigation of Graham Mitchell in 1963 (code named Peters) by refusing to approach Ministers in order to get authorisation for telephone tapping; refusing to let MI5 officers brief their opposite members in the CIA and FBI for cooperation on the case; and above all refusing to allow Mitchell to be interrogated despite overwhelming evidence that this was necessary and justified.

   (iii) thwarting the interrogation of Blunt soon after his

immunity had been granted in April 1964 by halting all interrogation of him for a vital two week period.

(iv) suspending and later effectively dismissing the head of MI5's Russian counter-espionage section in order to obstruct his work on both the Blunt and Mitchell investigations.

(v) destroying some significant raw material of the Mitchell investigation in 1964.

d) That as a result of great anxieties within the Security Services, and following a later review of the Hollis–Mitchell cases, Lord Hunt, the then Secretary of the Cabinet, in approximately 1975 asked his predecessor Lord Trend to write a report on the penetration of the Security Services. It is alleged that Lord Trend's report concluded that high level Soviet penetration had taken place and that Hollis was probably the Soviet agent responsible.

e) That Hollis and Mitchell between them recruited other unidentified Soviet Agents into the Security Services. It follows from this that our Security Services may still be severely penetrated today.

I hope it is right to assume that both you and the Home Secretary have already been fully briefed on the history of most of the items outlined in paragraphs a) to e) above. If that is the case, and if you have read both the Trend report and the important accompanying memoranda on which the report is based, then my letter to you will be largely superfluous, although I hope you will at least find it helpful to receive prior warning of possible press disclosures, principally from American sources.

However, since it emerged from the Blunt affair that Prime Ministers have not always been given the fullest possible picture of the workings of the Security Services, I hope you will

not think it presumptuous of me if I set out some further information which may be of assistance if you and the Home Secretary are not completely au fait with some of these matters.
Perhaps the most coherent way of doing this is to trace certain
threads of this story back from the situation that exists today.

Once you took the decision to confirm in your answer to Ted
Leadbitter's Parliamentary Question of 15th November 1979
that Blunt had indeed been a Soviet agent, there was frantic
activity by the media to follow up the story. During the week
immediately after the publication in Hansard of your written
answer, Blunt's close friend, the Kensington art dealer, Mr.
Brian Sewell, gave extensive interviews to the press. In the
course of these interviews Mr. Sewell gave away some vital
clues which indicated that Blunt was only the tip of a far more
sinister iceberg. Asked if there was a "Fifth Man" in the story,
Mr. Sewell confirmed that there was and that he and Blunt
had known him well. Mr. Sewell continued: "The man died
full of honours. I don't want to ruin yet another reputation but
if the Fifth Man is the Fifth Man then he is the First Man and
you have to start renumbering everybody" (see *Daily Telegraph*
19th November and various U.S. newspapers passim).

This disclosure was enough to launch one or two expert journalists, who have been following the British Secret Service
story for years, into a new series of investigations. It was obvious to them that Blunt could not conceivably have been allowed by his Soviet controllers to retire from espionage in
1945 unless there were other Soviet agents inside MI5. Moreover, information gleaned from certain Russian defectors, notably the CIA's Anatol Golystin in 1962, also confirmed the
existence of a high Soviet source within MI5. Who was he?
During the last three months, journalists have been chasing
the trail of the late Guy Liddell, a former deputy director of
MI5. However, it is now evident that Liddell was not a traitor,
for the suggestion that he was has enraged former British and
American intelligence experts into setting the record straight

publicly (see the interviews from Sir Dick White and William Skardon in *The Sunday Times* of 18th January), and has triggered off a new round of disclosures.

Now it has become clear that Liddell was not the Fifth or First Man, the thrust of press investigations may concentrate on other senior MI5 figures and reach the true story. You should, I suggest, ask to be fully briefed on the extraordinary saga of how Hollis and Mitchell came to be suspected, and of how Hollis first blocked the interrogation of Mitchell and then suspended and later dismissed from MI5 the head of the counter-penetration department, who had mounted the secret investigation of Hollis and Mitchell.

It is a story which has deeply concerned high ranking officers of the CIA, MI5 and MI6 for many years, and it is their concern which eventually led to the Trend report. I understand that Lord Trend's conclusions suggested that, although unprovable in a court of law in the absence of a confession, Hollis and Mitchell probably were Soviet agents. However, it also seemed likely that Soviet penetration of the Security Services had now ended, according to the report.

This sanguine view of the situation would be unlikely to satisfy American or British public opinion if the Hollis story were to become known. Already demands are building up for "an authoritative and comprehensive statement" on events within MI5 (see Robert Cecil's letter in *The Times* of 29th January) and these demands would surely explode into a major controversy if further disclosures occurred. My respectful suggestion is that you should at least prepare to forestall the expected explosion, and I would like to put forward the following ideas on how you might do this most effectively.

1) The paramount need is to set up a major independent inquiry into all these allegations, headed by a High Court Judge or Service Chief sitting in secret, supported by his

own independent staff drawn from outside the ranks of the Security Services.

2) As a first step for this inquiry, Graham Mitchell, who unlike Hollis, is still alive and living in retirement, must be interrogated in depth and if necessary offered immunity in return for his cooperation.

3) With or without Mitchell's cooperation all members of the Security Services recruited in the time of Hollis and Mitchell should be re-vetted on a much stricter basis.

4) All files relating to the alleged treachery of Hollis and Mitchell should be reopened and comprehensively reviewed, and the officers and former officers engaged on that investigation should be asked to cooperate with that review as part of the independent inquiry.

5) As certain judgements and disclosures made in your own speech to the House of Commons on 21st November 1979 may well be seen in a more critical light in the event of the Hollis story becoming known, I think it might be wise to prepare a House of Commons statement of great frankness to defuse all such potential criticisms. If you did not know of the Hollis story when you took the decision to go public on Blunt, then I believe you should say so even though this would inevitably amount to a serious indictment of the Security Services.

6) Any such statement should include the announcement of a major reform of the Security Services. The objective of such a reform would be once and for all to close the chapter on past treacheries and penetrations and to restore confidence in the Security Services. One option to be considered would be the uniting of MI5 and MI6 into a single Security Service with a new outside Director General drawn from the Armed Forces.

In making these suggestions it may be that I am taking too dramatic and pessimistic a view of the impact that the revelation of the Hollis story could have on public opinion. But even if my pessimism is only half well founded, then I am sure that the drama would still be a big one. Nevertheless if any such drama does occur it is imperative that it does not adversely affect you or the Government. There is no reason why this need be so. Indeed, a major reform of the security services could be seen both as the right policy for Britain and as a firm and well handled decision by the Government. I hope you will feel that this letter is helpful to you in deciding what is the best course of action to take.

With all good wishes.

Yours sincerely

Jonathan Aitken

Appendix B

Summary of secret British documents presented to the Sydney court, December 10, 1986.

▌▏ Their Trade Is Treachery ▏▌

The Security Intelligence Agencies received the synopsis on or a little before 14 December 1980.

The letter (MI6(D) to MI5) dated 15 December 1980 from a security organisation to the Security Service indicates that the writer had been informed that Chapman Pincher intended to publish, probably in February or March 1981, a book about the Security Service, a synopsis of which was enclosed.

It was generally agreed in the security and intelligence services that there would be no point in trying to encourage specific deletions or changes in the text, but no reasons are expressed for this view.

The security and intelligence services first became aware of the book on or a little before 15 December 1980. The manuscript was first read in February 1981 when it appeared that much of the information in it had come from former members of the security and intelligence services. By 12

March 1981 several sources had been identified, but it was stated in writing by an officer of the service to Sir Robert Armstrong that the service was a long way from obtaining hard usable evidence on sources and it was stated orally to Sir Robert Armstrong that the advance copy was obtained on conditions which made it impossible to take any action about it, which view was later recorded.

Sir Robert Armstrong and the Home Office learned of the fact that information contained in the book would have come from former members of the security and intelligence services on or about 12 February 1981. The documents do not show when the Prime Minister or the Home Secretary learned of these matters.

∎| Too Secret Too Long |∎

So far as the documents disclose, the Security Service first knew on 19 July 1984 of the report in *The Times* as to the forthcoming book. On 3 September 1984 the Security Service was informed that Chapman Pincher was claiming that he had received material from former MI5 officers. On 26 October 1984 the Security Service had a copy of the book. The documents do not state reasons for not seeking an injunction but state the view that the central argument is much the same as in *Their Trade Is Treachery* about whether Hollis was a spy, filled out with additional detailed comment.

Sir Robert Armstrong reported to the Home Office and, approached by a member of Parliament, was told that Chapman Pincher's next book was likely to be an anthology of espionage cases since the Second World War.

∎| Cathy Massiter Programme |∎

The documents do not state when the Government first learned of the Massiter programme or that it contained an interview with the former MI5 officer.

∎| Peter Wright TV Interview |∎

The Security Service had information by 4 May 1984 that there were plans for a *World in Action* programme in which Wright was assisting and might take part. The Security Service had information by 3 July 1984 that Granada TV intended to show an interview with Wright in which Wright would reopen the Hollis case and, in effect, present the case against him and so advised the Treasury Solicitor in a letter of that date. Following a report in *The Times*, on 16 July 1984, the day of the broadcast, the likelihood that Wright had breached the Official Secrets Act was noted and it was presumed that he had taken the precaution of remaining outside the United Kingdom jurisdiction.

Following the article in *The Times* the possibility of asking for a preview of the programme and seeking to restrain publication, if necessary by means of an injunction, was discussed on the telephone between the Treasury Solicitor's department and the Security Service. The view was expressed that, if a preview was refused, going for an injunction would undoubtedly be a hard fight and if a preview was agreed the Government could be put in the position of appearing to have approved it whether or not it asked for cuts.

After that discussion the view of the Security Service conveyed to the Treasury Solicitor's department was that the interests of the Security Service would be best served by not taking action at that stage (16 July 1984) although the question of taking legal action would need to be reconsidered if Wright returned to the United Kingdom jurisdiction.

This communication appears to have been made late in the day and the documents do not show that any further consideration was given to the possibility of restraining the broadcast of the programme.

Appendix C

Copy of a letter from Sir Robert Armstrong to William Armstrong. This letter was made available to the Sydney court.

CABINET OFFICE

70 Whitehall, London SW1A 2AS   Telephone
01-233 8319

From the Secretary of the Cabinet, Sir Robert Armstrong
KCB, CVO

Ref. A04524

23rd March 1981

Dear Mr. Armstrong,

    I have seen the extracts in the *Daily Mail* today from Mr. Chapman Pincher's forthcoming book "Their Trade is Treachery". The Prime Minister is in my judgement likely to come under pressure to make some statement on the matters with which Mr. Pincher is dealing. I believe you will agree with me that, if she is to make a statement, it is in the public interest that she should be in a position to do so with the least possible delay. Clearly she cannot do so until she has seen not just the extracts published in the *Daily Mail* but the book itself. I should like to be able to put her in a position where she could make a statement this Thursday (26th March), if she should wish to do so.

I should therefore be very grateful if you would be willing to make one or (preferably) two copies of the book available to me as soon as possible today or tomorrow.

I can understand your need and wish to protect the confidentiality of the book until publication date, which is (I understand) 26th March. I can assure you that, if you are able to comply with my request, that confidentiality will be strictly observed, that the copies will not go outside this office and the Prime Minister's office, and that until the book has been published there will be no disclosure to the Press or the broadcasting authorities of any part of the contents of the book.

I can also assure you that the only purpose of this request is to equip the Prime Minister to make a statement, if she should need or be minded to do so, with the least possible delay. The request is not made with a view to seeking to prevent or delay publication, and I can assure you that we shall not do so.

Yours sincerely

Robert Armstrong

William Armstrong, Esq.

I Notes and Sources I

I Chapter 1: A Momentous Message II

1   Affidavit sworn by Wright on November 8, 1986, in Sydney, New South Wales, Australia.
2   Lord Rothschild told me, on several occasions, that he had abstracted this chapter and he still has it.
3   Letter dated June 12, 1980.
4   Wright's affidavit.
5   The source was Jonathan Aitken, Member of Parliament.
6   As confirmed to me in a telephone conversation with Wright's attorney, David Hooper.
7   As stated to the House of Lords by Baroness Young.
8   For example, a letter from me to Wright dated March 4, 1983, stated: "I have never had anything to do with the payments, save for expediting." (N.B. In a letter to Turnbull's London attorneys dated May 12, 1987, Rothschild denied knowledge of any agreement between myself and Wright entered into in his house.)
9   Lord Rothschild stated, in July 1980: "Leaving aside a

small number of people who have got the subject in the brain, to the extent of paranoia . . . I wonder whether the anxiety and mistrust caused by those with their own motives for discrediting people and institutions are not being successful if experts such as yourself take up the cudgels. I am inclined to think one should let the dogs lie without comment."

10 In Wright's affidavit.

11 Wright's affidavit and Sydney trial transcript.

12 Wright's affidavit.

13 The book was called *Their Trade Is Treachery.*

14 John Sawatsky, in *For Services Rendered*, Doubleday, New York, 1982.

15 *Daily Express* article of November 26, 1986.

16 *Spectator,* June 14, 1980.

17 Statement in Wright's affidavit.

18 Information from Lord Rothschild.

19 *Daily Express*, November 26, 1986.

20 Wright's affidavit.

21 I have a copy of this letter.

22 Information from Lord Rothschild to the Metropolitan Police and checked by them.

23 £700, according to Lord Rothschild.

24 Wright's affidavit.

25 Ibid.

26 See *Daily Telegraph*, November 26, 1986.

27 Wright's affidavit.

28 Letter from Wright to Lord Rothschild dated November 3, 1976.

29 Wright sent me a copy of this letter from MI5. In his affidavit, Wright claimed that he began his book, which he called a "dossier," in 1979.

30 I gave evidence at the Vassall tribunal in 1963 (see Cmnd 2009) and during the D-Notice affair (See Cmnd 3309 June 1967).

31 Conversation with Sir Peter Ramsbotham.

■| Chapter 2: The Hollis Affair |■

1   I have established that there was no personal animosity between Angleton and Hollis.
2   I have a contemporary note of this conversation.
3   See Wright's affidavit.
4   See note 9, chapter 1.
5   None of this evidence ever pointed to Hollis as being the fifth man. That description makes sense only in relation to the Cambridge ring of spies in the 1930s. Hollis was at Oxford in the 1920s.
6   Trial transcript; see also *The Times*, March 25, 1986.
7   Statement in Justice Powell's judgment, p. 217.

■| Chapter 3: Encounter in Tasmania |■

1   The Dr. was genuine. I am an honorary Doctor of Letters.
2   The name of G. M. Wright had been given to me by the late Sir Frederick Brundrett, the chief scientist of the Defence Ministry, who told me about the countermeasure to Satyr after the U.S. authorities had revealed the existence of the Russian device.
3   Brundrett was a close friend of mine for many years and kept me well briefed on secret defense matters but he never mentioned Wright or any aspect of his own connection with MI5.
4   See *Too Secret Too Long*, St. Martin's Press, New York, 1985, for Operation Dew-worm in Canada and Operation Mole in Australia.
5   Wright told me that Rothschild did all he could to secure him a better pension, even taking the matter up with Edward Heath when he was Prime Minister in 1973. The Treasury informed Heath that Wright would be receiving his full entitlement and no more, as other officers were in the same position.

6   *Dilexi justitiam et odi iniquitatem propterea morior in ixilio.*
7   In connection with the case of Anthony Blunt, Parliament had been told that no such cavalier action was possible.
8   This was eventually made clear by Wright himself in his sworn affidavit, in which he stressed that he had been only one of several informants for the book and had never received any manuscript or even a synopsis.

▮| Chapter 4: Secret Intervention: Enter MI6 |▮

1   Among the omissions were details of Movements Analysis, operations such as Party Piece, and the names of serving officers.
2   Letters to me from William Armstrong.
3   Letter from Lord Rothschild, August 10, 1987.
4   Summary of documents in trial transcript (see appendix B), and various references in the Sydney trial transcript.
5   For these views, see Chapman Pincher, *Traitors: The Anatomy of Treason*, St. Martin's Press, New York, 1987.
6   Summary of documents in trial transcript (see appendix B).
7   Lord Longford was later to be accused of having handed over the script, which he hotly denied, assuring me that, other considerations apart, he would never have rendered any assistance to the Thatcher government!
8   Date given in the summary of documents (see appendix B) and by Sir Robert Armstrong in court.
9   Letter to William Armstrong dated January 19, 1981.
10 Letter from Sir David English dated September 14, 1987.

▮| Chapter 5: A Perilous Web of Secrecy |▮

1   The name of the legal adviser to MI5 has been given in the Wright trial.

2 *The Times*, December 11, 1986, and trial transcript.

3 Conversation with the Arbiter on April 20, 1982.

4 Trial transcript.

5 In evidence in court, he gave the date when he first became aware of the existence of the book as "about February 1981."

6 See trial transcript, summary of documents (appendix B), and *The Times*, account of December 11, 1986.

7 Suggestions that Wright has been back to the UK since 1980 are untrue. See David Owen, *Hansard*, December 3, 1986, col. 935. On March 18, 1987, Owen wrote to me admitting his error.

8 At the lunch in Farnham described in chapter 9.

9 This had been effected without his permission or agreement so soon after the public and Parliamentary row over the secret immunity granted to Anthony Blunt. See Blunt debate, *Hansard*, November 21, 1979.

10 Trial transcript and *The Times*, December 11, 1986. Memories of the meeting are dim. Sir Robert's was so vague that he claimed in the Sydney court to have forgotten it completely, and believed that the decision to permit publication of the book had been made solely by the Attorney General, who had not even been present!

11 Telephone conversation with Havers, December 2, 1986.

12 Trial transcript.

13 Ibid.

14 Sir Robert specifically said that he did not mean legally restrained.

15 Trial transcript.

16 Ibid.

17 Ibid.

18 *Observer*, November 30, 1986.

19 See Statement on the Recommendations of the Security Commission, Cmnd 8540, May 1982. The full report, which has never been published, contained a mass of secret recommendations.

20 Trial transcript.

▮| Chapter 6: A Letter from the Cabinet Secretary |▮

1 See appendix C.
2 Conversation with William Armstrong. See also *Daily Telegraph*, December 3, 1986. The two Armstrongs were introduced to each other in a London club in 1987. Sir Robert was most affable.

▮| Chapter 7: A Review by the Prime Minister |▮

1 The award was made by the Publishers' Publicity Circle.
2 Trial transcript.
3 Ibid.
4 Statement by Turnbull in court, and Wright's affidavit.
5 An attitude that was rather contrary to the fury inside the *Daily Express*, especially when Andrew Edwards, the *Express* chief lawyer, revealed that he had known all about the book because he had reviewed it.

▮| Chapter 8: The End of a Relationship |▮

1 Angus Macpherson. *Daily Mail*, March 25, 1981.

▮| Chapter 9: A Meeting with Sir Arthur Franks |▮

1 Franks was cleared in Parliament on December 18, 1986, of all allegations that he had supplied information on matters of state security (*Daily Telegraph*, December 19, 1986).
2 Trial transcript—various references.

■| Chapter 10: The Security Commission Reports |■

1 Cmnd 8540.
2 April 17, 18, and 19.
3 Whether he did so or not, MI5 clearly believed that he did.

■| Chapter 11: Enter Mr. Greengrass |■

1 Wright gave me the initials of the five, whom I recognized. I was very doubtful that any would appear, and none eventually did so.
2 Letter from Greengrass, July 16, 1984.
3 Wright's affidavit and information from Greengrass.
4 Transcript of *World in Action* program, *The Spy Who Never Was*, July 16, 1984.
5 There can be little doubt that similar efforts have been made since to secure more up-to-date information.
6 Statement by Robert Kaplan in press interview March 26, 1981, reported in the *Toronto Star* on March 27.
7 The Granada team had secured the code word for the meetings, *CAZAB*, and other information from American sources.
8 Letter dated July 16, 1984.
9 Trial transcript (see appendix B), and *The Times*, December 11, 1986.
10 *Within Whicker's World*, David & Charles, North Pomfret, Vermont, 1983.
11 Letter from Greengrass, November 8, 1984.
12 Statement by Greengrass at lunch, November 7, 1984.
13 *Listener,* August 6, 1987.
14 *A Spy's Revenge*, Richard V. Hall, Penguin, London, 1987.
15 *Sunday Telegraph*, July 19, 1987.

▮| Chapter 12: The "Dossier" |▮

1 A device I have used myself in the past.
2 Conversation with Sir Anthony Kershaw, August 7, 1984.
3 Conversation with Kershaw, October 19, 1984.
4 *The Times* and *Daily Telegraph*, August 3, 1984.
5 Letter dated January 18, 1985, and produced by Wright in evidence at his trial.
6 He sent me a copy of his speech, to which I suggested amendments that he accepted.
7 Conversation with Kershaw, September 25, 1984.
8 According to Richard V. Hall (*A Spy's Revenge*), Heinemann Australia had already made a deal with Wright in November 1984.

▮| Chapter 13: The Lunch That Never Was |▮

1 Trial transcript—various references.
2 Ibid.
3 Justice Powell's judgment, March 13, 1987, p. 124.
4 *The Times*, April 24, 1987.
5 Contemporary notes of a lunch with Kershaw on August 7, 1984. Letter from me to Kershaw, September 13, 1984.
6 Telephone conversation with Kershaw, September 25, 1984.
7 Notes of conversation with Kershaw, October 19, 1984.
8 Letter from Kershaw, November 12, 1984.
9 Summary of documents; see appendix B.

▮| Chapter 14: *Spycatcher* |▮

1 Letter reproduced in *People*, November 23, 1986.
2 Wright's affidavit.
3 Telephone conversation with Hooper, October 25, 1985.

4   Trial transcript and conversation with Kershaw.
5   *The Times*, April 28, 1987.
6   *Sunday Telegraph*, May 3, 1987.
7   *The Times*, May 4, 1987.
8   Conversation with Goldsmith on June 11, 1987, at Cliveden; and conversation with Lord Rothschild.
9   *The Times*, August 7, 1987.
10 I had recorded this in *Too Secret Too Long* in 1984. Even cabins in liners and seats in aircraft have been bugged to secure information considered valuable.
11 During Anthony Eden's premiership, a delegation from Argentina was in London to discuss supplies of meat at Lancaster House, and Eden suggested that their anteroom be bugged to learn the lowest price at which they were prepared to settle. The bugs were not inserted because several MI5 officers refused, as the project had nothing to do with security.
12 I was among several journalists who received forged bank statements said to belong to Edward Short. The incident was fully investigated by Scotland Yard. There was no evidence that MI5 had been involved.
13 Information from a confidential source.
14 *Sunday Telegraph*, July 19, 1987.
15 *The Times*, August 5, 1987.
16 *The Times*, August 13, 1987.
17 Noel Annan, *New York Review of Books*, September 24, 1987.

∎∎ Chapter 15: The Climate of Secret Suspicion ∎∎

1   For example, I took no action on the false bank statement attributed to Edward Short, except to warn him. A mass of information reached me in three anonymous letters from Tenerife, alleged to be from an American intelligence officer on vacation there. I passed the letters on to Sir Maurice Oldfield of MI6, who declined to give me

the results of his inquiries. The information was not used. One specific allegation said, "Members of the Wilson Cabinet were put under wire tap and electronic surveillance both by the CIA and your intelligence networks." Another stated that "US Intelligence has wiretapped the homes of prominent politicians and trade union leaders in Britain." This was alleged to have happened during 1973 and 1975. The letters seemed to be too amateurish to have derived from MI5. In the unlikely event of an inquiry, they should still be on file in MI6.

2 As trusted adviser and confidant to Jomo Kenyatta, McKenzie had developed far-flung intelligence connections. He was, for example, instrumental in setting up the Israeli raid on Entebbe airport, in Uganda, through his contacts with Mossad, the Israeli intelligence service. He had an estate in Surrey and was a neighbor of mine until his assassination in May 1978. Harold Wilson rated him so highly that he wrote an obituary notice for *The Times*, which declined to print it because it was so critical of Idi Amin, who had almost certainly been involved in planting the bomb that destroyed McKenzie's aircraft during a return flight to Nairobi from Entebbe.

3 *Daily Express*, July 29, 1977.

4 *Daily Telegraph*, April 21, 1987.

5 See *The Times*, May 7, 1987; *Hansard*, May 6, 1987.

6 Information from Lord Mayhew, November 15, 1979. See also his memoirs, *Time to Explain*, Hutchinson, London, 1987.

7 Notepaper from 10 Downing Street and the Prime Minister's name and influence were alleged to have been used by members of Wilson's office to secure land for development. Wilson involved himself by rising to the defense of the person concerned in Parliament.

8 *Listener*, August 6, 1987.

9 The evidence of Cathy Massiter, a former MI5 officer, is relevant here. It emerged as a result of a *20/20 Vision*

television program, *MI5's Official Secrets*, screened on March 8, 1985.

10   For example, Lord Mayhew told me that Hollis had asked him to report on his Labour colleagues and that he had declined.

11   There were several occasions when, at the request of MI5 or MI6, I induced editors of the *Daily Express* to refrain from publishing information. The editors were also sometimes approached directly.

12   See Douglas Hyde, *I Believed*, Heinemann, London, 1951.

13   Information from a confidential source.

14   *Daily Telegraph*, January 2, 1981.

15   Information from a confidential source.

16   For details, see Chapman Pincher, *Inside Story*.

17   One well-known trade union leader was known in the prewar Comintern traffic by the code-name Mask. In the 1960s, he was often in touch with the wife of a Swedish diplomat known to be a Soviet agent and serving as a cutout. Mask's wife was known to have been a Comintern courier. Prime ministers saw reports on this man, but it was considered too dangerous politically for him to be more thoroughly investigated.

18   The details of my conversation with Brown on this subject are recorded in a memo I sent to Lord Beaverbrook, dated August 1, 1961.

19   Letter from Peter Wright.

20   Frank Haxell and Jack Frazer, who agreed to be scapegoats. The communist union president, Frank Foulkes, was also disgraced. See Frank Chapple, *Sparks Fly*, Michael Joseph, London, 1984.

21   *Security Procedures in the Public Service*, Cmnd 1681, 1962.

22   For details see Chapman Pincher, *Inside Story*.

23   Conversation with Lady Falkender. Lady Plummer died in June 1972.

24   Original information from Peter Wright and Lord Wilson.

25   Information from George Wigg. See also *George Wigg* by Lord Wigg, Michael Joseph, London, 1972.

26   On August 6, 1987, Stonehouse, then sixty-two, called for an inquiry into MI5's "dirty tricks," intimating that he had been framed by the defector Frolik and that he was not a spy.

27   Information from Lord George Brown.

28   MacDermot letter to *Sunday Times*.

29   *Observer*, May 10, 1987.

30   Barbara Castle, *The Castle Diaries*, Holmes & Meier, New York, 1981.

31   Jan Sejna, *We Will Bury You*, Sidgwick and Jackson, London, 1982.

32   For details, see Chapman Pincher, *Traitors: The Anatomy of Treason*, St. Martin's Press, New York, 1987.

33   The names of the two MI5 officers mainly involved in this official operation have been given as Harry Wharton and Tony Brookes. *Observer*, May 10, 1987.

34   Conversation with Kagan on July 23, 1981. Witnessed by Michael Ivens.

35   When I was researching a prospective book on the extreme-left infiltration of the Labour Party, several senior Labour figures listed this event as one of the major factors facilitating infiltration.

36   The letter was written in 1977 to David Yorck, a veteran of the American Office of Strategic Services.

37   Joe Haynes, *The Politics of Power*, Coronet, London, 1977.

38   "The Infiltrators" was never completed because Lady Falkender was unable to supply the documentary evidence required.

39   Barrie Penrose and Roger Courtier, *The Pencourt File*, Harper & Row, New York, 1978. *Daily Express*, February 2, 1978.

40 Letter from Lord Dacre, dated August 24, 1977. *Daily Express*, February 2, 1978.

41 The government's decision to deunionize GCHQ owed much to pressure from Washington on behalf of the NSA.

42 See James Bamford, *Puzzle Palace: A Report on America's Most Secret Agency*, Penguin, New York, 1982. Archival material is said to show that GCHQ and the NSA jointly tapped telephones in the UK. Bamford also revealed that GCHQ was providing the Americans with "non-verbal" intercepts.

43 For details, see Chapman Pincher, *The Secret Offensive*, St. Martin's Press, New York, 1986.

44 *Daily Mail*, January 4, 1985.

45 *The Times*, April 24, 1985, and letter to *The Times* from Lord Orr-Ewing, April 26, 1985.

46 Script of *20/20 Vision* program, *MI5's Official Secrets*, March 8, 1985.

47 Commissioned by the Coalition for Peace through Security.

48 *The Times*, May 7, 1987.

▮▮ Chapter 16: The Web of Deceit in Australia ▮▮

1 By John Mortimer, the writer who interviewed him, *Daily Telegraph*, February 14, 1987.

2 Article by Malcolm Turnbull, *Sunday Times*, March 15, 1987.

3 Mortimer, note 1.

4 The Director of Public Prosecutions was not allowed to read the book because Turnbull would not give permission for it to be shown to him!

5 *The Times*, August 21, 1986.

6 Turnbull himself has stated that *Their Trade Is Treachery*

was to become the central issue of the case. *Sunday Times*, March 15, 1987.

7   *Hansard*, November 26, 1986, col. 243.
8   Trial transcript.
9   *Sunday Express*, November 16, 1986.
10 The friends were Professor Harry Messel of Sydney University and his wife.
11 *Daily Telegraph*, December 18, 1986, and trial transcript.
12 Trial transcript.
13 Information from a confidential source.
14 *Hansard*, cols. 707 and 708.
15 Turnbull called early on the morning of November 22, 1986. I could hear someone prompting him with questions.
16 *Daily Telegraph*, November 26, 1986.
17 Ibid.
18 Ibid., and trial transcript.
19 Transcript of Codd's affidavit, sworn November 14, 1986. *Sydney Morning Herald*, November 18, 1986.

▌▌ Chapter 17: A Statement under Oath ▌▌

1   Affidavit sworn November 8, 1986.
2   Justice Powell's judgment.
3   I made these comments in an article in the *Sunday Express*, published before I had seen Wright's affidavit and before he had given evidence.
4   *Daily Telegraph*, November 26, 1986.
5   Trial transcript.
6   Interview, *Daily Mail*, December 18, 1986.

▌▌ Chapter 18: Echoes in Parliament ▌▌

1   *Hansard*, November 20, 1986, cols. 263–265.
2   *Hansard*, December 15, 1986.
3   *Hansard*, July 21, 1986.

4 *Hansard*, November 28, 1986, col. 392.
5 *Hansard*, December 3, 1986, col. 678.
6 *Hansard*, December 8, 1986.
7 *Hansard*, November 27, 1986, cols. 426 and 427.
8 The so-called "Zircon affair"—a prospective television program. The police searched Campbell's home and removed research material.
9 I gave details of this conversation to Havers in a letter dated January 1, 1987.

▮| Chapter 19: The Vindication of Lord Rothschild |▮

1 This action could not have been in connection with the eventual police interviews because they were not asked to see Rothschild until December 17. Solicitor General's statement, *Hansard*, February 6, 1987.
2 Trial transcript, p. 508.
3 For details of the Alister Watson case, see Chapman Pincher, *Too Secret Too Long*, St. Martin's Press, New York, 1985.
4 Ibid. See also Chapman Pincher, *Traitors: The Anatomy of Treason*, St. Martin's Press, New York, 1987.
5 Lord Rothschild, *Meditations of a Broomstick*, Collins, London, 1977.
6 Lord Rothschild, *Random Variables*, Collins, London, 1984.
7 Rothschild says he now has proof that MI5 has no letter showing that he introduced Blunt into MI5, as has been claimed.

▮| Chapter 20: The Charmed Life of Arthur Martin |▮

1 *Hansard*, November 28, col. 392.
2 For Movements Analysis, see Chapman Pincher, *Too Secret Too Long*, St. Martin's Press, New York, 1985.

3 Trial transcript.
4 Barrie Penrose and Simon Freeman, *Conspiracy of Silence: The Secret Life of Anthony Blunt*, Farrar, Straus & Giroux, New York, 1987.

▌| Chapter 21: Enter the Police |▐

1 Sydney press conference. *Daily Telegraph*, November 26, 1986.
2 Statement to police by William Armstrong.
3 Ibid.
4 Information from William Armstrong.
5 *Hansard*, May 7, 1987, col. 527.
6 *Hansard*, July 9, 1987, col. 207.
7 *Daily Telegraph*, April 28 and 30, 1987.
8 See Chapman Pincher, *Traitors: The Anatomy of Treason*, St. Martin's Press, New York, 1987.
9 The first installment about Oldfield appeared on April 19, 1987.

▌| Chapter 22: Judgment and Appeals |▐

1 Judgment in the Supreme Court of New South Wales, Equity Division. No. 4382. Friday, March 13, 1987.
2 *The Times*, editorial, March 14, 1987.
3 Allegedly after an intervention with Lord Blakenham, the chairman of Pearson, the British owners of Viking Penguin. See *Sunday Times*, July 19, 1987.
4 The case of Sgt. Clayton Lonetree, who was convicted by court martial.
5 *Daily Telegraph*, May 15, 1987.
6 *The Times*, June 30, 1987.
7 *The Times*, July 13, 1987. *Sunday Times*, July 19, 1987.
8 On July 13, 1987.
9 *The Times*, July 15, 1987.

10 Paul Johnson, *Daily Mail*, July 18, 1987.
11 *Daily Telegraph*, July 18, 1987.
12 *The Times*, Law Report, July 18, 1987.
13 *Daily Telegraph*, July 23, 1987.
14 *The Times*, Law Report, July 25, 1987.
15 Ibid.
16 *The Times*, July 29, 1987.
17 Lords Brandon, Templeman, and Ackner were in the majority, with Lords Bridge and Oliver dissenting.
18 *The Times*, Law Report, August 14, 1987.
19 *The Times*, August 14, 1987.
20 *Daily Mirror*, July 31, 1987.
21 *Sunday Times*, August 2, 1987.
22 *Observer*, August 2, 1987.
23 *News on Sunday*, August 2, 1987.
24 *Daily Telegraph*, August 5, 1987.
25 Ibid.
26 *Sunday Times*, August 2, 1987.
27 *Observer*, August 2, 1987.
28 *Sydney Morning Herald*, July 31, 1987.
29 Against the *South China Morning Post*.
30 *Daily Telegraph*, September 25, 1987.
31 Ibid., and BBC interviews.
32 *Daily Telegraph*, editorial, September 25, 1987.
33 See *Mail on Sunday*, September 27, 1987.

▮❙ Chapter 23: Damage Assessment ❙▮

1 *Hansard*, December 3, 1986, col. 961.
2 Noel Annan, *New York Review*, September 24, 1987.
3 Trial transcript.
4 Letter dated March 29, 1987.
5 Letter to M. L. Saunders, legal secretary, Law Officers Department, dated March 30, 1987.

❚❙ **Chapter 24: Lessons to Be Learned** ❙❚

1   *The Times*, August 8, 1987.
2   *The Times*, March 2, 1985. Edward Gardner, Merlyn Rees speech, *The Times*, August 8, 1987.
3   The improvements were outlined by the Home Secretary, Douglas Hurd, *Hansard*, December 3, 1986, col. 943.
4   *London Standard*, January 30, 1987.

|Select Bibliography|

Hall, Richard V. A *Spy's Revenge*, Penguin, London, 1987.

Penrose, Barrie, and Freeman, Simon. *Conspiracy of Silence: The Secret Life of Anthony Blunt*, Farrar, Straus & Giroux, New York, 1987.

Pincher, Chapman. *Inside Story*, Sidgwick & Jackson, London, 1978.

————. *Their Trade Is Treachery*, Bantam, New York, 1983.

————. *Too Secret Too Long*, St. Martin's Press, New York, 1985.

————. *The Secret Offensive*, St. Martin's Press, New York, 1986.

————. *Traitors: The Anatomy of Treason*, St. Martin's Press, New York, 1987.

Sawatsky, John. *For Services Rendered*, Doubleday, New York, 1982.

West, Nigel. *The Circus: MI5 Operations Nineteen Forty-Five to Nineteen Seventy-Two*, Stein & Day, Briarcliff Manor, NY, 1983.

Wright, Peter. *Spycatcher*, Viking, New York, 1987.

| Index |